GRAYSHOTT

THE STORY O[

Cover photo: Headley Road, Grayshott, circa 1905

Grayshott

THE STORY OF A HAMPSHIRE VILLAGE

J. H. SMITH

B.A. (London), M.Ed. (Manch.)
Author of "Churcher's College,
Petersfield" (1936)

GRAYSHOTT

First published 1978 by Frank Westwood, Petersfield Bookshop

This edition published 2002

Typeset and published by John Owen Smith
19 Kay Crescent, Headley Down, Hampshire GU35 8AH
Tel/Fax: 01428 712892
E-mail: wordsmith@headley-village.com

ISBN 1-873855-38-9

Printed and bound by Antony Rowe Ltd, Eastbourne

Publisher's Note

In producing this new edition to mark the centenary of the civil parish of Grayshott in 2002, we have reproduced faithfully the text and format of Jack Smith's original work published in 1978 with a few minor corrections.

We had initially considered 'updating' his work with references to today's village, but eventually resisted the temptation. It would have depended upon finding people with enough knowledge on each of the subjects covered, and would probably have resulted in an uneven treatment. Instead, we have left open the possibility of creating a new work in the future to continue the story from the point at which this one ends.

Although the text is unchanged, we have augmented the index found in the previous publication, and added some of maps showing the general area and the centre of the village at two stages in its initial period of growth.

Thanks are due to Barry Penny, Chairman of Grayshott Parish Council in its centenary year, for the Foreword to this publication.

We should also like to thank Grayshott Parish Council and Frank Westwood of Petersfield Bookshop, joint copyright holders of this work, for their permission to republish.

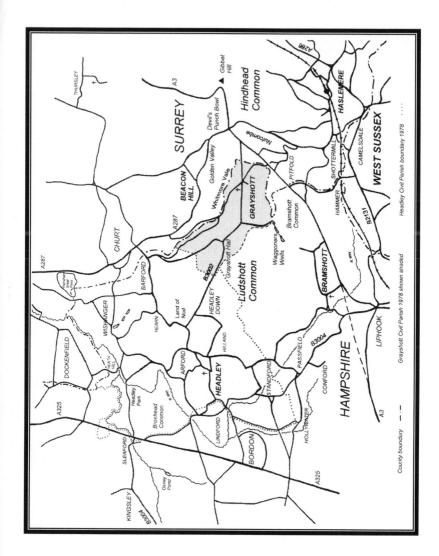

General map of
the Grayshott,
Haslemere,
Headley and
Liphook area,
1978

Contents

Illustrations

Foreword

Jack Hayden Smith was a local boy, who was born in the village and later returned to live here in his retirement. From humble beginnings he went on to obtain degrees from both London and Manchester universities and pursued a career in education. In his retirement years he became immersed in local affairs: the Church, Parish Council and the Grayshott Stagers being among his interests. It was during this period that he wrote the first part of this book.

He had no family of his own, and on his death he generously left a legacy to the Parish Council together with half the copyright of his book. The legacy has been used over the years to improve village amenities. The Parish Council has also used it to provide an annual prize for a pupil of Grayshott School for some outstanding achievement, the winning child receiving a book.

As the year 2002 marks the centenary of the Civil Parish of Grayshott, the Parish Council were pleased to receive a request from John Owen Smith to republish this work. Over the past ten years or so, he has written and published a number of books and plays based on the history of this area.

While sharing a surname and the love and interest of local history, he and Jack Smith are not related.

Grayshott,
February, 2002   BARRY PENNY

Here follows a facsimile of Jack Smith's book of 1978,
with minor corrections, footnotes and maps

Preface

The genesis of this book was the celebration in 1962 of the Diamond Jubilee of the civil parish of Grayshott, when I was persuaded into organising an exhibition illustrative of the village and its history. I was amazed at the amount of material available. It seemed a good idea to attempt an account of the development of what is essentially a modern village which had not originated as an ancient agricultural settlement, and which had an isolated and somewhat tenuous connection with the ancient agricultural village of Headley, Hampshire, of which it was for centuries a part. Grayshott and Headley were separated by some three miles of wide stretches of uncultivated 'waste of manor'. Indeed, it was not long after the growth of the new Grayshott began that its inhabitants sought independence from Headley in matters spiritual and temporal.

Born in Grayshott, I have known the village intimately for more than seventy of the hundred years during which it has developed, and also many of its inhabitants who contributed much to it.

Much of the material concerning the earlier years comes from my memories and those of other old residents, and this would be lost if it were not soon written down. The last three Chapters lean very heavily on Parish Council records and may seem to some readers rather dull—and at times even trivial. My defence is that these records were readily available over long periods and were very well kept: they form a reliable account of most things, large and small, which went to the formation of our village community.

The exigencies of an otherwise busy life caused this work to be spread over a number of years, and I am thankful to have had friends who from time to time prodded me on, particularly Rev. Canon A. R. Winnett, sometime Vicar of Grayshott.

Grayshott,
March, 1978

J. H. SMITH

Chapter 1

The Early Grayshott

A. THE EARLY HAMLET

The present village of Grayshott is of quite recent growth and has had a
separate existence, ecclesiastical and civil, for only about 75 years. And yet the
name is found as early as the 12th century. The explanation lies in the fact that
there was an early settlement of that name lying about a mile west of the
modern Grayshott village, a small outlying hamlet of the ancient parish of
Headley. This small settlement was in the neighbourhood of Grayshott Hall
and Grayshott Hall Farm (formerly Bull's Farm), while the site of the modern
Grayshott was open waste land of pine, heather and gorse, though there were
a few small farms and squatters' cottages in Stoney Bottom and Whitmore
Vale or Bottom, the valleys running in an easterly direction up to the higher
land of Hindhead. Some of these more ancient habitations still exist, though
most have been modernised out of recognition. That the modern village
developed so late was due, no doubt, to its remoteness on the high land of
Hindhead, to the poorness of its soil, to the fact that until the middle of the
nineteenth century its site was part of the unenclosed common land of
Headley — and, perhaps, to the reputation for lawlessness which its few
scattered inhabitants possessed.

The first Grayshott lay wholly within the parish of Headley, a Domesday
parish, which before the Norman Conquest was part of the manor of Bishops
Sutton in the possession of Earl Godwin of Wessex. It passed at the Conquest
into the possession of Eustace, Count of Boulogne. King Stephen (1135–1154)
married Matilda of Boulogne and the manor became Crown property for a
short time. Stephen, however, exchanged his manor of Sutton for that of
Merton, which belonged to his brother, Henry of Blois, Bishop of Winchester.
Thus the manor of Bishop Sutton, and Headley with it, came into the
possession of the Bishops of Winchester who held it for centuries as Bishops
Sutton. In course of time, this huge manor was sub-divided, one of the sub-
divisions being the manor of Wishanger in which was comprised part of
Headley, including the old Grayshott. After many changes of ownership it
came to the Speed family, who sold it in 1797 to the Miller family of Froyle. In
turn, they sold it in 1868 to John Rouse Phillips, and from him it was bought
in 1884 by Joseph Whitaker of Yorkshire and Palermo.

The first references to this earlier Grayshott are found in the records of the
Bishopric of Winchester. In the Pipe Rolls of 1185 it is mentioned as
Gravesetta and in the Bishop's Register of 1200 as Graveschete, the name
signifying a clearing in a wood. There is, indeed, archaeological evidence of
even earlier settlement as far back as Neolithic times. Traces of settlement of
this period were found when the Hindhead Golf Links were being made, and

in 1949 a Bronze Age flint flake about four inches long was unearthed during ploughing in a field by the stream at Purchase Farm in Whitmore Vale. An expert's opinion of this flake was quoted in the *Papers and Proceedings of the Hampshire Field Club and Archaeological Society*, Volume XVII, Part I, p. 54; "A fine flake with serrated edges which, I believe, may confidently be assigned to a Bronze Age industry. This I judge more from the shattered scar of percussion than from the state of the object. The denticulations appear to me to combine both retouch and wear. The edge still shows the signs of continuous utilisation."

During medieval and later times the name of Headley appears in different forms. In the 11th century it is Hallege, in the 13th Hertelegh, in the 14th Hedle and Hetlegh, and in the 15th Hedley. Later we find other variants: Hethle and Hethelie (16th century), Hedleigh (17th century) and Heathley (18th century).

In the Bishop's Register in the County Records Office at Winchester there is the record of a perambulation of the parish of Headley in 1533 which contains the following reference to the early hamlet of Grayshott: "There is a wood of hethe and waste being in a wood containing 240 acres, lying in length on the east of Graveshotte, in length between Kingeswode Bottom on the south and Graveshotte and Shirley Dene on the north, and on the west abutting on Brokesbottom, and on the east abutting on Les Merke Okes, of which the wood contains 140 acres and the waste 100 acres. There is another waste containing 100 acres, lying on the east of Hetheleshyll and north-west even to Graveshotte."

Some of these place names make it clear that 16th century Grayshott lay between the 100 acres of moor above Headley Hill and the 240 acres of moor and wood which then covered the site of the present village, i.e. on some cleared land round the present Grayshott Hall and Grayshott Hall Farm. They also testify to the longstanding use of the term "bottom" to denote a valley and to the antiquity of the name Kingswood. Indeed, Canon Capes of Bramshott in his *Rural Life in Hampshire* suggests that Kingswood Firs may well have been a royal plantation going back to early Tudor times.

In 1766 Sir Thomas Gatehouse of Headley was worried because of un-certainty concerning the rents payable to the lord of the manor by the tenants. He made investigations, no doubt in the episcopal records, and found and copied out a survey of the Tithing of Headley made in 1552. This copy has survived in the Blount Papers in the County Records Office. The survey has notes of mid-16th century landholders at Grayshott. Richard Heyes held some 5 acres, some of it adjoining the land of William Graveshotte, who, as well as having land at Barford, held "Bull's Toft" of 18 acres in Graveshotte. By 1760 this holding had become sub-divided and the holders then were Cane, Richard Holloway and Richard Messingham. In 1552 John Newman, who held Barford Mills, also had a small holding at Graveshotte; in 1760 this was in the hands of Richard Pim. In 1552 Robert Harding (9 acres), William Langford (12 acres), John Warner who held "in right of Johanne his wyfe" (23 acres), Robert Luckin "in right of Elizabeth his wyfe (21½ acres), Richard Chetty who held "a messuage garden and certain lands called Higher Graveshotte" (22 acres), and Richard Gill were other landholders. The combined acreage of the nine landholders named may have extended to about 150 acres. Some of the successors of these in 1760 were Richard Holloway,

Robert Mayhew and William Triggs. In a later entry Gatehouse noted that Richard Chetty's holding of Higher Graveshotte had become Keyne's (Cane's) Estate, which had been purchased by John Rooke for £510 and sold by him to Robert Mayhew in 1773 for £600.

In the 1552 survey the word "toft" is used frequently and was explained by Gatehouse as a piece of land where a house had formerly stood, which had since fallen into decay. This, together with the name Graveshotte used as a family name (e.g. John of Grayshott becoming in time John Grayshott) as well as a place name, indicates a settlement going back a long time before 1552, as, indeed, do the 11th and 12th century references mentioned above.

Among names of the small farms in 1552 we find Bull's Toft, Graveshotte, Higher Graveshotte, Homehouse, Barneland and Grafseat, while the old lanes were Graveshotte Lane (probably taking the same position as the modern Headley Road in the section by Grayshott Hall and Grayshott Hall Farm), Oldland Lane (quite possibly now Hammer Lane), Barnefield Lane, Bull Lane, later called Green Lane (possibly the old road leading from the top of Hammer Lane down into Whitmore Vale).

B. SOME GRAYSHOTT 16th CENTURY WILLS

A search of the 16th century episcopal registers at the County Records Office resulted in the discovery of some Grayshott wills of the period. The testators seem generally not to have made a will until they became seriously ill, since they normally describe themselves as sane but sick. When death occurred, the neighbours came in to take an inventory of the goods and chattels. Some of these inventories were filed with the wills and make interesting reading. Among the wills are those of members of the family called Grayshott.

In 1543 John Grayshott made his will, as follows:-

"In the name of God Amen the second daye of Aprill in the yere of our Lord God one thousand five hundred and forty three I Jhon (sic) Grashott the elder of Hedley sycke of boddy and whole of mynd and of perfect remembrance do make this my last wyll and testmentt in maner and forme following, First and chefly above all thyng I bequethe my solle to allmyghty God my Redeemer to our Lady Seynt Mary and to all the holy company of heven my boddy to be buryed within the churchyard of Hedley, Item I bequethe to the mother church of Wynchester ii d, Item I give and bequethe to Margarett my wife x pounds in redy money iii kyne xii shepe xii hyves of bees and her chambers stuff and aparell thereof, Item I give and bequethe to Johan my daughter vi pounds xiii shillings iv pence in redy money iiii pewter platterys i brasse potte and i coffer, Item I give and bequethe to Johan Moryer my goddaughter iiii d, Item I give to the reparcyon and amending of the belles of Hedley viii d, Item I wylle that my executor bestow x d for a trentall of masses to be sayed for my sole, Item I wylle that my executor cause v masses to be seyd and sung for my sole att tyme of my buryall, the rest of my goods and chattells nott before given nor bequethed I give and wholy bequethe unto Jhon Grashot my younger son whom I make my whole and sole executor of this my last wylle and testyment to dispose thereof according to hys dyscrecyon for

15

my soles helthe for wytness wereof these being present Rychard Rous Jhon Valour and Jhon Alwey."

It is possible that John Valour was an ancestor of the Voller family of Grayshott and that John Alwey was an ancestor of the Holloway family mentioned as landholders at Grayshott in 1760.

This John Grayshott, having made his will on 2nd April, 1543, died a few days later aged 60 and was buried at Headley on 9th April.

Three years later another John Grayshott, son of William Grayshott, made his will on 6th January, 1546. He is described in the Headley registers as the son of "Wyllyam and Alys Grayshot," and was buried on 12th May of the same year at the age of 30. When making his will this John Grayshott referred to himself as "whole of mynd and sike in body of good and perfect remembrance, not knowing the houre and tyme of my deth but at the will and pleasure of almyghtie God." He also bequeathed his soul "to almyghtie God my only Savior and redeemer and to our lady Seynt Mary and to all the company of hevyn." He left vi d to the mother church of Winchester and provided, by a bequest of two sheep, for funeral torches, bells and masses at Headley, and for annual dirges and masses by a bequest of iii s and iiii d. To Agnes his sister he left one "heffer bullock," to the overseers of his will, Richard Rous and John Turner, "ii of my best oxen and xxvi shillings and viii pence of money" and "i shepe" respectively, and to his other sister Joan the residue of his estate.

Agnes Chaddler, a Haslemere girl who had married into the Grayshott family and of whom there is a story to relate presently, made her will in 1575 "the xiii th day of Maye in the xvii th yeare of the raigne of our Soveraigne Lady Elizabeth by the grace of God of England Fraunce and Ireland quene Deffender of the Faithe." She bequeathed her soul to "Almighty God my Maker and Redeemer." It is interesting to note that in the Grayshott family wills of 1543 and 1546 the soul was bequeathed to Almighty God, to the Virgin Saint Mary and to the company of heaven, and provision was made for the saying of masses, whereas in the later wills there is no mention of the Virgin, the company of heaven, and masses. This could reflect the progress of the Protestant Reformation, having reached the remote hamlet of Grayshott a little late.

Agnes also died shortly after making her will, on 30th May, 1575. Her will is a short one. She gave 20 d to the "poor mens box of Haslemere"; to Agnes her god-daughter she left "my best kettle," and to Joan Lawrence "my two next best kettles," the residue of her estate going to her brother-in-law, John Warner. The will was endorsed "to be sent to Hedley in Hampshire to the parson for John Warner there" — i.e. to the John Warner who was a Grayshott landholder.

On her death on 30th May three of her neighbours, including John Warner, made the inventory of her goods and chattels as follows:–

"one flocke bed and all things belonging to hit	x	s.		
two short planks a churne and a forme			viii	d.
one brasse pott	iii	s.	iv	d.
three kettles			ix	d.
three coffers			xvi	d.

a platter a candlestike ii porringers ii sacers		ii s.		x d.
ii tubbes with other lumbery stuffe		v s.		
a panne with other old iron		ii s.		
one axe a byll a hatchett and a hammer				xvi d.
a spynnyng whele and the rele				iiii d.
her apparell		xiii s.		iiii d.
ii ladders with certayne chestes				xx d.
vii bordes		iii s.		iiii d.
summa totalis (sum total)		liiii s.		ii d."

The three kettles valued at 9d which she left in her will were, of course, large iron pots which were suspended over the fire.

One more Grayshott will. John Turner made his will on 8th August, 1584, and on 17th August of the same year he died and the inventory of his goods was taken by his neighbours. He seems to have left a widow, one son and five daughters to all of whom he made specific bequests, including "one heyfer bulloke of iii yere of age the which I will shall be equally devided amongest all my sayd children." His inventory shows him to have been of some substance:–

"iiii kyne and ii bullokes praysed at	£vi	x s.		
one olde mare and ii small coults		xx s.		
xvii shepe and eyght lames	£ii	xiii s.		iiii d.
fyve yonge hogges		xiii s.		iiii d.
vi stalles of bees with other emtie hyves		xvi s.		
all the rie in the barne		xxx s.		
all the ottes in the barne		xxx s.		
one lode of hay		x s.		
a table a forme and one old chayre				xv d.
ii old flocke beds with what belongeth to them		xx s.		
iii old coffers		iii s.		
all the brasse and pewter		xiii s.		iiii d.
iii small hogges		x s.		
in butter and cheese		vi s.		viii d.
a brothe a frying pan a grydyron and				
a payre of pothangers		ii s.		
certen wodden vessells as tubs and others		v s.		
one axe a bill a spitter and one hammer				
with a thatcher's forke		ii s.		vi d.
one olde pannell with a bridle and halter				xii d.
sacks and a bagg				xii d.
all his aparell		xiii s.		iiii d.
in money in his purse		xx s.		
gese duckes and other poiterie		v s."		

Some of the inventories attached to wills illustrate the rise of prices caused partly by the influx into Europe of Spanish-American silver. Thus cattle valued in 1584 at about £1.1.0 apiece had risen by 1637 to about £1.15.0., while sheep priced at 3s.0d. each in 1563 and 2s.8d. in 1584 had risen to 6s.6d. in

1637. Hives of bees show a similar increase: 1s.0d. in 1568, 2s.8d. in 1584, and 6s.8d. in 1637.

C. THE STORY OF JOHN CHANDLER AND AGNES GRAYSHOTT

We have noticed the will of Agnes Chandler. Robert Chandler, yeoman of Haslemere, had two sons, John and Robert, and entered into a marriage alliance with the family of William Grayshott. The arrangement was for John Chandler to marry Agnes, daughter of William Grayshott, and a marriage settlement was agreed, the alleged terms of which caused subsequent trouble between the two Chandler brothers and resulted in a lawsuit in the Court of Chancery.

This lawsuit is not exactly dated but must have been between 1558 and 1579. It began with a bill of complaint laid by John to "the Right Honourable Sir Nicholas Bacon, Knight, Lord Keeper of the Great Seal." Describing himself as a "husbandman" of Haslemere, John alleged that Robert, his father, in consideration of a sum of money and "for other consideration" (evidently the marriage dowry) agreed with William Grayshott "to bring the marriage into effect" and further, "in consideration of the said marriage and for an advancement thereof," promised to leave to him, John, a farm in Haslemere of 200 acres of land, meadows and pasture, with eight oxen and two horses amongst divers other goods and chattells." John said that "upon trust thereof your said orator shortly after married and toke to wyfe the said dowghter of the said Greyshott."

John Chandler complained that fairly soon after the marriage "Robert Chaundler younger brother of the saide John by senester labor and undewe meanes procured his said father lyinge on his dethbedd by his last will and testament to assure and give to him as well the said ferme oxen and horses as also much other his goods."

John appears to have been at hand at this deathbed scene, for he asserted that he "humbly requested his father to have dewe consideracion to his said promise unto him." Nevertheless, the father "being seduced as is aforesaid and therfor not myndinge to perform the said promise requested your orator to hold himself content and no further move him to alter his will and in doing so he said your orator shold well perceive that he shold have at the hands of the said Robert his said brother as good a porcion of his other goods and chattels as the said Robert or any other your orator's brothers or sisters shold have. And the said Robert Chaundler the younger standinge by and heringe the said request and promise of his said father promised also for himself that his brother, meninge your orator, thus doinge he wold see his said father's promise therein justly performed."

John reported himself as the dutiful son and trusting brother: "whereupon your said orator more regardinge his dutie and obedience and the extremitie his father was then in than any comoditie and trustinge to the promise aforesaid so faithfully made held himselfe therwith contented and quietly departed without more troublinge his father and shortly after his father died."

Then came John's disillusionment. Though he "divers and sundry times" besought his brother "to perform the first promise made by his father" (to leave the Haslemere farm to John) "or ells the second promise made not only by his father but by the said Robert himself" (the deathbed promise), Robert utterly refused to perform either "and yet doth refuse."

In his answer to the Court, Robert stood firmly on his father's will and denied that his father made the deathbed promise or that, even if he did, it could upset the terms of the will. He denied that he himself had made any promise to John, who, he said, had brought the case to Court in order to put him, the defendant, "to travayle coste charge and expense in lawe without juste or lawfull cause and for none other purpose and intent."

John Chandler's "replicacion" to his brother's Answer merely reiterated his original allegations. There is no record of how the case ended, but it is clear that Robert Chandler retained the Haslemere farm.

D. THE HEADLEY REGISTERS

The Headley Registers, which commence in 1539, contain records of the baptisms, marriages and deaths of families of the small hamlet of Grayshott. Unfortunately in some cases they are fairly recent copies of the original registers and they seem to be incomplete. Another difficulty is that many of the families evidently had branches in different parts of the extensive parish of Headley. Instances of this are the Hardings and Fullicks, whose names abound and it is not possible to identify those actually living in the old Grayshott.

The entries relating to the family called Grayshott are confined to the 16th and early 17th centuries. During this period the family greatly favoured the names of William and John and it would be almost impossible to disentangle a line of descent. They intermarried with other families living at Grayshott such as Mill and Warner. Thus in 1546 John Mill the younger married Alice Grayshott and there are entries of the baptisms of six of their children, Alice (1542), Mary (1544), William (1545 — he lived only six days), Denyse (1550), Margaret (1551), and Joan (1553). In 1546 John Warner married Joan Grayshott but there is no record of their children. The last entry of the Grayshott family name is in 1613 when Joan Grayshott, wife of John Grayshott, was buried.

Another interesting small group of entries notes the baptisms of three children of Matthew Bull "gentleman" — Timothy (1605), Elizabeth (1608) and William (1613). These are the only entries of the Bull family, but we have already noted that as early as 1552 there was a Bull Lane and a Bull's Toft. The name persists as is evident from the Blount Papers. In 1609 the Roll of the Quit Rents mentions tithes paid to the Rector of Headley amounting to £5.14.0. for "84 acres at Piggott's Hill and Bulls," and in 1761 a survey of the Tithing of Headley notes John Keyne (Cane) as holding 18 acres at Bulls and the subdivision of his holding between Richard Holloway and Robert Missingham. By 1802 the ownership of Bulls had passed to Samuel Locke and William Voller was the actual occupier. In 1826 it was mentioned in a land tax assessment as belonging to Edward Slade. Certainly until recently the present Grayshott Hall Farm was called Bulls Farm. It is by no means unlikely that the ancestors of Matthew Bull, gentleman, had long been landowners in Grayshott and gave their name to a particular holding. It is, perhaps, a pity that the re-naming of the farm has obscured its probable ancient origin.

Other Grayshott family names with the earliest dates of entries in the Registers are Harding (1549), Boxall (1541), Cleere or Cleare (1597), Robinson

(1639), Morer (1626), Cane (1719) Trigg or Triggs (1681), Rook (1758), Pook or Pooke (1760—this family probably gave its name to Pook's Hill), and Belton (1845—described as a broomsquire of Waggoners Wells). Most of these names occur frequently down to modern times. The families who hold land continuously in the 18th century were Elliot, Triggs, Mayhew and Hammond.

The curious name Land of Nod is mentioned as a holding belonging to John Hammond in 1761, having previously been part of the lands occupied by the Cane family. Was there some circumstance concerning the Cane occupation of this site to recall the story in Genesis that Cain "went out from the presence of the Lord and dwelt in the land of Nod on the east of Eden"? In 1800 it was owned and occupied by Thomas Boxall, but by 1804 it had passed into the ownership of Mark Coombes and was occupied by James Barnett: some twenty years later, though still occupied by Barnett, it was owned by William Voller. It eventually became part of the Grayshott Hall or Wishanger Estate, sold by the Miller family of Froyle to John Rouse Phillips in 1868, who in turn sold it to Joseph Whitaker of Palermo in 1884. The tenant at the Land of Nod in 1868 was Henry Powell. It is now in the possession of Major Jeremy Whitaker.

E. LIFE IN THE OLD GRAYSHOTT

Life in the old Grayshott pursued, no doubt, its quiet rural way, but it could not have been easy to derive more than a sparse living from the holdings. Occasionally events happening in the world outside touched the lives of the inhabitants. In 1644, during the Civil War, Parliament deprived the Rector of Headley, Rev. Averil Thompson, of the living, which was a Crown living to which Charles I had presented him in 1631. He was reinstated in the living by Charles II at the Restoration in 1660. Charles gave six livings, of which Headley was one, to Queen's College, Oxford, who had supported him "in his troubles" by giving him all their plate. The living has remained in the gift of Queen's College.

Some additional local employment may have been created when in the 17th century the Hooke family, lords of the Manor of Bramshott, dammed a local stream, which is one of the headwaters of the River Wey, to form the Waggoners Wells (or Wakeners Wells) ponds. It is not certain whether this operation was carried out to form fishponds or to provide a head of water to operate the Hooke iron works at Hammer. If the latter, this was an example of the great iron industry which stretched across Sussex in those days, but which gradually died out in these southern areas with the denuding of the woods which supplied charcoal for the furnaces and with the development of smelting by coal and coke. Whatever the object, the commoners of Ludshott complained bitterly at the interference with the stream. It may be worth noting that the Hooke family originated as clothiers (i.e. cloth sellers) of Godalming. It was Henry Hooke who developed the local iron mill. His son John was elected Member of Parliament for Haslemere in 1658 but was unseated by an election petition.

The Grayshott landholders were tenants of the manor of Sutton, at first under the Bishop and, after 1797, under the Miller family who had bought the Wishanger Manor, a sub-division of the Manor of Bishop Sutton, from the Bishop. As tenants, the Grayshott inhabitants had certain customary rights which were upheld by the Court Leet and which enabled them to take certain things from the common land. Two examples are taken from the Register of the Fines of the Manor of Bishop Sutton:

1724 "We present the tenants of Headley to have the right to cut turff in the Common to burn in their houses and not elsewhere."

1732 "We present that the coppeyholders in the tything of Heathley may cutt what turfe they will burn in their houses, but not to burn on the Common or on their enclosed lands for if they do so they shale pay two pounds and ten shillings to the Lord of the Manor and fifty shillings to the informer. We present that no coppeyholders in the same tything shall cutt any firz or heath to burn lime to carry out of the tything upon the forfeit of ten shillings to the Lord of the Manor and ten shillings to the informer."

Similarly the Blount Papers contain the following note made in the 18th century:

"The copyholders under the Bishop have an Immemorial Right of cutting whatever shrubwood they have occasion for in Whitmore Bottom and also in the Bottom near Wakeners Wells ponds for making outside fences but no other."

Some interesting jottings in the Headley Parish Registers give prices paid for particular jobs. There is an account of 1761 for cutting "Kiln Plott coppice":

"Cutting Poles: 1/- per 100 and 8d per 100
Making Faggots: 1s. 8d. per 100."

There is also the following account dated later in the 18th century:

"Expenses for a Common Kiln of Lime.		
For digging one load of chalk	2s. 0d.	
For bottle and bag-nose work	1s. 0d.	
7 times this sum repeated for 1 kiln	3s. 0d.	£1. 1s. 0d.
To carriage of 7 loads of chalk	£3. 10s. 0d.	
To cutting 5 loads of heath	12s. 6d.	
To the Keeper's fee 1/6 per load	5s. 0d.	£4. 7s. 6d.
To the Lime Burner	5s. 0d.	
To an Assistant	3s. 0d.	
For Victuals and Drink	4s. 0d.	12s. 0d.
		£6. 0s. 6d.

My Kiln on the Common will hold 10 or 11 loads of chalk which will be sufficient for Four Acres, i.e. about 12 Dungcarts full. It must be observed that there is a full load difference in Placing in the chalk and the only way to Reconcile that matter is by a Cup of Ale now and then to the Burner."

There is another note in the Headley Registers of about the same date: "The digging a Load of Chalk is only 1/6, and three pence per Load instead of Bread and Cheese, which is much the cheapest way. On the other Hand you commonly send 2 or 3 Quarts of Drink, 2 pounds of Bread and one Pound of Cheese." The carts had, no doubt, to be sent to the Petersfield district to procure chalk for converting into lime for the fields.

In spite of commoners' rights life must have been difficult in the days of large families, even though children went to work at a tender age, particularly when the increase of population and the impact of the long French Wars drove prices upwards, and when there was no Welfare State to cushion hardship. The result was that many of the "labouring poor" lived under the dread of having to depend on poor relief.

Poor Law Relief became a great problem in the latter part of the 18th and the early part of the 19th centuries. Gilbert's Act of 1784 had sought to incorporate parishes into poor districts or "unions," each district being grouped round a workhouse. Under that Act the parishes of Headley, Bramshott and Kingsley were formed into the Headley Union, where there was a workhouse, which is clearly shown in the centre of Headley village in a map of 1808/9. But the main relief, particularly after 1795 under the Speenhamland System, was out relief consisting of a dole of money from the poor rates, the amount depending on the size of the family and the fluctuating and continually rising price of bread. The units of dole were usually fixed by the local magistrates. Inevitably under this system the poor rates increased until they became a heavy burden on the landowners, particularly on the smaller ones, since they employed little or no labour but had to pay poor rates: and so to some extent subsidised the larger owners who were thus able to employ labour at artificially low wages. The poor rates at Headley, as elsewhere, rose considerably in this period until the Poor Law Reform of 1834 ended the Speenhamland System of outdoor relief and forced the very poor into the workhouses where the standard of living was deliberately spartan in order to discourage recourse to that form of relief. From figures given in the *Report of the Select Committee on Poor Relief 1844,* the Headley poor rates had expended the following amounts on poor relief:

1777 — £185	1815 — £1,909
1803 — £629	1824 — £1,913

Even without relief many families must have been far below an adequate subsistence level. In his *"The State of the Poor and Parochial Reports 1797"* Sir Frederic Morton Eden noted that in 1795 in the Petersfield District wages were 9/- a week without board, while typical prices were: beef, 5½d. per lb; mutton, 5½d. to 6d. per lb; bread, 11d. per quartern loaf; wheat, 10/- a bushel; bacon, 10d. to 11d. per lb; milk, 1½d. per quart.

Low wages and increasing prices caused rising discontent among farm labourers in the years immediately following the French Wars and led to rural uprisings, often brutally suppressed by the yeomanry, and leading to an aftermath of executions and transportations to the convict settlements. The manifestation of this discontent occurred in Headley in 1830, when a riot led to the partial destruction of the workhouse. It is worth noting that these agrarian riots were a rural counterpart of the Luddite Riots in manufacturing districts where the introduction of machinery was immediately threatening the livelihood of hand workers.

When the chronically poor were forced, after 1834, into the workhouses, that their standard of living was kept deliberately low can be seen from the dietary of the Petworth Workhouse, as quoted by the Select Committee of 1844. There is no reason to believe that that of the Headley Workhouse would have been more generous. On each day of the week breakfast consisted of 8 ozs. of bread and 1½ pints of gruel for men, and 7 ozs. of bread and 1½ pints of gruel for women and children over 9 years of age. For dinner, men, women and children alike received on Sundays, Tuesdays and Thursdays 5 ozs. of cooked meat and ½lb. of potatoes. On Mondays, Wednesdays and Fridays the ration was 1½ pints of soup, with 14 ozs. of suet or rice pudding for the men and 12 ozs. for the women: while on Saturdays they had 1½ pints of soup and no pudding. For supper the men had 8 ozs. and the women and children 7 ozs. of bread on each day. On four days this supper ration was accompanied by 2 ozs. of cheese—on the other three days by 1½ pints of broth, men, women and children being served alike on these items. The only alleviations of this monotonous and inadequate provision were that old people over 60 could have 1 oz. of tea, 7 ozs. of butter and 8 ozs. of sugar instead of the breakfast gruel. Children under 9 were "to be dieted at discretion," whatever that implied, and the sick were to be dieted "as directed by the medical officer." *White's Directory* of 1859 mentions that the workhouse had accommodation for about fifty paupers, Mr. James Bridger being Clerk to the Guardians of the Poor, and Mr. Benjamin and Mrs. Elizabeth Bridger being respectively master and matron of the workhouse. The Headley Workhouse continued until 1870. After that date paupers from Headley went to Alton Workhouse.

In spite of poverty, Headley prided itself on its health record. In the Headley Church Registers there is a quotation in 1773 from a newspaper: "In Headley Parish are 700 inhabitants as computed accurately in February, 1771," and the newspaper calculated the annual death rate in Headley as 1 in 54, as compared with 1 in 30 in Norwich, 1 in 18 in London, 1 in 22 in Rome, 1 in 19 in Berlin, and 1 in 50 in Madeira.

Chapter 2

The Headley Enclosure—1859

So far we have been thinking only of the small but ancient hamlet of Grayshott round Bulls Farm, together with isolated small farms and squatters' cottages in Whitmore and Stoney Bottoms. The site of the modern village had remained for centuries quite undeveloped on common land of the manor. Until this land ceased to be common land and came into private ownership the modern development was impossible.

By the middle of the 18th century improved methods of agriculture and the desire of many landlords to introduce these more efficient and financially profitable improvements led to the passing of a very large number of private Acts of Parliament, each dealing with the enclosure of an individual parish or group of parishes, in order to do away with the conservatism of the open field system, to amalgamate the scattered holdings of the larger landholders, and to take in desirable parts of the common land. This was the second great wave of enclosures, the first taking place in the Tudor period. The whole process of this second wave and its effects on rural life were described by the Hammonds in The Village Labourer. But the method of promoting separate private Acts was slow and costly, and eventually the landlord-dominated Parliament passed General Enclosure Acts so that parishes up and down the country could be scheduled for enclosure.

In 1846 one of these General Enclosure Acts had been passed under which, in their Annual General Report of January 1849, the Inclosure Commissioners recommended enclosure for a number of parishes, of which Headley was one. In consequence an Annual Enclosure Act was passed in March 1849, of which the preamble is as follows:

"Whereas the Inclosure Commissioners for England and Wales have in pursuance of an Act passed in the Ninth Year of the Reign of Her present Majesty instituted an Act to facilitate the Inclosure and Improvements of Commons and Lands held in common, the Exchange of Lands, and the Division of intermixed Lands, to provide Remedies for defective or incompleted Executions and for the non-execution of the Powers of the general and local Inclosure Acts; and to provide for the Revival of such Powers in certain cases, issued Provisional Orders for and concerning the several proposed Inclosures mentioned in the Schedule to this Act, and have, in the Annual General Report of their Proceedings, certified their Opinion that such Inclosures would be expedient; but the same cannot be proceeded with without the Authority of Parliament: Be it enacted by the Queen's Most Excellent Majesty by and with the Advice and Consent of the Lords Spiritual and Temporal and Commons in this present Parliament assembled and by the

Authority of the same, That the said several proposed Inclosures mentioned in the Schedule be proceeded with."

The Schedule to the Act listed 22 places for enclosure in 15 counties widely scattered through the country.

In their Annual Report the Inclosure Commissioners said that the date of application for the Headley enclosure was 24th February 1848, and that it was for the enclosure of Headley Common and other lands in the parish of Headley containing over 1,667 acres of "waste of manor." They recorded the following opinion: "We consider this proposed enclosure expedient, on the ground that by draining and cultivation, a considerable portion of the land may be rendered very productive, and useful employment, of which the labouring population stand in need, afforded to them."

The Assistant Commissioner had held an Inquiry in April 1848, the Commissioners had issued the Provisional Order for the Headley enclosure on 18th September 1848, and reported that consents to the Provisional Order had been received by 16th December 1848. Their report provided that, in the case of the Headley enclosure, 4 acres of land should be allotted for "exercise and recreation" and 40 acres for "allotments for the labouring poor."

And so the Act of 1849 was passed.

The County Record Office at Winchester has a copy of the Headley Enclosure Award. The first valuer appointed by the Commissioners was John Dowe, who was sacked in 1851 for neglect of duty and replaced by Edward Hewett, a land surveyor of Winchfield.

Some of the land, including some on the site of the present village, was sold in 1851 to meet the costs of the Inclosure Commissioners. These are shown in a map and catalogue given to Grayshott Parish Council in 1928 by Mr. G. L. C. Warren of Standford. Lot 1, of about 75 acres which lay on the south side of Headley Road between Ruffit Lane and Grayshott House, was sold for £137. Of this Lot, Mr. Warren's grandfather had noted in the catalogue: "I should say this is a great bargain, tho' the situation is adjoining a nest of rather rough customers called the Hindhead Gang, but I should apprehend no mischief from them as I have always found them civil and well-behaved. There is, I hear, an excellent spring of water on the property." This note is a reflection of the character for lawlessness which the district then possessed. Lot 2 was the land immediately east of Lot 1, on the south side of Headley Road between Ruffit Lane and the Fiveways corner. It amounted to over 58 acres and fetched £76, which caused Mr. Warren to note: "This of course must be equally cheap." Lot 3 was part of the triangle of land between the Headley, Crossways and Boundary Roads. On the catalogue Mr. Warren wrote, "High, dry, sandy ground I think, but cheap." It amounted to over 28 acres and was bought for £64: perhaps we can agree with Mr. Warren's assessment when we realise that this became the very heart of the village. The average price of these three Lots was about £1.14.0. per acre, though in Lot 3 the average price was £2.5.8. per acre.

In 1859 the enclosure was completed. Among people to whom awards were made were:-

Henry Fullick who paid £4.19.0. for over an acre in Stoney Bottom;
William Lawrence who paid £130 for about 20 acres in Whitmore Bottom;

James Baker of Frensham Hall who gave £140 for some 80 acres;
Charles Andrewes of Farnham who paid £220 for about 32 acres.

The discrepancies in price are probably accounted for by previous use and development of the land or otherwise. The lands bought by James Baker and Charles Andrewes changed hands at steadily increasing prices in succeeding years.

As we have seen, some land was set aside for recreation and for allotments. The public footpaths were noted and safeguarded, including Hill Road and the path through Stoney Bottom to Waggoners Wells.

No doubt it was the conversion of Grayshott's "Waste of manor" into private ownership, together with the opening of a railway service between Haslemere and London in 1859, and the growing reputation of the Hindhead district as a health-giving resort, that made possible the development of the modern village and rendered it eventually inevitable that Grayshott should split away from its parent parish of Headley.

Chapter 3

The Beginnings of the Modern Village, 1859–1900

The enclosure made the modern village possible. That it quite quickly grew into an organised village with a community life of its own is due, in the main, to the work of a few of its early wealthy inhabitants who possessed a strong public spirit.

Grayshott is a late example of a village growing under the influence of a benevolent autocracy represented, though not exclusively, by the I'Ansons, the Whitakers and the Lyndons. Writing in 1899, George Bernard Shaw could refer to the work of rescuing the people of Grayshott from "the barbarism of twenty years ago," even though he could have wished that the neighbourhood had developed under the stricter feudal control of a Duke of Bedford or a Duke of Devonshire in order that the "miserable eruption of ugly little brick houses" might have been prevented.

To the families mentioned above, Grayshott owes its early institutions — the Parish Church, the village school, the Village Hall, the Fire Brigade, and even its public house.

In 1861 Mr. Edward I'Anson bought Grayshott Park Estate, part of Lot 1 of the sale of 1851 referred to in the last Chapter. A family tradition credits Mr. I'Anson with having ridden on horseback from Clapham to Grayshott to view the land. He built a house called "Heather Lodge," which was later bought by Mr. Vertue, a Roman Catholic, who re-named it "The Court." In his days and those of his widow it became the centre of the local Roman Catholic community and is now the Convent of the Cenacle. At the time of Mr. I'Anson's purchase, as Thomas Wright wrote in his book *Hindhead*, published in 1898, Grayshott consisted of "some scattered huts" and two of three substantial houses, including Grayshott House and Grayshott Hall. When Mr. I'Anson started to build in 1862 he was warned, Wright says, "that he would not succeed in completing it, or in living there, the few cottagers of the hamlet bearing the character of being lawless folk who would never allow a stranger to settle among them. The predecessors of the squatters were runagates — persons who had fled from justice, and in the dense woodland they skulk like the badger or the fox." But, as Wright acknowledges, Mr. I'Anson not only succeeded in building "Heather Lodge," but he and his family lived peaceably there, eventually moving to "Pinewood."

That the whole district of Hindhead was wild and lawless becomes vividly evident in a story of probably the middle of the century, told in *Frensham Then and Now* (Baker and Minchin: published 1938):

"As to the buildings called "The Hut," now known to us as the Huts Hotel, it is safe to say that they constituted one of the oldest habitations on Hindhead, comprising a little inn of a very primitive type, with a brewery

27

attached. The brewery, now dismantled, was in action as recently as 1870, John Elliston being the last to brew ale there. His successor, the late Benjamin Chandler, started the first motor-bus service from Hindhead and Grayshott to Haslemere ... it is equally certain that up to the middle of the last century many of the squatters who sparsely inhabited the Hindhead valleys ... eked out a hand-to-mouth existence by sheep stealing and highway robbery. They were frequented too by fugitives from justice, from whose depredations nothing in the immediate vicinity was safe.

My father used often to tell the story of how he once narrowly escaped being robbed and maltreated ... He was sent to an important cattle fair at Haslemere to sell some cattle — the business done, he started on his return journey, but calling at Frensham Hall on his way and leaving his horse there, the afternoon was far advanced before he resumed it.

'At this time' — so my father told the tale — 'the commons were unenclosed, and large numbers of forest ponies, cattle and deer grazed on the unenclosed wastes of the Manors. No defined road existed, and my way from Frensham Hall to Simmondstone was by a track crossing the Portsmouth Road near High Pitfold, traversing the centre of Wagner's Wells Bottom, emerging thence near where Grayshott Hall now stands, and so leading on to Barford and Simmondstone.

It was now dusk. Immediately on entering Wagner's Wells Bottom, I passed a drove of ponies lying down in the fern, and had only proceeded a few hundred yards when I heard a shrill whistle from my rear. Startled by the sound, the ponies I had just passed came galloping down on me. At once I realised that I had been marked down at the Fair. As they overtook me I managed to grasp one of them by his mane and neck and ran beside him. Almost immediately I saw figures emerging from the high furze bushes which grew densely in the narrowest part of the valley. But with the ponies all round me I broke through them safely, and reached Simmondstone sound in limb and pocket. I learnt afterwards that the gang who waylaid me were from Blackdown, over the Sussex border, that I had been shadowed at the Fair, and had been heard to say that I was taking the money to Simmondstone that night, instead of cutting short my journey at Frensham Hall. It was the custom of the Blackdown Gang to work Hindhead, whilst Hindhead went further afield."

In an Appendix to the same book there is the following account of the apprehension caused to Frensham people by the Hindhead Gang:

"It[†], who am now well over the allotted span, can remember when a boy being told by my Grandmother tales of the goings-on of that rough Hindhead Gang who were so noted for sheep stealing and highway robbery. I still have a staff which was regularly carried by my Grandfather when he went out after dark. I myself remember tales of these rough gangs going round and smashing up threshing drums, as they were very embittered against these inventions, thinking they would do away with their winter's work. These old drums were but small affairs driven by

† *Written by William E Legg, a builder of Greatham, and grandson of Edward Harding of Frensham.*

28

horse gear. Old Mrs. Sturt kept a shop at the crossroads opposite Earle's Farm [at Frensham]. On very rough, windy nights they were afraid to go to bed. Sometimes old Mrs. Sturt would rush across the road in the morning and say, 'Oh, Harriet, they have been again; they have taken our cheese, butter and everything; it is that Hindhead Gang and they have cleared us right out'."

Again, in 1867, when Tennyson took a lease of Grayshott Farm, now Grayshott Hall, he wrote to Francis Palgrave that he had been warned about the local inhabitants. Nevertheless his stay was a success.

The first postal delivery to Grayshott started in 1864. The post was brought on horseback from Bramshott to Mr. I'Anson's house, where people called for their letters. In later years the mail came to Grayshott from Shottermill.

In the 1870s there was a small village shop kept by Mr. Henry Robinson at "Mount Cottage" – this was later bought by Mr. I'Anson and Mr. Robinson moved in 1877 into Crossways Road (then Hindhead Road) in what was called Upper Grayshott and built a shop there, which then became the place of call for letters and itself became the Post Office in 1887. It remained in the hands of Mr. Robinson and then of his widow, Mrs. Hannah or "Granny" Robinson for many years. It is now a cleaner's shop.

We have seen in the previous Chapter that land rapidly changed ownership after the enclosure. In September, 1879, Henry Brake, Estate Agent and Surveyor of Farnborough, issued a plan showing for sale practically the whole site of the modern village, bounded by Headley Road, Hill Road, and Stoney Bottom Road (then Haslemere Road) and bisected by Crossways Road. This area was divided into neat freehold plots of about 20 ft. frontage on to the roads and of about 200 ft. in depth at £6.10.0. per plot. On the plan some plots with frontage on to Stoney Bottom Road were marked as already in the ownership of Messrs. Heather, Allen, Leuchars, Pocock, Freyd and White, and of Dr. Plympton. Mr. Heather was a well-known local bootmaker, Mr. White became a baker at Grayshott in the shop now known as Flair, and Mr. Leuchars owned what is now Apley House. The plan gives no other indication of owners or purchasers, but the offer for sale of this area marks, no doubt, an important stage in the development of the village.

The Whitaker family came to Grayshott in 1884 when Mr. Joseph Whitaker bought Grayshott Hall, which was largely re-built two years later by his son, Mr. A. Ingham Whitaker (see next Chapter). Mr. Ingham Whitaker and his wife were generous benefactors to the developing village for many years, and succeeding Chapters will carry many references to them. About ten years later Dr. Arnold Lyndon and his wife, Charlotte, came to Windwhistle House and entered enthusiastically into local affairs and in helping to mould the early development of the village.

During the last two decades of the century the permanent population of Grayshott was rapidly increasing. Estimated at about 100 in 1872, thirty years later at the census of 1901 there were 143 habitable houses and a population of 666. This permanent population was considerably augmented by many summer visitors, because, apart from its natural beauty, the Hindhead district had a great reputation as a health resort ever since Professor John Tyndall, who built a house at Hindhead in 1883 and lived there until his death in 1893, had extolled the purity of its air as equalling that of the Swiss Alps. Tyndall was a noted mountaineer.

Many years later, in 1935, Sir Frederick Pollock in his *For My Grandson* remembered Tyndall as a genial man and "one of Huxley's fellowship" who "loved Hindhead for its solitude and spaciousness (qualities which had made Cobbett call it the most accursed spot that God ever made) but he did not reflect that to dilate in print on the beauties of an undeveloped site is to invite the speculative builders. One must go further afield nowadays to find anything like what the Hindhead region was in Queen Victoria's days."

Tyndall, who resented the threat to his solitude, constructed an enormous heather-thatched screen around his grounds to protect his privacy. This screen survived him by some years, being destroyed in a storm in 1901. He himself had died tragically through taking an overdose of chloral in mistake for magnesia. His name is perpetuated in properties to the south of the Hindhead cross-roads, on the north side of the road from Haslemere.

By 1891 the increase in population had made it necessary to build a temporary church of corrugated iron (now at Liphook), but within a very few years this had become inadequate and it was resolved to build a permanent church.

The Grayshott people were distinct from their distant neighbours at Headley, not only by physical separation, but also in character. At Grayshott the residents consisted of shop-keepers, employees of a growing building firm, and well-to-do residents and their servants, not to mention boarding-house keepers. They were more "progressive" than their neighbours and did not share the predominantly agricultural pursuits and interests of the Headley folk. In these circumstances the movement for the creation of a separate parish was bound to grow rapidly. It achieved success in the opening years of the next century.

This Chapter represents an attempt to give a brief and factual survey of the events between the enclosure and the end of the century. Later Chapters will deal with individual topics during that period. Meanwhile it may be of interest to sketch village life in the last decade of the century.

The local paper was then *The Haslemere and Hindhead Gazette*, whose first issue came out on 16th September 1896, and which was amalgamated in June 1897 with *The Weekly Herald* of Farnham — as *The Haslemere and Hindhead Herald*. Some advertisements in these early issues make interesting reading and give an indication of the increasing pace of development. In 1896, Messrs. Pannell of Haslemere and Grayshott advertised as follows:–

Men's Nailed Boots: 3/11 to 12/6

Repairs:	Soled Only	Heeled Only	Soled and Heeled
Men	2/- to 2/9	8d to 1/-	3/6 to 4/-
Small boys	1/9 to 2/3	6d to 8d	2/9 to 3/3

In the same year another advertisement read:–

Contractor: Mr. E. H. Chapman

Superintendent of Joinery Department: Mr. Oliver Chapman

Properties for Sale and to Let.

(Mr. Oliver Chapman later became Postmaster and Church Organist, while Mr. E. H. Chapman's business developed into Messrs. Chapman, Lowry and Puttick).

Advertisements of the same year included two estate agents well-known for many years—Reginald C. S. Evenett and C. Bridger and Son. In 1898 advertisements appeared of the Grayshott and Hindhead Sanitary Laundry "to conduct all its working operations in a perfectly sanitary way, and this, too, without sacrificing efficiency." This laundry was conducted for many years in premises adjoining the village school, and has only quite recently been converted into a pottery. The proprietor in 1898 was a Mr. P. B. Brain.

In the Grayshott and District Magazine in March 1898, the following tradesmen were advertising:-

W. G. Chapman, Stationer, Post Office:
"variety of Goods suitable for Presents, including Hymn Books, Prayer Books, Bibles, etc."
(That Post Office is now the Sports shop in Crossways Road).[†]
J. A. Prince, Baker and Confectioner. Mr. Prince's original shop was in Crossways Road, then later in Headley Road, these later premises still being a baker's shop.
W. G. Deas, Family Grocer:
"Agents for Fremlin Brothers, Maidstone Beers, and Royal Exchange Fire and Life Assurance; Patent Medicines, etc."
H. Mitchell, Family Butcher:
"Purveyor of English meat only."
(This shop is still a butcher's shop in Headley Road).
Pannell's Boot Establishments, Haslemere and Grayshott:
"the best repairing houses in the district."
(This was in Crossways Road).
E. Coxhead, General Ironmonger; This firm became the modern Messrs. Coxhead and Welch and was in the same premises as at present.
A. J. Moore, Grayshott Mews, Livery and Bait Stables:
"open and closed carriages for hire."

In the next year Mr. B. Chandler of the Royal Huts, Hindhead, had also started Livery and Bait Stables at Grayshott: "Landaus, Broughams, Victoria, etc. on Hire. Horses and Carriages Jobbed by the month or year."

Only a few years earlier, as the late Mrs. George Cane remembered, the chief means of communication with the outside world for ordinary folk was Stephen Boxall's cart. He had a very large black horse and his cart acted as hearse for funerals at Headley, there being no churchyard at Grayshott. The coffin rested in the cart, with any mourners unable to walk to Headley sitting on the rails of the cart. Stephen Boxall (an ancient Headley and Grayshott family name) was also a broomsquire and a hawker of whortleberries as far afield as Guildford. Another well-known Grayshott broomsquire was Body Hill in Hill Road in an old brick cottage, afterwards pulled down and re-built as "Lowlands." An old and faded photograph of about 1880 shows him and his wife, Nancy, at the door of the low cottage—he with a low round brimmed hat, a smock and leather armguard for the left arm, she in a long

[†] *This was where Flora Thompson worked 1898-1901. The building was demolished in 1986 and replaced by 'Pendarvis House'*

31

black dress with apron and shawl. Other well-known broomsquires were the Beltons of Stoney Bottom and Waggoners Wells and the Mooreys of Stoney Bottom.

In 1899, T. Puttick and Sons of Headley Road were advertising as House Decorators. They joined with Mr. Chapman to form Messrs. Chapman and Puttick (later Messrs. Chapman, Lowry and Puttick). Another well-known trader of those days and for long after was B. C. Hoy, Fishmonger and Poulterer of Headley Road: "Fresh Fish every morning."

Queen Victoria's Diamond Jubilee caused some anxiety. A Committee, of which Mr. Edgar Leuchars and Sir Frederick Pollock were members, was set up to arrange for a celebration bonfire. The apparent need for careful organisation arose from the recollection that the Golden Jubilee bonfire of 1887 had led to an extensive common fire. This anxiety about the continual risk of common fires had led in March, 1897, to the formation of an Association for the Prevention of Heath Fires, of which the Joint Secretaries were Mr. Leuchars of Grayshott and Mr. S. Marshall Bulley of Westdown. The Association would seek an amendment to the existing law enabling the magistrates to detect offenders and bring them to trial. What success the Association had does not appear. Nor do we know whether the Jubilee bonfire was a success, but we do know that the village children were taken in Mr. Whitaker's farm wagons to a treat at Headley, each child receiving a Jubilee mug.

There is ample evidence of a vigorous beginning of organised social life in the village. In 1897 a Band of Mercy (which inculcated in children kindness to animals) had already been formed, and Grant Allen (the novelist) lectured to it on "Spiders," Rev. J. M. Jeakes operating the magic lantern. Two years later George Bernard Shaw lectured "discursively" on "Animals" to the same body, which flourished for many years and held an annual show of horses, ponies, traps and pets. Again we read of Technical Classes in 1897 which led to the issue of certificates to some who attended, and of the formation of a local Lodge of the Manchester Unity of Oddfellows by the efforts of Rev. J. M. Jeakes and Aneurin Williams, M.P. (he lived in Tower Road). This Lodge was active for many years, and only comparatively recently was amalgamated with a Lodge at Haslemere. Also in 1897, Dr. Lyndon was running St. John's Ambulance Classes, the Grayshott Choral Society was starting its second season, a Church Lads' Brigade was formed, and an entertainment at the Working Men's Club (not the present building but a temporary building in Headley Road) included three one-act plays.

On New Year's Day, 1898, a "Social Evening" was organised by Mrs. Lyndon in the Working Men's Club. These Social Evenings became an annual feature, eagerly looked forward to, of village life for many years. After 1902 they were held in the Village Hall, usually on the last day of the old year and the first day of the new year, and achieved a real mix of social classes.

In 1898 the Choral Society gave a performance of Farmer's Oratorio "Christ and His Soldiers," under the conductorship of Mr. Eyre, organist of the Crystal Palace. He gave a number of concerts in the village, usually in aid of St. Luke's Building and Endowment Fund. We also hear of further entertainment at the Working Men's Club, consisting of a farce, "Domestic Economy," musical items and four tableaux. In the next year there was a Day School Treat given at Grayshott Hall by Mrs. Whitaker, and a Sunday School

Treat given by Miss I'Anson. These also were annually recurring highlights for the children for many years.

It is easy to recognise the rapid, vigorous development of the village in the closing years of the century, and the growth of a village society which would soon render inevitable the attainment of separate corporate organisation.

If, in imagination, we could stand in the centre of Grayshott, say, in early 1898, the scene would be far different from what it is to-day. The following reconstruction, which claims neither completeness nor absolute accuracy, is based on notes written by the late Mrs. George Cane, supplemented by the memories of the late Mr. Tom Johnson and others. Along the Headley and Crossways Roads some development had taken place, but, compared with to-day, there were large gaps still filled with the woods and heath of the old "waste of manor": photographs of the time show both roads as poorly surfaced and shaded at frequent intervals by trees, mostly fir.

In those days St. Luke's Church had not been built and its site was an expanse of fir trees and brushwood owned by Miss I'Anson, though there was a small temporary church of corrugated iron near where the present church toolshed stands. Opposite the site of the future church Mr. Edgar Leuchars had recently built Apley House. The present village green was then a small, rough, rather scruffy field surrounded by a tall unkempt holly hedge. Here for a number of years a small fair made infrequent appearances. This field had recently been purchased by Alton brewers with a view to erecting a public-house. On the opposite side of Headley Road the present Children's Recreation Ground was still a piece of waste land.

Up the Headley Road on the left-hand side of the road there were no houses until, just before Avenue Road, there was a small house occupied by Mr. Oakley, and then Alfred Wells' forge and smithy which occupied the site of the present Grayshott Garage. The smithy was set well back from the road, and here "Alfy," a great consumer of pints of beer, plied his trade in a splendid shower of sparks and a wealth of language, often profane. On the land in front of the smithy a "cheapjack" called Nixon held periodic sales of his goods. A little further along there was a small stone cottage inhabited by Mr. and Mrs. George Cane. It had been previously occupied by a Mr. and Mrs. Hale who built a larger-house with cement walls, which they called "The Oaks," later "Village House." This house and its large grounds have disappeared in recent years, to be replaced by "The Square." Further along, still on the same side, was a cottage where Mr. Jack Sandall, a carrier, operated somewhat spasmodically, and it was said that on his journeys between Grayshott and Haslemere he had difficulty in passing the Royal Huts Inn. Mr. Sandall's cottage was on the site now occupied by "Headley House." Just beyond this cottage Dr. Plympton had recently built "Hurstmere," now converted into flats. He was a London surgeon and a pioneer in early X-ray apparatus.

Looking up Headley Road from the Five Ways cross-roads, on the right-hand side of the road, just beyond the present Children's Recreation Ground, two shops had already been built on a site previously occupied by a small wooden house where Mr. and Mrs. "Dumpy" Winchester lived — he was a

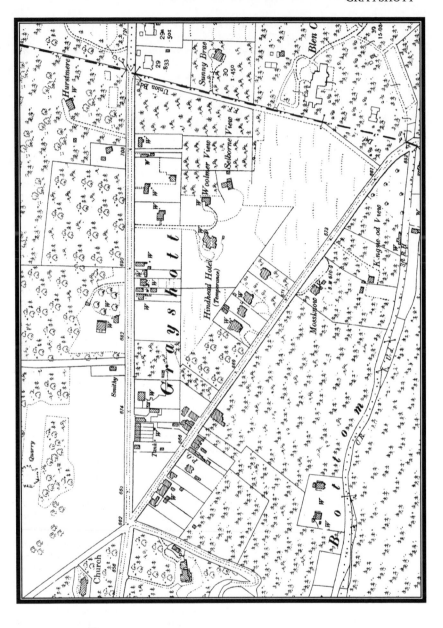

Centre of
Grayshott
circa 1895

great digger of wells before the days of a public water supply. In one of those shops, now "Gaynews," Mr. and Mrs. Frost had a stationery and barber's business. For many years Mr. Frost fulfilled a sanitary purpose in collecting and disposing of "night soil." Then came "Hindhead Terrace," a range of four shops, two housing Mr. and Mrs. Cornish's grocery and drapery businesses, then a sweet shop kept by Mrs Hart, and finally Mr. Sayers' butcher's shop. Just past these shops, and behind where the present International Stores now stand, was Mr. Moore's, "Grayshott Mews," livery and bait stables. There was at the entrance to the yard a temporary building used as the Working Men's Club. This Club subsequently moved to its present premises in Hill Road. Above this again was "Wayside," recently demolished, then occupied by a curate of Bramshott who was the first resident clergyman in the village. Beyond "Wayside" were the three cottages still standing there. Further along, after a gap, were two shops, one of which (the present wool shop) was the chemist's shop of Mr. Gane Inge who also had a shop at Haslemere, and the other Mr. Charlwood's saddler's and boot business (now the Tuck Box). Then there was another gap until Mr. Mitchell's butcher's shop (now Hill's). Beyond Mr. Mitchell's shop were two cottages, where Mr. Benham's and Mr. Mattin's shops now stand, and behind them, in premises now used as a builder's yard and offices, were Mr. Ben Chandler's livery and bait stables, in what was then called Smith's Yard. Beyond these cottages were Mr. Coxhead's ironmongery business — one of the few premises to have carried on the same trade in Grayshott continuously, and Mr. Hoy's fish shop (now Mr. Burden's). There was nothing beyond these shops, except two small cottages, until just before The Avenue, where Mr. and Mrs. J. Fry lived in an old house on the site of the present Rardley Motors premises. Mrs. Cane remembered them as a "very religious" couple. "How often I had called on them to find them with a candle reading the Bible and eating kippers for their tea. And, too, how often he told me that as he passed the Royal Huts homeward bound he had to run past as the Devil tempted him so hard to go inside."

Beyond The Avenue there were three or four houses built by a Mr. Bevis, and Mr. Barnes' house and workshop — still there, but in different ownership. There was a small boot repair shop where the British Legion now have their Headquarters. The land on which the Village Hall and Fire Station now stand was then quite undeveloped. There were a few houses along The Avenue which had been built by a Mr. Barrett.

If we follow Crossways Road from Five Ways towards Pook's Hill, on the right-hand side was a small house built by a Mr. Cover, long since demolished and replaced by three shops. Next to this Mr. Pannell of Haslemere kept a boot shop — in recent years it reverted to the same business under Mr. Tickner until his removal to the shop at the corner of Hill Road. Next again was "Granny" Robinson's little general shop, and at that time the post office, with some adjoining cottage property. An old wooden cottage stood where are now Messrs. Barker's and Murphy's shops. Jubilee Lane and Jubilee Cottages, built by direct labour by their owners, were in existence. Immediately beyond Jubilee Lane was Mr. Walter Chapman's house, which later became the Post Office and which is now a sports shop. Then came "Grayshott Terrace," a range of three shops, the first of which was Mr. Prince's bakery, now Mr. Ford's shop, then Mr. Munday's greengrocery shop, soon to be occupied by Mr. Johnson, the hairdresser, when Mr. Munday moved to Headley Road. The last shop in the Terrace was an "off licence" kept by Mr Upex, and later for many years by Mr. Milton. The premises recently occupied by the "Continental" greengrocers had also been built. They were then Mr. Deas' grocer's shop and dwelling house. Beyond the shops, on the same side, "Windwhistle" and "Ensleigh" had both been built: the Lyndons were occupying the former and Miss Agnes Weston the latter. Between "Ensleigh" and Hill Gate, standing well down the slope, was an old cottage which has been converted into a dwelling and studio by Mr. and Mrs. F. Seyd. At the top of the reverse slope of Pook's Hill there was a small stone-cottage built, no doubt, by squatter's right at the beginning of the nineteenth century. This cottage has been attractively extended in recent years.

On the other side of Crossways Road, coming from Five Ways, there was "Victoria Terrace" a range of small shops, two of which—and ultimately four—were occupied by Madame Warr† before she later moved into new premises in the Headley Road (now Peter Mattin's and Augusta Rolfe's). One of her shops was a stationers and book shop. The present shop at the far end of that range is a later addition. A very few years later than the period we are now describing the land on which it stands became the entrance to Mr. Lewis' coal yard—he occupied a shop, with a watchmaker, Mr. Owen, as his neighbour in an adjoining shop, both shops having been converted from a villa. They were combined in more recent years into an antique shop. Then came Mr. Chapman's builder's yard. A few of the older residences further along the road—"Rake," "Heathside," and "Kings Mead"—had also been built, but just before Boundary Road is reached there was a wild corner of heather and gorse traversed by a rough path leaving Crossways Road and joining Boundary Road almost opposite St. Edmund's School, then a private residence named "Blencathra." This corner is now being developed.

A little further afield there were squatters' and other cottages in Hill Road and in Stoney Bottom and Whitmore Bottom, some of those in Stoney Bottom having the reputation of being used in former days for smugglers' traffic. In Stoney Bottom there was also an iron building which had been built as an Institute on I'Anson land. This was later transferred to School Road to the site now occupied by the nurse's cottage. There it was used as a Band Hut. Still later it became the Scout Hut. In more recent years it was again moved on to the Playing Fields for use as a storage shed, and here it remains to finish out its days.

The village school had been started, but opposite to it all the land now occupied by Council and other housing was a wild copse, delightful to play in after school. The laundry (now the pottery) had already been built by Miss I'Anson as a means of providing employment for local girls. In Whitmore Vale Road, where there are now houses opposite the church land, there was then a rough field, called Ward's Field, separated from the road by a tall hedge.

There are also a few interesting contemporary descriptions of Grayshott at the end of the century. Thomas Wright, in his book *Hindhead* published in 1898, wrote:

---

† *Referred to as Madam Lillywhite by Flora Thompson in 'Heatherley'*

"A bye-road [i.e. the Pitfold Hollow Road from Shottermill] brought us to Grayshott, which consists of a street of new spruce looking shops situated near a spot where five roads meet, and a number of handsome private residences and palatial lodging houses dotted about in the remains of a forest of glorious larches and Scotch pines. Hind Head, of which Grayshott is only a part, is now one of the most fashionable health resorts within forty miles of London.

Grayshott looks like a doll's village, not so much because of the size of the houses, but because of their quaintness. The upper storeys are covered with lozenge shaped bright red tiles, made at Haslemere. It has a temporary look, and there is the feeling that one could upset it like a village built with a pack of cards. The tiles, which the damp, south-west winds render necessary, are secured to walls built not of brick but of wood covered with felt. The houses are all new, having been erected during the last five or six years. Numbers of persons of distinction reside or have resided at or near Hind Head — famous poets, scientists, novelists, sculptors, journalists, painters. The "oraculous doctors" never tire of recommending life-giving Hind Head."

In 1862, when Mr. I'Anson decided to build a house at Grayshott, he was warned that he would not succeed in completing it, or in living there, the few cottagers of the hamlet bearing the character of lawless folk who would never allow a stranger to settle among them. The predecessors of the squatters were runagates — persons who had fled from justice, and in the dense woodlands they skulked like the badger or the fox. The place was a rural Alsatia. However, the house was not only begun, but finished, and Mr. I'Anson and his family took up their abode in it. The praiseworthy ambition then seized his eldest daughter, the present Miss I'Anson, to civilise and lift up the degraded outcasts among whom her lot was cast. The task was no light one. It took a considerable time before the cottagers could be convinced that in visiting them she had no ulterior object. She started a Sunday School, but few could be enticed into it. However, the opposition of the parents disappeared "and the children brought their little empty heads to be filled up."

There were two schools of thought about working men building their houses through their own labour. On 14th October 1896, the following letter, signed "One of the Worms," was published in *The Haslemere and Hindhead Gazette*:

"Can you advise in law how to stop the following nuisance: or if it can be stopped? Two labouring men are building a mud house. They do the main part of the work after they have done their ordinary day's work and on Sundays. Sometimes at about ten o'clock at night a hammering begins and lasts up to one o'clock in the morning and then there is no sleep for the wicked or the good."

This letter eventually produced a reply, signed "Cement Concrete," on 20th January 1897:

"I have been and looked at the so-called mud house that the 'Worm' refers to in his complaint, and to my surprise I find it built very substantially with stone and cement concrete. Now Sir, the 'Worm' speaks of two labouring men building this so-called mud house; he is quite right in this — they are labouring men and I think it is credit to them, for they are setting many of their class a good example in providing a place of shelter instead of spending every penny in waste."

The early slightly haphazard development of Grayshott evidently offended George Bernard Shaw's aesthetic sense, for in a letter published in the local paper on 11th March 1899 — and which will be quoted much more fully in a later Chapter, he said:

"For my part, I heartily wish Grayshott had arisen under feudal management. Does Mr. Anderson Welles suppose that if Hindhead had been part of the Bedford or Devonshire estates that miserable eruption of ugly little brick boxes, varied by something that looks like the cast-off cabin of a condemned excursion steamer, which has turned one of the prettiest village sites in England into the beginnings of a Hoxton slum, would have been allowed to depreciate, as it soon will, all the property within eyeshot and noseshot of it?"

This, then, was what Grayshott looked like in the closing years of the nineteenth century, and these were impressions of it and fears for its future development. It is fortunate that the lay-out of the roads forced development into a relatively compact pattern, and that during the next few years the public spirit and forethought of some of the residents ensured that the nub of the village around the Five Roads crossway should be provided with green and pleasant open spaces.

Chapter 4

Grayshott Hall

Grayshott Hall was originally Grayshott Farm and was, no doubt, one of the small farms in the early Grayshott hamlet. In the early 19th century Grayshott Farm was known as Triggs Farm, the tenant farmer being of that name. Somewhat later the tenant was Stephen Langford. About the middle of the century a man named Robinson was the tenant. His son was Henry Robinson, who married Hannah Moore of Purchase Farm, and who has already been mentioned as owning the first shop in the modern Grayshott. The late Mr. B. P. Chapman recalled that Henry Robinson left Grayshott Farm because he refused to pay a higher rent demanded by the landlord. He then "squatted" at Mount Cottage.

Grayshott Farm is described in the 1860s as a two-storeyed stone and brick house with small low rooms, windows with diamond panes and doors with bolts and bars. The tenant was then Edmund Cornewall who rented rooms to Alfred Tennyson for over a year from the Spring of 1867. In September 1866, Tennyson and his wife came to Haslemere to visit Mrs. Gilchrist. Tennyson, being tired of the tourists at Farringford and seeking solitude, was looking for land on which to build. At one time he seems to have thought of building on the Devil's Jumps. However, as a base for exploring the district, he chose Grayshott Farm. Mrs. Gilchrist wrote: "The Tennysons ... have taken a house at Grayshott, Grayshott Farm, that will serve their purpose for a time, enabling them to judge how the climate suits and to be on the watch for any land that might be on the market. I have undertaken to see to the furnishing of the house."

Later, in March 1867, she reported: "I am still busy furnishing Grayshott and hence, of course, very frequent letters from Mrs. Tennyson. I hope it will turn out well—but there are drawbacks. I think they are eager to try it and will come as soon as it is ready." On 23rd March 1867, Tennyson himself wrote to Francis Palgrave: "In this farm house I have taken rooms for ourselves and three servants for two years. We go there in about a week. I do not give the name of the place because I wish it to be kept secret. I am not flying from the cockneys here to tumble among the cockneys there, though some of my friends tell me it will be so and that there will be cockneys of a worse kind. But I do not believe them, for the house is quite solitary and five miles from town and village." Later, he wrote: "We arrived at Grayshott Farm where we spent the early summer. In the woods the nightingales were singing; the anemones were out in all the woods." It is said that he was inspired at Waggoners Wells to write the tiny poem:

> "Flower in the crannied wall,
> I pluck you out of the crannies:—
> Hold you here, root and all, in my hand.

Little flower—but if I could understand
What you are, root and all, and all in all,
I should know what God and man is."

Tennyson's object of finding a suitable site on which to build was fulfilled on Blackdown. In June 1867, Mrs. Tennyson described their first expedition from Grayshott to the Aldworth site: "We went there in an odd procession, Lionel on a donkey with a lady's saddle, I driving in the basket carriage, the rest walking. The wheels spun round on the axles without touching ground in some of the deep ruts, and the carriage had to be lifted over, William leading the pony carefully. At last we reached the charming ledge on the heathery down. This looks over an immense view bounded by the South Downs to the south, by Leith Hill on the north. Copse wood surrounds the ledge and the hill protects it from the north-west. The foxglove was in full bloom." Tennyson bought the site and the building of Aldworth House proceeded. By August 1869, he was resident there. Of their stay at Grayshott Farm, Mrs. Tennyson wrote that "notwithstanding the drawbacks of Grayshott" it was a great success. "Tennyson likes the country and the people and enjoys his walks."

In 1868 the Wishanger Estate was sold by the Miller family to John Rowan Phillips, "with the Manor or Lordship of Wishanger." In the sale catalogue it was described as comprising 1,794 acres, the cultivated land being divided into five principal holdings, Upper Hearn Farm, Lower Hearn Farm, Wishanger or Manor Farm, Land of Nod Farm, and Grayshott Hall Farm. It extended from "Hind Head Common" on the north to Frensham Pond on the south and was extolled as "presenting to the Capitalist the opportunity of acquiring a large and compact tract of land in a beautiful country, ... while its many enjoyable features ... and its dry Sandy Soil would suggest the erection of a Mansion." That the country was still relatively wild is indicated by the statement that the shooting included Blackcock, Wild Fowl, Partridges and Pheasants. The land tax on the whole estate was £52.18.6. per annum and the tithe charges £214.4.11. Full possession was offered at Michaelmas Day, 1869.

It is perhaps worth noting that on a section of the Ordnance map bound with the catalogue the name is spelled Greyshott. For many years this was the more usual spelling, but there seems little doubt that Grayshott is the older and correct form—the medieval and Tudor family and place names clearly indicate this.

Grayshott Hall Farm was a substantially built residence of stone and slate which had recently had additions. On the ground floor were a drawing room and a dining room, each 16 ft. square, a breakfast room, kitchen, dairy, knife room and pantry. On the first floor four front and four back bedrooms, a linen closet and a water closet. The outbuildings included a two-stall stable and coach house, a barn, stabling for four horses, a cow shed of wood and thatch, and a coal house. The land attached to the farm, mainly arable, amounted to over 224 acres. The present tenant, Mr. Edmund Cornewall, paid a rent of £120 per annum and held tenancy up to Michaelmas 1869.

The Land of Nod Farm was tenanted by Mr. Henry Powell at £25 per annum until Michaelmas 1869, and had over 76 acres of land. The house, with parlour, sitting room, kitchen, wash house and three bedrooms, had been recently erected of stone and slate. There was stabling for four horses, a cowshed, a thrashing room, a hog house and loft, and a root house.

The other properties attached to the Grayshott Hall estate included Purchase Farm of about 27 acres in Whitmore Bottom, whose tenant was John Moore at £15.6.0. per annum; a two-roomed cottage with four acres under the tenancy of Alfred Harding at £6 per annum; another two-roomed cottage with one acre whose tenant—P. Rook—paid £4 per annum; a three-roomed cottage in Whitmore Bottom with seven acres under the tenancy of George Crawt at £6 per annum; and a garden and pasture of two acres held by R. Cane at £2.6.0. per annum.

In 1882 the estate was again for sale and it is clear that Grayshott Hall Farm had, indeed, become Grayshott Hall, since the estate is described in the catalogue as "an important and valuable freehold property, known as the Grayshott Hall and Wishanger Estate, comprising a newly-erected moderate sized mansion called 'Grayshott Hall' ... "with the Manor or Lordship of Wishanger." Bound into the catalogue are two charming water colours, one of Grayshott Hall, the other of Wishanger Lodge. The area to be sold was nearly 1,900 acres, and there were still Blackcock, Wild Fowl, Partridges and Pheasants for the shooting, while "a large quantity of Store Trout can always be obtained from the Stream which flows through Whitmore Bottom from Hind Head to Frensham Pond." Moreover, "Rabbits breed in very large numbers every year, and there is now a large supply." It is also noted that "The Coach which runs from London to Portsmouth calls at the 'Royal Huts' about 1½ miles from Grayshott Hall." This coach must have been near the end of its activities as London and Portsmouth had been for some time linked by rail.

The Hall was described as a "picturesque modern residence or small mansion ... well and substantially erected within the past five years of Bargate stone (quarried on the Estate) with Red Brick Dressings and Weather Tiles and Strong Red Tiled Roofs." There were a good carriage drive, a large level lawn, a "capital walled kitchen garden," and a "large ornamental Entrance Lodge." The house itself had an ornamental outer porch leading to the inner lobby from which, through a glazed screen, there was access to the entrance hall and corridor. On the ground floor the main apartments were a breakfast room, a large dining room with a serving window from the kitchen, a drawing room (24'6" by 23'2") with a bay window, and a conservatory at the end of the corridor. On the first floor there were a billiard room with french windows opening on to a balcony, seven principal and secondary bedrooms, three dressing rooms, a linen closet and a housemaid's closet with sink and water supply. The second floor had two principal bedrooms, a dressing room, and a large water tank. There were also notable examples of domestic progress—both the hall and the first floor having a water closet, and the latter a bathroom also.

The domestic offices were extensive, including a store room, larder, boot cupboard, wine closet, dairy, butler's pantry with hot and cold water, kitchen, servants' hall, beer cellar, scullery, knife house, coal cellar and ash house. In the basement were ale and wine cellars. But, alas, those were not egalitarian days: the domestic staff had to make do with earth closets.

In the stable yard at the rear of the house were—all recently built of stone and brick—a coach house for six carriages with a loft, stabling for five horses, a large loose box with four stalls and a loft, a harness room with a man's bedroom adjoining, and a bottle shed.

Then, again to the rear of the stable yard, there were the farm buildings: a stable for six cart horses, two open sheds, two loose boxes, a dog kennel, a piggery, a four-bay cart shed with loft, a large open cart shed and a wood house.

The land and gardens amounted to five acres. Water was pumped to the house from Whitmore Bottom by a ram. In those days the rough road from Grayshott to Headley passed close by the front of Grayshott Hall. Mr. Whitaker got permission to close this, dedicating land for the diversion of the road on to its present course in the Grayshott Hall area.

There were subsidiary properties involved in the sale. Bulls Farm was by now divided into two tenements. Some of the names of fields attached to this farm were Kiln Field, Warpole Field and Burnt House Field (now Grayshott Hall Park) and Eel Field (opposite Grayshott Hall). In Whitmore Bottom George and Stephen Crawt were tenants of a "cottage dwelling" with 19 acres of land at £25.10.0. per annum: Daniel Crawt had "a small occupation" of 9 acres at £15 per annum, and John Moore tenanted Purchase Farm at £13 per annum, and 6 acres of arable land at £5 per annum. Purchase Farm itself had 16 acres and was described as a new farm house with four bedrooms, a parlour, a sitting room, kitchen, pantry and wood house, and farm buildings consisting of a cow house, a stable and a two-bay barn.

The whole estate was purchased in 1884 by Mr. Joseph Whitaker, who had large estates in Yorkshire and Palermo, and who was a wine importer. He purchased an estate for each of his three sons, giving Grayshott Hall to Alexander Ingham. In 1886 Mr. A. Ingham Whitaker again largely rebuilt Grayshott Hall and, about twenty years later, added a small tower. In 1895 he married Miss Berthe de Pury, grand-daughter of Edward I'Anson and at that time resident with her parents at Grayshott House. Under him and his wife Grayshott Hall became the source of much of the public spirit which went to the formation of the new Grayshott. Though Mr. Whitaker sold much of the Grayshott Hall Estate in 1921, he continued to live at the Hall until 1928. Many changes of ownership came after Mr. Whitaker left: Sir George Hennessy, Mr. E. P. Jucker, Mr. J. S. Beard, Mr. Rubin and Mr. Stalbow. But Grayshott Hall itself did not alter very much. It no longer played such a prominent part in village life as it had done. This was, no doubt, partly owing to social changes. It is now a Health Centre, and hence has a social significance — but with an entirely different emphasis.

Chapter 5

George Bernard Shaw
at Grayshott

When Shaw came to Grayshott it had not yet become a separate parish, either civil or ecclesiastical. He lived on the Surrey side of the county boundary but within the area of Surrey which became part of the ecclesiastical parish. He had already achieved fame as dramatic critic for the *Saturday Review* (1895–1897), for his attacks on the prevalent naturalistic drama and for his ardent support of plays dealing with urgent social themes. He was, for instance, an enthusiastic supporter of Ibsen.

Shaw's first contact with the district was in 1898, while he was on his honeymoon. Lord Beveridge, the author of the great Beveridge Report on which was framed the modern British National Insurance Scheme, in his book, *India Called Them* (1947), related how his father, Henry Beveridge, a Bengal Civil Servant, bought the house called "Pitfold" — he partially rebuilt it in 1899. He and his wife settled there largely because Mrs. Beveridge's sister was Mrs. James Mowatt, who had been living at "Kingswood Firs," Grayshott, for some years. In the summer of 1898 there arrived at "Pitfold" a Miss Payne Townsend to arrange a tenancy, as the Beveridges were going away for a time. The tenancy was agreed, when Miss Townsend announced that she was about to be married to Shaw and that they would spend their honeymoon there. The Shaws and Beveridges became close friends. Shaw presented to Mrs. Beveridge a copy of his *The Perfect Wagnerite* which he inscribed to "perhaps the cleverest lady and the wickedest in her opinions that I have ever met." In spite of this friendship their opinions sometimes clashed, and Henry Beveridge "once expressed his views of Mr. Bernard Shaw's *Candida* by burning the volume containing it upon the lawn."

"Kingswood Firs," mentioned in the previous paragraph, is one of the older houses in Grayshott. In 1884 James Mowatt bought from two different owners the Kingswood Firs estate which lay between Kingswood Lane and Stoney Bottom and extended from the ford at Waggoners Wells to Crossways Road from its junction with the Stoney Bottom lane to the A3 road. The whole estate, which was then in the Parish of Bramshott, was purchased for less than £6,000. It was mainly wood and heath land with some grazing in the area near Waggoners Wells. At the western end Mr. Mowatt built a large house in 1887 which he called "Kingswood Firs." He was predeceased by his wife and family and bequeathed the whole estate to Gonville and Caius College, Cambridge, to which it passed on his death in 1931. The College sold about 8 acres at the Waggoners Wells end to the National Trust in 1934 and the remainder to Mr. Fordham in 1937, who sold it in the same year to Mr. Nixon. After another change of ownership the large house and surrounding land was purchased in 1948 by the present owner, Mr. L. Franks, and was re-named

"Hunter's Moon." The house was built in red brick with a tiled roof and with partially tile-hung walls—a common feature of the older Grayshott houses. It is, perhaps, even more attractive inside than out. The whole of the original Kingswood Firs estate was transferred in 1932 from the Parish of Bramshott to that of Grayshott.

Later in 1898 Shaw rented a house "Blencathra," now St. Edmund's School, and resided there until he left the district in 1900 owing to its remoteness from London. The nearest railway station is about three miles away at Haslemere, whence the railway journey is about 40 miles to London. At "Blencathra," Shaw wrote the third act of *Caesar and Cleopatra* while recovering from a badly sprained ankle. His indisposition and progress were regularly noted in *Fabian News*:

January, 1899:   a report that he was slowly getting better and that he had just published *The Perfect Wagnerite*.

February, 1899: he was somewhat worse but had been lecturing in Haslemere.

March, 1899:   Shaw had written to say that his numerous sympathisers were wasting their emotions: "In spite of alarmist paragraphs in Fabian News and elsewhere his condition is not in the least serious. He is still a cripple and continues to sprain his ankle from time to time; but his general health is good. He lectured last month at Haslemere and delivered a vigorous oration at the Peace Meeting at Hindhead."

July, 1899:   a report that Shaw "seems at last on the way towards recovery."

August, 1899:   "Bernard Shaw is well. We have the pleasure to state that no more bulletins will be issued."

In February 1899, Shaw, as reported in the local paper, had written a characteristic letter to a Scottish newspaper whose London correspondent had stated that Shaw's condition continued "to be far from satisfactory, and since the end of last week he has grown slightly worse. The malady is of a particularly insidious character." Shaw wrote, "For the sake of precision will you allow me to add that the change in my condition at the end of last week began and ended with a sprained ankle, but not, I trust, a specially 'insidious' one. Scotland may, therefore, dry its tears: there is still hope for yours truly, G. Bernard Shaw."

According to Minute Books of Hindhead Congregational Church, the Peace Meeting referred to in Fabian News in March 1899 was held in the Hindhead Congregational Hall on 28th January, and had been arranged in support of W. T. Stead's Crusade in favour of the Czar's Rescript and the ensuing European Conference on National Armaments. The Minutes record that "the meeting was well attended and was freely noticed by the Daily Papers in consequence of the presence and support of well-known literary men. Dr. Conan Doyle (in the chair) and Mr. Bernard Shaw were the principal speakers. Amongst others were the Revs. Professor G. A. Christie of Hampstead, G. H. Aitkin of Haslemere, and J. M. Jeakes of Grayshott (then Curate-in-charge, later first Vicar of Grayshott).

On 17th February 1899, Shaw lectured in the Haslemere Educational Hall at the opening of a new session of the Microscopic and Natural History Society and took as his subject, "Why I am a Socialist." The local paper reported as follows:

"The Educational Hall, as well as the adjoining ante-room, was simply packed on Friday evening last, when Mr. G. Bernard Shaw opened the new session with a lecture on 'Why I am a Socialist.' The subject was not more attractive than the speaker, who is well-known as an entertaining lecturer; hence the large attendance. The lecture was a bright one, and contained smart flashes of wit, which kept the audience in good spirits. The discussion was, however, far and away the best part of the meeting, and, if it were only for the smart passage of arms between the Rector and Mr. Shaw, and the lecturer's delicious sarcasm on Mr. Blount's speech, it would have been well worth the trouble of attending.

Mr. Bernard Shaw said he had undertaken to explain why he was a Socialist, but on finding himself confronted with so numerous and distinguished an audience, he felt he was not egotistical enough to talk about himself for an hour, and that it would be more modest and becoming on his part to explain to them why they should be Socialists. (Laughter). He wished them to understand clearly at the outset that he advocated a Socialist policy precisely as any one of them might advocate a Conservative or Liberal policy, by the ordinary constitutional methods, and the ordinary Parliamentary means. Far from desiring to add to the divisions already existing in politics by a new party, he hoped that Socialism in Parliament would have the effect of re-uniting many people who were now taking sides against one another in the name of Liberal and Conservative principles which they did not understand. (Laughter). Mr. Shaw then gave a sketch of the historical changes from the medieval social order, with its strict regulation of duties and status, to the modern order, brought about by the downfall of the medieval system, under the influence of Liberal ideas. Bad as our social condition was—and it was very bad indeed—it had been established under an honest belief that if Government refrained from interfering with industry, and protected property acquired under perfect freedom of contract, the result would be that men would prosper in proportion to their industry and integrity, and that the division between rich and poor would be a righteous difference between the hardworking and the idle, the thrifty and the wasteful, the temperate and the drunken. The lecturer proceeded to demonstrate by an elaborate series of examples that no such result could possibly follow. Taking such varied cases as those of the crossing sweeper, the shopkeeper, the banker, the wheat importer, the farmer, the mine owner, etc., he showed that, although all of these might be equally industrious, the widest disparity might be produced in their gains by differences in the circumstances under which they exercised their industry. The fortunate possessors of the best soils, minerals, and urban sites must become enormously rich without contributing any labour, and their monopoly, at first a monopoly of land only, must produce a monopoly of capital, which the lecturer defined as spare money, and consequently of social opportunities and education. The resultant inequality in the distribution of the national wealth did not tend to disappear as we progressed; on the contrary, our industrial progress made it worse, and must continue to do so unless checked by Socialism. But the remedy had begun. The people, through their Parish, District and County Councils, their Municipal Corporations, and School Boards, were taking industry out of the hands of private speculators, and acquiring land which was ultimately paid for by taxation; and taxation was being thrown more and more on the five hundred millions which were annually paid away as rent and dividends in this country.

In reply to a question, Mr. Shaw said, speaking of traders, that some kind of competition must be submitted to, and if it was not from a public body raising its capital from the rates, it was from great companies with huge working capitals derived from the rich classes. By competition with the latter many traders had already been crushed out of existence. The small shopman would be infinitely better off employed as a salesman than in business on his own account. When the County Councils and other authorities took over the trade, more hands would have to be employed, for the simple reason that the present remorseless sweating would not be allowed to continue."

The report of the discussion which followed Shaw's lecture is as follows:

"The Rev. G. H. Aitkin observed how very interesting and amusing Mr. Shaw had been. He did not, however, think that he had quite tackled the subject. He had not that evening told them so much as what a Socialist was. What he [the Rector] took Socialism to mean was that the whole of the means of production must be in the hands of the people. He was not a Socialist because he did not think they were near enough to the goal aimed at. The road Socialism was taking he felt to be the right one, but in pointing it out Mr. Shaw had not been giving them Socialism, but Progressivism. It was no use at present preaching Socialism; all the inherent selfishness was against them, and that would take a lifetime to extinguish. The question of character must be taken into account. Reform was needed, but, above all, it must be a reformation of character. With regard to Mr. Shaw's remarks about saving, if a man spent all his money as he earned it, where would he be when the pinch came? Why, he would become absolutely dependent on the poor law; or, what was worse, on private charity. True friends of the workman told him that, things being what they were, he would be doing the best for himself and his if he put something by out of his earnings. Money was power, and what he felt was that, by saving, a man was preparing to hold up his head, and at the same time, strengthening the backbone in his character, and preparing himself for a higher place in the world. He thanked Mr. Shaw, who had made them think of those things and care for them. Tolstoi and Ruskin put Socialism before the world in its true sense, and he hoped that those who took an interest in it would carefully read and study it. Let them be Christians first, and then, perhaps, nothing else would be necessary.

Mr. C. E. McLaren, M.P., observed that Socialism, in the sense of dividing the money, seemed to be the popular idea. They did not, any of them, except Mr. Shaw, care to be called Socialists, but they could not deny that things were pointing in that direction. They felt that the power municipalities were assuming was one step; another was that joint stock companies were working industrial concerns. Fifty years ago capitalists took 50 per cent; now they were fortunate if they obtained five. Wages were five times as high, and workmen might save, and if they didn't the money went into the pockets of the village shopkeepers. Then there was the tendency of Parliament to tax the rich instead of the poor. The whole of the taxation of the country, with the exception of that on beer and tobacco, which working people need not have unless they wished to, was upon the rich classes, in the form of income tax, death duties and commercial taxation. It seemed to him that if Socialism proceeded on those lines no one need be afraid of it. He could not help feeling that they must look for salvation on somewhat similar lines as that treated that evening. Mr. Godfrey Blount maintained that the world should proceed on the lines upon which it was at present moving. No system of Socialism could eradicate the feeling of individuality. England was great, and that greatness had been built up by individuality, to which he believed Socialism to be opposed.

The Rev. E. R. Hawker referred to Socialism as found in the country of Australia. The Government had acquired land on the river Murray, and passed an Act of Parliament by which all who went to those settlements were given a piece of land, had the implements of agriculture, and provisions for a certain time given free. The results of the labour and the profits were also equally divided. He had no doubt that Mr. Shaw would think that an equitable arrangement. But a large number of the people would not work, and the industrious ones lived to bear the burden of those who were indolent. He thought it very questionable if the idea of the State taking over all enterprise was a correct one. He thought the illustration he had given was the only one in the history of the world, and that had proved a failure.

Mr. Shaw, alluding to Mr. Hawker's remark that he would probably agree with the experiment tried in Australia, would say it was the most idiotic ever invented, and as for the supposition that it had never been tried anywhere else, why, it was tried by some fool or other every seven years. It was exactly as if the Government came to them and said, 'Here are the rails, the sleepers, and the tools; there is a railway to be made; go and make it.' It was not of the slightest use expecting the thing to be made in such a manner. Socialism was not responsible for such idiotic procedure as that. Mr. Blount had harped a great deal on individuality. He had said that he (the speaker) was crushing individuality. Take the case of the working of a train. Individuality would not be of much use there. It would not be of much use to put up signals where they looked the prettiest, Men must act in unison with one another. The leaders of mankind, admirals, statesmen and generals, had all performed their greatest feats when acting conjointly with other persons. Mr. Blount seemed to think Socialism would eradicate individuality, but he need have no fear. Mr. McLaren had said nothing he need disagree with; and then he came to Mr. Aitkin. Now he took it that that gentleman had been a trifle hard on him. While others had been talking about the millennium he had been particularly careful not to advance a single theory. Nothing he had mentioned was anything but facts. Mr. Aitkin had pointed out that he did not advocate theories, like Mr. Burrows; the explanation was that he did not agree with that gentleman. ('Hear, hear' from the Rector). Mr. Burrows belonged to the Social Democratic Federation; he belonged to the Fabian Society. With regard to the Rector's statement that money was power, how much power was £100? It would not make a despot or Napoleon of anyone. Four thousand sixpences! How long would it take a working man to save that sum? Of how much would he have to deprive his children? And when he had saved it would the money be power? Such a statement people felt to be uttered with reckless thought, and without realisation of what it meant. The question of Socialism was more an economic one than anything else. A beginning must be made with healthy surroundings. The poor, moreover, must not depend upon the upper classes for their education. They had to form their character for themselves."

Shaw's Haslemere lecture created quite a flurry of correspondence in the local paper. In the issue of 4th March 1899, a Mr. Anderson Wells of Grayshott wrote a robust letter:

"I have been vainly hoping, before trespassing on your space, that now Hindhead has become a veritable literary Ghetto, some of our shining lights in the world of literature might have entered the lists against the recent attempts to diffuse a Socialist propaganda in the neighbourhood. Our Parish Magazine, I see, just touches on both sides of the question in a few remarks, which, however, are hardly convincing.

One of the high priests of the Socialist Cult has, with considerable persistence, been telling us that he is a Socialist, being apparently impressed with the idea that it is to others as supremely an interesting fact as it evidently is to himself

In inculcating the why and wherefore, I fail, however — when his sentences are stripped of the 'exuberance of their own verbosity' — to discover a true definition of what Socialism really means.

Succinctly, Socialism spells slavery; individualism, freedom. The latter breeds men of the stamp who have made the British Empire what it is; the former, slaves with none of the absorbing interests of ambition, their lives reduced (from loss of individuality) to the dull monotony of sheep browsing in a clover field.

Individual liberty and personal property were the very first fruits of the overthrow of the Socialistic tendency of feudalism; and to anyone who has a love for the aspirations and traditions of all that is best in the British nation, are the very best salt of life. If the first principles of liberty are abandoned, all that justifies existence dies.

The end of the nineteenth century is, thank goodness, too enlightened, too honestly progressive, to give up the right for men to do as they like, as long as they do not, in the best sense of the word, encroach on the freedom of others.

What but the interference with individual freedom, and a general programme of grand-motherly legislation, has been the cause of the reduction of the great Liberal party to a moribund monster, grovelling in the mud, with no brain left for organisation, or belly for a fight?

Life to most is a battle (except to those living in luxury on 'the unearned increment'), and to win the prizes of the fight we must strive for ourselves individually, trust to ourselves individually.

Apparently one of the great fetishes of the Socialist creed is the common property hotch-pot, with a special desire to compulsorily draw the harmless, but necessary, landlord into the stew!

This is euphemistically called 'the nationalisation of land' by our Socialist friends; in more vigorous Saxon, 'robbery under arms.' Thief, though, is perhaps after all a word basely invented by those selfish persons who have a misguided and immoral hankering after private ownership.

Quite apart from the natural shrinking of honest minds from the immorality of the spoilation of one particular class for the supposed benefit of the many, anyone with a smattering of economics must stand aghast at the absolutely Gargantuan appetite for company promotion with which these gentry are endowed; an appetite which would even appal a Hooley! What would the leviathan National Joint Stock Land Company's shares stand at if the nation had kindly forcibly bought out the landowners when wheat was 60s. a quarter?

The value of the land of this country must be so stupendous that the mind can hardly grasp the sums involved, and one could foresee the possibility of the national exchequer being so involved that British credit would no longer be measured by 2½ per cent.

And why fix on the poor landowner always to compulsorily 'buy out'? Why not nationalise beef and beer? Has not Mr. Whitaker the same right to resent the moving of his landmarks as Mr. Mitchell the forcible distribution of his joints of meat? There is, after all, much in the crude idea that a Socialist is one who dislikes to see anyone with the leisure to have his hands in his own pockets, and has a violent longing himself to have his in other people's.

However, the haranguing of a mob by cranks never did much harm yet. As in the old jackdaw legend, 'No one was ever a penny the worse.' If they only won't mix up ethics and economics, we can forgive much, for then they are about as dangerous to society as a serpent on the spree.

I have diffidently touched on no more than the very fringe of the subject of Socialism and individualism in as few words as possible, in the hope that some of those whose shoe-latchets I am unworthy to unloose may follow after me, and may contribute more fully and less crudely to the subject."

In the next issue of *The Herald*, Shaw, foregoing any criticism of Mr. Anderson Wells' style, wrote the following amusingly ironical letter:

"The lot of a Socialist on Hindhead is not an easy one. I have come here to get some rest from Socialist propaganda and to recover my broken health. But the inhabitants insist on my lecturing to them, both in Grayshott and Haslemere, and will not hear of any other subject than Socialism. I devotedly cause myself to be carried to both places, ascend the platform on crutches, lie down on two chairs, and feebly do what I am asked to do. And then Mr. Anderson Wells—ungrateful Mr. Anderson Wells—rebukes me in your columns for thrusting my gospel impertinently on a respectable reluctant neighbourhood, and sarcastically asks me whether I think the fact that I am a Socialist 'as supremely interesting to others as it evidently is to myself.' I can only reply that it evidently is about ten times as interesting to everybody in the place—including Mr. Anderson Wells—as to myself. If not, why does he write half a column in the 'Hindhead Herald' about it? He is positively boiling over with it, whereas all I ask is to be let alone. He declares that he is fully occupied with 'the absorbing interests of ambition' and that I am reduced to 'the dull monotony of a sheep browsing in a clover field.' Well, for the moment I ask nothing better. Why will not Mr. Anderson Wells let me browse peaceably, and go on his own ambitious, British, Imperial way? Is it manly, is it Imperial, to wantonly attack a poor disabled sheep who never harmed him?

I will not attempt to defend Socialism against Mr. Anderson Wells, or even to put in a plea for the 'veritable literary Ghetto' consisting of a Canadian and two Irishmen, against whose right to live on Hindhead equally with himself his Imperial instincts so haughtily revolt. But I confess I am curious to know why he should be so very hard on feudalism with the example of Hindhead before his eyes. As far as my observation goes, everything that is decent and orderly and public-spirited in the place is the work of a few ladies and gentlemen who have voluntarily assumed feudal duties towards their poorer neighbours. For example, the whole work of rescuing the people from the barbarism of twenty years ago by founding a school and getting the children into it has been done by a lady, who, on antifeudal principles, might have greatly increased her income by investing for her own benefit the money and personal work she has spent on the education of the people. Everybody in the place gains by her work: the children, the employers for whom they work, and Mr. Anderson Wells himself, who has to depend on the civilisation of the neighbourhood for escaping getting burned out occasionally by what is euphemistically called a 'heath fire.' And yet, at the Parish Council [the Headley Parish Council] election this week, there were Grayshott men—only a few, I am happy to say—who were not ashamed to refuse to vote for this lady on the ground that they 'did not hold with women doing public work' as if she had not for years been doing for them the public work which they were too selfish or too stupid to do for themselves.

Another example. When I first came to this neighbourhood I tried the vicinity of Shottermill [the parish in which Pitfold was], which seems to enjoy to the fullest degree the 'freedom' which, as Mr. Anderson Wells patriotically observes, has made our empire what it is. In fact, every man there was so free to dispose of his house refuse, without any regard to his neighbour's health that the place smelt insufferably; and I moved up the hill to Grayshott, to a house with three gates. One gate had (and has) a stinking pond in the public road just outside it. [This refers to a small stagnant pond which used to exist at the foot of Pooks Hill]. Another opened on a road which was impassable [Boundary Road]. Fortunately the third was on the Portsmouth Road, which, owing to the tyranny of the authorities against which Mr. Wells' freeborn soul revolts, is one of the best roads in the country. The impassable road has just been put into tolerable repair by a few of my neighbours, at their own private expense. Though I am not a feudal baron, I am a Socialist; and I have shared the cost with the others. Mr. Anderson Wells now has the use of that road for himself, his carriage, and his tradesmen, without paying a farthing for it. And the use he makes of it, apparently, is to stride along it with expanding imperialist bosom, and then write to the local newspaper describing me as a person with 'a violent longing to have my hands in other people's pockets.' In doing so he is acting, he says, as a man 'of the stamp who have made the British Empire what it is.' No wonder the British Empire is somewhat unpopular with polite foreigners.

For my own part, I heartily wish Grayshott had arisen under feudal management. Does Mr. Anderson Wells suppose that if Hindhead had been part of the Bedford or Devonshire estates, that miserable eruption of ugly little brick houses, varied by something that looks like the cast-off cabin of a condemned excursion steamer, which has turned one of the prettiest village sites in England into the beginning of a Hoxton slum, would have been allowed to depreciate, as it soon will, all the property within eyeshot and noseshot of it? Not a bit of it; the thing would have been intelligently planned and financed, so as to make the best and prettiest of a big opportunity. What I want to see is the people of Hindhead, through their Parish and District Council, taking the same care of the place as the Duke of Devonshire or the Duke of Bedford would if they had bought the hill as a private speculation. The absence of such intelligent planning and financing is not British freedom, but British anarchy – good, old-fashioned, lazy, idle, short-sighted, penny-wise, pound-foolish, British letting things slide. Mr. Wells may wave the British flag at me, and pretend that he likes to see the air of Hindhead sold by speculators and forestallers to the highest bidders, the view from his windows wantonly disfigured, his neighbour's cesspool draining into his well, a filthy pond instead of a lamp in the road to drive into on a dark night, labourers forced to drag six hours' honest work out into nine or ten hours because they can only get 4½d. an hour for it, and nightly fires threatening his house without a fire engine in the village, all in the name of freedom. I will not insult him by affecting to take him seriously. I have no idea of what his politics are; for though the principles he enunciated are unmistakably Anarchistic, his tone about the British Empire is not that usually taken by professed Anarchists. He rages at feudalism like a Whig, at Liberalism like a Tory, and at Socialism like a gentleman in the worst sense of the word. But it is clear that he vaguely supposes that I, a new arrival in the neighbourhood, have come to oppose and disparage his politics, and that he is bound to raise, in your columns, in defiance of me, the amazing cock-a-doodle-do which has just frightened the village from its propriety. Now I confess I have no political bias either for or against him. I care even less for party politics than I do for other popular English sports. But I dislike diphtheria, and ignorance, and poverty, and squalor, and had much rather live on a small income in a place where they did not exist than on a large one in a place where they were the lot of four out of five of my neighbours. If Mr. Anderson Wells is of the same mind, then he need not fear my 'attempts to diffuse a Socialistic propaganda in the neighbourhood.' If not, let him say so, and see how much support he will get outside Bedlam. But of course he will not say so, or think so, either; so why on earth should we quarrel about nothing?"

The lady mentioned in the second paragraph of Shaw's letter was Miss Catherine I'Anson, whose father had founded the Grayshott Church of England primary school in 1871, and who herself largely managed and financed it. "The veritable literary Ghetto" apparently comprised the novelist, Grant Allen (a Canadian) and Shaw and Richard Le Gallienne, the novelist (an Irishman).

Mr. Godfrey Blount of Haslemere joined in the controversy on 18th March with the following letter under the heading *Socialism and Individualism*:

"This discussion, by its confinement to Hindhead, is in danger, I fear, of being lost in the clouds for want of clearer definition. Mr. Bernard Shaw lectured at Haslemere on the same subject, and as your reporter considered that his 'delicious' satire on my remarks was the *pièce de résistance* of that entertainment, perhaps you will allow me to say a few words.

From the nature of your correspondent's argument it is difficult to discover what Socialism or Individualism means. Mr. Shaw diplomatically evaded his advertised title 'Why I am a Socialist,' nor can I find a definition of that creed in the "Daily Chronicle's" account of last Thursday's banquet, which Mr. Shaw's health prevented his attending, but at which the Social Democratic Foundation, as well as the Fabian Society, the Independent Labour Party, and the advanced Radical Party, agreed to sink their differences, and unite in welcoming their foreign comrades, Liebknecht, Jaures and Vandervelde. Vague commonplaces like the Rev. Stewart Headlam's message to the diners, 'Good Luck! Land is the mother, and labour the father of all wealth,' or Mr. Herbert Burrows' 'Socialism stood for the abolition of privilege, and democratic equality before the law, for equal opportunities for all, and for the idea that the highest individual life is not attained by trampling, etc.', cannot surely help the cause by making its objects clearer, and although it is unfair, perhaps, to expect too much distinctness after a banquet at the Holborn (and no one, I am sure, will grudge the Socialists their fling if they can afford it), such sentiments as these are apt to leave the outsider rather in the dark.

Does Socialism mean the actual possession by the State of all the means of production, or, as they put it themselves, the acquisition by everybody of everything for the use of everyone; or does it only describe some people's desire for that state of things? In the latter case a Socialist is only an idealist, and can call himself what he likes; but, in the former case, and until the State builds our houses, clothes our bodies, fills our stomachs, and tells us what we must and what we must not do, he has no right to the term, because we can have no idea what a Socialist is till everybody is, or is forced to become one. In this respect Socialism is inferior to Christianity as a theory of life, because it is quite possible to be a Christian without your neighbour being one too.

Now, Sir, an Individualist, on the other hand, does not necessarily think, as your reporter says I do, that the present state of things is a good one. An Individualist, I take it, only wants to help himself, and occasionally other people, in his own way; and the majority of Individualists have agreed, and try in various ways to prevent his pursuing his hobby to the inconvenience of others. History demonstrates how inadequate many of those ways are, or rather how much cleverer the children of this world are than the children of light; but there is surely all the difference in the world between giving your policeman more power on his beat and inviting him into your house to order your dinner and carve it for you?

Nature is not with Socialism, in spite of Mr. Bernard Shaw. Nature, it seems to me, is for inequality always; for giving the best crossing to the best sweeper; the most money to the one who loves money most; and the greatest happiness to the one who loves it least. All honour to Socialists for their enthusiasm, for their pity and sympathy with the oppressed. Their strength lies in that, and in their protest against modern conditions of labour, which are bad enough to account for any aberration, but their panacea seems to me as impossible and as impracticable as that of the extreme Individualist, the Nihilist, who mistakes a bomb for the Gates of Paradise.

Our times are doubtless diseased, but their worst symptom is our lack of faith in individual honesty of purpose or imagination, and in the substitution of a bloodless constitutional fetish for that human inspiration which is our most sacred possession.

Socialism, as I said, is the political reflection of a mechanical age, which is not only eliminating all individuality from our labour, but all belief that labour can be anything but slavery. What should we gain, however, by a mere change of taskmasters? The human one often has a heart, the official one never. Our bodies have already become machines; Socialists would make machines of our very souls.

Mr. Bernard Shaw takes it for granted that the people of Hindhead, if they were Socialists, would cherish their neighbourhood as a duke his model village. The supposition is quite open to doubt. We at Haslemere have with difficulty escaped the adoption of Socialist building bye-laws, and long, unlovely streets, and you, Sir, would not be allowed to publish my letter if those 'good days coming' of the Socialist Utopia were already here. I still, however, have the honour to remain, Your humble servant."

Mr. Blount, too, had the honour of a reply from Shaw:

"Mr. Godfrey Blount's letter is not one that will distress any Socialist because the spirit in which it was written is not the spirit that comes into conflict with practical Socialism. The fact is, the issues that arise are not between Socialism and individualism, but between alternative methods of supplying public needs. Let me illustrate this by a case in which the same issues have arisen within the sphere of ordinary competitive trade. When railways were first started, the companies simply employed contractors to make the permanent way and build the stations. Then they bought engines, carriages, and trucks, and ran trains. But this involved their paying, not only the actual cost of what they bought, but the profits of the firms from which they bought them. To save these profits, and to effect the economics of centralised production under their own control, they have set up engineering and manufacturing departments of their own; and now they make, not only engines, but canal boats, steel bridges, cranes, hydraulic jacks, capstains, harness, coal scuttles, lamps, and innumerable other things, down to etched glass lavatory windows and artificial limbs for the maimed in the shunting yards; not to mention that they run their own docks, canals, ferries, steamships, and hotels. Mr. Blount will not, I think, contend that the railway companies are violating any principle of Individualism in supplying themselves with everything they want at their own shops in the most economical way.

Now take the same issue as it presents itself to a modern municipality. One town (say London) buys gas from a joint stock company, and pays 3s. per thousand feet, with the risk of being plunged into darkness by a strike among gas-workers receiving the lowest competition wages. Another town (say, Bradford) manufactures its own gas, and supplies it at 2s. 3d. per thousand feet, with the lighting of the streets thrown in for nothing, and constitutional remedies open to discontented gas-workers. Will Mr. Blount contend that it is Bradford's duty to adopt the London plan in the name of individualism; and if he will, is there any chance of the citizens of Bradford agreeing with him for the sake of having their gas bills increased by 33 per cent., and paying an extra rate for street lighting? These are the real issues that are being decided in favour of municipal Socialism in this country, and Mr. Blount will see at a glance that they have put quite out of date the old discussions as to the abstract principles of Individualism and Socialism, with the demand for definitions and all the old academic ceremonies. Whatever Individualism may mean, it certainly does not mean that the English citizen must do nothing for himself, but must get everything done for him at a profit by a contractor or a joint stock company.

I am rather taken aback by Mr. Blount's assertion that 'Socialism is inferior to Christianity as a theory of life, because it is quite possible to be a Christian without your neighbour being one too.' Pray how? I have had to pay my contribution to the expenses of the late massacre of Dervishes in the Soudan, culminating in the digging up and mutilation of the body of the Mahdi. So has Mr. Blount. Have we acted as Christians in doing so? I think not. But we have been forced to do it because our neighbours, including the Dervishes, are not Christians."

About a fortnight earlier than his Haslemere lecture, Shaw had lectured in the Grayshott Clubroom, and the Grayshott and District Magazine for February contained the following account:

"Last and not least among a number of activities mentioned comes Mr. Bernard Shaw's lecture, "Socialism: What it was and what it is." It means either a great desire to hear Mr. Shaw, or a very keen interest in his subject, that the Clubroom was nearly full, and that everyone in it must have travelled over a road which recalled the "very miry slough of despond" in which Bunyan's two pilgrims "wallowed for a time, being grievously bedaubed with dirt." And, indeed, had not Mr. Lowry caused a path of heather and planks to be laid over a portion of the road, the only thing possible would have been an open-air meeting at the corner, a situation which would have been, perhaps, even more after Mr. Shaw's heart.

According to an old story, two men disputed about a shield. One said it was black, the other white. There was truth on both sides, for they had been looking at it from two points of view, and it was black on one side, white on the other.

Remembering this old story we have asked two friends who look at this subject from different points of view, to give us their impressions of the lecture. Here they are; and we heartily thank both our correspondents.

1. *By a Socialist:-* "Those who were present at the institute on Friday evening, January 13th, were rewarded, and let us hope enlightened, by the lecture which Mr. Bernard Shaw gave on Socialism.

   Mr. Shaw is a comparative stranger to Grayshott, but he soon made himself at home with his audience, and if his remarks did not always gain the approbation of his hearers, he never failed to secure their interest.

   Mr. Shaw gave a short sketch of the growth of Socialism in England during the present century. Robert Owen, the chief exponent of Socialism in its early days, was a wealthy manufacturer who endeavoured to put his principles into practice by founding communities to be run on Socialist lines; his example was followed by others, but these communities were sooner or later doomed to failure. Then succeeded a period of revolutionary Socialism, when the poor and oppressed, having no legitimate way of fighting their wrongs, made fruitless attempts to gain their ends by force. We have now reached the stage of constitutional Socialism. The term 'Socialist' is no longer one of reproach, but a vast amount of ignorance still prevails respecting the aims and objects which Socialists have in view. The Socialists of to-day belong chiefly to the middle and upper classes; but it is to the working classes we must look if the present system of competition is to be replaced by co-operation, and Socialism supplant individualism.

   At the close of his address Mr. Shaw invited discussion, and several questions were asked and answers given, which afforded a good deal of amusement. One of his audience was heard to remark rather disconsolately, she had not expected the lecture to be comic. Can Mr. Shaw take a hint, and when he next appears before a Grayshott audience, assume what will assuredly be, to him, a new role—that of being dull as ditch water and dry as dust. May we be there to witness the attempt.

II. *By an Individualist:-* It is not often that one has the opportunity of listening to such fluency of language as that with which Mr. Shaw addressed a Grayshott audience on the most interesting and intricate subject of Socialism, and if indeed it was necessary for the fuller exposition of his views to apply strong, uncomplimentary epithets to those who are endowed with this world's riches, Mr. Shaw's ready humour helped to soften down any irritation thereby caused, and probably most of his hearers, including such as did not agree with him, were very greatly interested, and came away with their minds full of food for reflection.

   It is a matter for congratulation for us that in these days an audience, however composed, is not roused to exasperation at the mere suggestion that those who have hitherto been regarded as good and useful neighbours are only thieves and vagabonds, and that it is able to discriminate between the theoretical and practical value of suchlike terms of opprobrium. Yet it is questionable whether needless ill-will and discontent might not thereby be created in the minds of such as are unable themselves to fully grasp the difficulties of the Social problem, and to whom it would appear that the individuals accused are themselves responsible for all the hardship and misery that undoubtedly exists. Mr. Bernard Shaw in narrating the progress of Socialism told his audience in graphic manner of the futile attempts to establish Socialist communities in the early part of this century, and of the revolutionary methods subsequently adopted in furtherance of the same cause, all which he condemned as useless, pointing out how in these latter days it is possible by legitimate and constitutional means to attempt to remove some of the evils still existing.

It would, no doubt, be interesting to learn from Mr. Shaw what in his opinion would be the state of things when the levelling processes of Socialism should have rendered all luxuries impossible, and how, in the absence of these, employment could be found for everybody in the production only of the simple necessaries of life, without bringing us back to a state which present ideas connect with barbarism rather than civilisation. One would also like to know what advantage, if any, the good and industrious would have over the bad and idle, and whether ability of any description would earn but a short and passing reward, since according to theory no permanent investment of benefit would be allowed to accumulate. Many such questions occur to one's mind, but it is not necessary to agree with Mr. Shaw in all that he said, to feel a keen satisfaction at the thought that, whether it be due to Socialism or not, very much has been done latterly to secure for the labouring classes a more happy and prosperous existence; and if in this respect we are in advance of others, it is to be hoped that the advantages will in due time be extended to the whole of the civilised world, while in our country we may trustfully long for a sure though gradual development.

We must remember, however, that things move but slowly. Broadly speaking, individualism exists and has existed from time immemorial, and might even be said to be indissolubly connected with civilisation; and it remains to be seen in what manner and to what extent it can advantageously be replaced or supplemented by Socialism.

Mr. Bernard Shaw told his audience that they would after hearing him, go away Socialists, and that they would all plan out various schemes of Socialism, which would all be equally bad and impracticable. We should set ourselves a less fruitless task and confer more benefit, if individually we follow the precepts of One before whom Robert Owen's name fades into insignificance, and while accepting the circumstances in which we are placed with the duties attaching thereto, adopt as our Socialism the full and conscientious performance of that Commandment which bids us do unto others as we would that they should do unto us."

The issue of *The Herald* of 25th March 1899 illustrated that Shaw was taking a very active part in local interests. On 14th March he had attended a lecture by Rev. R. C. Fillingham, Vicar of Hexton, on "Disestablishment" [i.e. of the Anglican Church] and his contribution to the discussion brought forth the following note:

"As an outcome of his speech at the lecture on 'Disestablishment' on Monday in last week, Mr. George Bernard Shaw has been accused of taking the side of the Ritualists. He has explained his true position in a long letter, published in *The Echo* of Tuesday, which concluded:- "My alleged 'defence of the motives of the Ritualists' had nothing to do with their doctrines. Mr. Fillingham, in a very lively description of the origin of the Church Defence Organisation, laid himself open, perhaps accidentally, to the construction that he believed and alleged the motives of his opponents to be altogether sordid. Now, no Socialist who knows what Socialism owes to the Guild of St. Matthew, the Christian Social Union, and the side of the clerical life which found expression in these bodies, could possibly sit silent at a public meeting where Ritualistic clergymen were accused of caring for nothing but their pockets. If a Ritualistic lecturer had brought the same charge against clergymen, Established or otherwise, of the type of Dr. Clifford, I should publicly have assured him, as I assured Mr. Fillingham, that he was gravely underrating his opponents. Any attempt to identify the line of cleavage between High and Low Church with the line of cleavage between high and low personal motives is as false to the facts as it is shocking to every brave man's sense of honour in controversy. I do not accuse Mr. Fillingham of having intentionally gone so far; on the contrary, in one of the best passages of his address he expressly set character above creed; but as the subsequent debate was not quite up to the level of that passage, the protest he elicited needs no apology."

Shaw had also in the same week been present at a lecture on photography under the title, "Sunlight and Shadow," in which the lecturer had made a somewhat slighting remark on the taking of snapshots. *The Herald* notes: "Mr. G. Bernard Shaw, in a humorous speech, proposed a vote of thanks to the lecturer. Referring to snap-shotting, he said that, in his opinion, it required a good deal of patience; and if the lecturer thought otherwise he would be pleased to lend him his Kodak."

What ferment Shaw and his opinions caused among the adults of Grayshott and a wider district is seen from the above. That he had also an impact upon the minds of children is shown by the following note in the *Grayshott and District Magazine* of July 1899:

"The following extract from a child's letter gives an account of the last Band lecture [i.e. a lecture to the Grayshott Branch of the Band of Mercy, a children's organisation promoting kindness to animals] which was given on May 26th by Mr. Bernard Shaw; "We children had, for once, a glorious but brief triumph, when Mr. Shaw came and talked to the Band, for he entirely took our side. 'We were better than our parents,' he said, 'we were not naturally cruel as grown-ups were'; 'we were always to answer back and insist on having reasons.' Then he went on to talk about a great deal, we agreed afterwards, we could not understand, and which seemed to us to have nothing to do with a Band of Mercy, so I won't trouble you with it. By the way he did say something else important, 'that meat-eaters were cruel,' and I do certainly feel a little uneasy since I have met him, and I am very carefully eating as much vegetable food as possible, though everyone knows any sensible and reasonable child who isn't a prig detests all greens as much as possible (except peas, by the way!) and that if we had our way we should live on jam-tarts, meringues, and meat. Milk puddings are abominable things, and every grown-up says they are wholesome, as if that were a good reason. Now, when Mr. Shaw told us to ask for reasons, we are quite sure he did not mean we were to have doctors' reasons, for they always give us horrid medicines, and we cannot answer back to them because we only have them when we are so feeble we can scarcely speak! By the way, that was perhaps why Dr. Lyndon was rather cross with Mr. Shaw. But Miss Moir [the headmistress of a girls' private school] made us feel a little uneasy at believing all Mr. Shaw said, for it is true, as she said, he did not know anything about children, so that is rather a weak point in him. I don't think father would go to a man who said he knew nothing about horses, and ask him to be his groom. But then Mr. Shaw had the last word. I heard Miss Moir say this was rather hard, because he was like a 'cork' and an 'eel.' Why, I can't imagine. But he completely smashed her by saying he would not bother his head about naughty children — (I forgot to tell, she would like to see him with a dozen naughty ones) — he would run away from them and leave them alone. So we cheered him heartily, and we have been as disobedient as possible since; only, as we are not used to it, it is a little difficult. But our Latin Exercise Book says, 'omne initium est difficile'; and then we can always blame him if anyone says we are wrong. It just occurs to me, if we are naturally good, how is it that grown-ups are so cruel? They must all have been children once. When did the cruelty begin?"

In the same year Shaw was one of the founders of the Grayshott Brass Band which, the Grayshott Magazine remarked, "could be a decided acquisition." This continued for some years and regularly performed at the local flower shows, garden parties, Band of Mercy shows and similar events. In a list of the initial subscribers, of whom there were 40 subscribing a total of £40. 17. 6., Shaw appears as giving £10. Whether this Band ever scaled musical heights may be doubted, since, when four years later land was given for the purpose of building a Village Hall, the donor inserted, perhaps in order to protect owners of adjacent property, a restrictive covenant prohibiting any 'band practice' on the land. One remembers such stalwarts as Albert Berry and the Halsteads, father and son.

On one occasion Shaw exercised his powerful, and sometimes devastating, gifts of dramatic criticism in this locality. In the summer of 1899 funds were being collected for the building of Haslemere Cottage Hospital [now Haslemere Hospital], and amateur open-air performances of "As You Like It" were given, the first in Haslemere Rectory Garden on 6th July, the second in Sir Frederick Pollock's woods at Hindhead. The latter performance provoked the following letter from Shaw, printed in *The Herald* of 15th July under the title, "As You Don t Like It":

"May I, as a dramatic critic of some experience, be allowed to volunteer a pronouncement on the late open-air performance of "As You Like It" in Sir Frederick Pollock's woods on Hindhead? I need not add any compliments to those which have already been paid to the merits of that achievement. Often as I have seen the play performed by the most accomplished comedians of England and America, I have never before heard such rapturous and unanimous praise lavished by an apparently delighted audience on everybody concerned. I foresee two possible results of this. One is that the performers will at once abandon their present profession and ruin themselves by going on the stage. I have known that happen on less provocation. The other, and the only one I propose to take into account now, is that they will repeat the effort. My dread lest they should do so under the very erroneous impression that their last attempt cannot be improved upon nerves me to venture on a word of criticism. I feel I must disappoint them at the outset by saying nothing about the acting, except that I have seen all the parts worse done at one time or another by professional actors at first-rate London theatres. Let that suffice for such flattery as can be extracted from it in view of the present condition of the English stage. But I must add that I have never seen a more exasperatingly amateurish presentation of the play. What is an amateur actor? In the proper sense of the word he (or she) is an actor who plays for love instead of for money. But in the sense which has been fastened on it by the misdeeds of the amateurs themselves, it means an actor who is not merely a bad actor (plenty of professional actors are that), but one who is bad with the special and unbearable badness produced by imitating the theatre instead of imitating life. The able professional in all the arts tries to conceal the artificiality of the technical processes he is forced to employ. The author tries to avoid being 'literary,' the actor dreads being 'theatrical.' The amateur does exactly the reverse. The more he can denaturalise himself, the more literary he is, the more painty he is, the more theatrical he is, the nearer he feels to success. On the stage he will not speak with his own voice, will not behave with his own manners, will not wear clothes that fit him, will persist in trying to identify himself with the unreal character in the play, instead of giving that poor phantom life by identifying it with his own real self. He is, therefore, often better when he is deliberately imitating his favourite professional actor than when he is trying to disembody himself into what he calls his "conception" of his part. In short, he believes that an actor is one who successfully pretends to be somebody else, like a criminal evading a policeman by means of a disguise. An actor is really one who has cultivated and intensified himself to such a degree that he can persuade audiences to pretend that they see other people embodied in him. Thus acting, in the amateur sense, is the one thing that the skilled actor avoids above all things. And acting, in the skilled actor's sense, is a thing that the amateur would regard as the abnegation of acting.

Whoever grasps this distinction will understand why it is that no fairly presentable performer ever fails as Hamlet or Rosalind. Every man believes himself to be a Hamlet; every woman a Rosalind. Consequently, in playing the parts, they do not "act" in the amateur sense; they try to be their best selves, and generally succeed, whereas in Othello and Lady Macbeth they generally make themselves ridiculous. "As You Like It" was carefully written by an experienced dramatist to make the most of this natural law; consequently a version of "As You Like It," with all the seriously unflattering characters left out, as they were on Hindhead, could not but act itself," even with amateurs. "Thank you for nothing" is not a polite speech; but it is not the business of a critic to be polite. Good manners in him consist in sincerity, not in smooth speech.

And why do I call the representation amateurish when I admit that the play, as cut, carried the actors safely over that pitfall? I will explain. Weary of the theatre and its conventions, its unreal scenes, and false lights, and stuffy air, I went to the Hindhead performance full of pleasant anticipations. "Here," I said to myself, "Rosalind will tread, not on nailed boards, but real mossy soil. Here there will be no footlights and battens, but a real sunlight—no enemy but winter and rough weather. Here the banished duke will really sit under the shade of melancholy boughs, and breathe scented airs high above the sea level. Birds will sing; crickets will chirp; Sir Frederick's woods, not being amateurs, will not pretend to be anything but what they are, and I, consequently will be able to pretend that they are the forest of Arden." Full of these joyous hopes, I hastened to the place of performance, and behold—a cottage piano! My heart sank; I knew that people who would put a piano in the forest of Arden would do anything. I turned with a pang of dread to look for footlights; and there, sure enough, was an imitation "float," ridiculously made of bracken leaves, and white soup plates full of cut roses. Then I knew what I was in for; and the event fulfilled my worst apprehensions. Amiens sang, "Blow, blow" to the piano, the setting being ultra-19th century, in the style of Blumenthal. Orlando's sonnets were represented by sheets of the smartest Bond Street notepaper, with the address and the nearest railway station neatly printed at the top, the page being otherwise virgin. Some of the men's costumes were too absurd for even an opera chorus. Silvius, a personable gentleman who spoke his lines excellently, struggled in vain against the comic effect of a tunic made for a much shorter man. The indigent Corin, who might quite fitly have worn the gaiters and smock which are still to be seen on old agricultural labourers in England, wore a thin Cheapside tunic with two rows of velvet, and, of course, tights. Everybody wore tights. It is impossible to persuade an amateur that he is acting unless he has tights on. It may be obvious to any gamekeeper that no man could possibly face the wear and tear of a forest life and keep his voice, or for the matter of that his life, without good boots, breeches and buckskin. But the amateur, because he has seen this ignored in some silly or impecunious theatre, ignores it in Sir Frederick Pollock's woods, and stands there, like a ghastly travesty of a medieval tailor on strike, making sensible men long for a hearty shower of rain to wash away his folly. Need I add that the foresters' weapons were of the most aggressively theatrical absurdity? The man who killed the deer had providently borrowed an assegai; but all the rest had the familiar tin-headed impostures which pass muster poorly enough by gas light, but which, under the sun of heaven, simply insult the spectator's understanding. The village carpenter and blacksmith would have been glad to turn out a few credible pikes for the sum charged by the costumier for the hire of his stagey arsenal; but no, that would not have looked like the real—theatre! Is it to be wondered at that men thus made ridiculous could not walk the woods like real foresters, and could only stand staring in fascinated desperation at the very persons it was their chief duty to ignore; to wit, the audience?

After all this, it did not need the wanton mutilation of the text to put one out of temper. Even the late Mr. Augustin Daly had more respect for Shakespeare than to cut out the best dialogues of Touchstone, and many of Rosalind's most quaintly pretty lines. It will not bear remembering this version of the play; I find that even after a week it still makes me splenetic, I went to it in the most amiable disposition towards everybody concerned; at the end no prudent person would have trusted me with a thunderbolt. Do me the justice, Mr. Editor, to remark that I am complaining of nothing that can be excused on the ground that the wrong-doers were amateurs. The acting was as good, and in several instances more than as good, as I expected or had any right to expect. If Shakespeare had been present to superintend the rehearsals, and the amateurs could have been persuaded to do what he told them, he could have produced a quite adequate performance with the talent at his disposal. But this is no excuse for faults due to a wilful disregard of sincerity and good sense. Our Hindhead and Haslemere population makes an almost oppressive parade of its devotion to art. Go where I will in the neighbourhood, I cannot escape from Bedford Park architecture, photographs from the early Italian masters, Morris or pseudo-Morris wall papers, and clangorous grand pianos ready for Schumann and Brahms at a moment's notice. My opinion of a good deal of this ready-made art I shall keep to myself until I return to town. But I cannot help asking what is the use of staring at photographs of the figures of Benozzo Gozzoli, if, when it comes to dressing a Shakespeare play, you cannot see that your shabby tunic is several inches too short for you, and your spear as foolish as the baton of an undertaker's mute? What does your knowledge of music come to if you cannot sing in the forest of Arden without a piano banging a modern drawing-room accompaniment on the grass? What is the current fashionable chatter about poetry and Shakespeare worth, when gentlemen who would rather die than walk down Bond Street in my hat, will wear any second-hand misfit in one of Shakespeare's plays? What sort of devotion to Nature is that which tries to make a real wood look like a real stage?

It is time to pause for a reply, Mr. Editor. The best form the reply can possibly take is a repetition of the performance with its follies left out."

Shaw's severe criticism of the production led to correspondence in *The Herald*, one letter being written by the producer and another by Mr. Bernard Hamilton, who also claimed to be a critic, but since Shaw did not answer either, there is little point in quoting them.

We have noticed at some length in this Chapter the considerable part that Shaw for a short time played in the political and cultural life of the developing district of Grayshott and Hindhead. There is, however, another aspect of this development in which he took an active interest—the foundation of the Grayshott public house, The Fox and Pelican, which will be dealt with in a later Chapter.

Chapter 6

Other Literary Associations

In the later years of the 19th century and the early years of the present one the Hindhead district contained quite a colony of literary celebrities. Professor John Tyndall, physicist, mathematician and mountaineer, had built a house at Hindhead in 1883 and had praised the purity of the air as equalling that of the Swiss Alps. The Hindhead of those days was almost entirely undeveloped and in a state of wild beauty. Tyndall described his house as "four-square to all the winds of heaven." His praise of the neighbourhood attracted others and, to his dismay, his beautiful solitude was becoming dotted with large new houses.

Among those who came to Hindhead and Grayshott were Shaw, Conan Doyle, Grant Allen, Richard le Gallienne and many others. The previous Chapter describes Shaw's impact on local thought and prejudice and an earlier one Tennyson's brief sojourn at Grayshott Hall Farm. The present Chapter makes no attempt at literary criticism but picks out a few writers who have played a part in village life.

When ARTHUR CONAN DOYLE arrived at Hindhead he was already well-known as an author: he had already produced some good historical novels and *Sherlock Holmes* and *Memories of Sherlock Holmes*. He came to Hindhead in 1896 for health reasons. His wife suffered from tuberculosis, and it was feared she might have to live abroad. However, Conan Doyle met the novelist, Grant Allen, who had scandalised the Victorian world by publishing *The Woman who Did*, a free-thinking book which dealt frankly with sex problems, and who already lived at Hindhead — at "Moorcraft" and later "Little Croft," where he had been able to keep his own tuberculosis at bay. Hence the coming of the Conan Doyles. Grant Allen died in 1899.

Conan Doyle chose a site at the head of Nutcombe Valley, which a little later was to become part of the ecclesiastical parish of Grayshott. He lived in the Moorlands Hotel (now a Bank Training Centre) from January 1898†, to supervise the building of "Undershaw" into which he moved in the October of that year. He named the house from the hanging grove of trees beneath which the house lay. It looked across a wide valley which he described as "like a scene in a German folk tale." Here he continued his writing with the second series of the Brigadier Gerard stories and further Sherlock Holmes stories which were published as *The Return of Sherlock Holmes*. He volunteered for service in South Africa in the Boer War and later wrote a book on the causes and conduct of that war. His patriotic gesture prompted a local testimonial to him. There were 160 subscribers, including Sir Henry Irving, Professor Williamson and Sir Frederick Pollock. He was presented in March

† *Probably 1897*

1901 with a mahogany writing table, a silver bowl and, of course, an illuminated address.

In January 1899, Conan Doyle had taken the chair at a meeting in the Hindhead Congregational Hall in support of W. T. Stead's campaign in favour of the Czar's Note on National Disarmament and the consequent European Conference on the matter. The Hindhead meeting was well attended and Bernard Shaw made a speech which he later declared had cured Conan Doyle of sentimental pacifism and had left him a raging Jingo.

As part of his patriotic enthusiasm Conan Doyle founded the Undershaw Rifle Club which remained under his direction for two years. Its members wore "broad-brimmed hats turned up at one side with the initials U.R.C." It used a rifle range firing over a distance of 600 yds across the valley. By 1902 there were daughter clubs at Haslemere, Churt, Grayshott, Godalming and Liphook. In May 1903 there was a competition for a silver trophy among 19 clubs from Surrey, Sussex and Hampshire; it was won by the London South Western Railway Club, with Undershaw coming second.

Conan Doyle also took a keen interest in local sporting activities. In a local cricket match in 1903 he assisted Grayshott to beat Linchmere who had been undefeated in four successive seasons. He founded the Undershaw Football Club which played on the Royal Huts field and provided the first organised football in Hindhead. The Rifle and Cricket Clubs made him a great friend of Ben Chandler, the landlord of the Huts, by reason of their common interests. Ben Chandler was the proprietor of the first regular omnibus service between Grayshott and Haslemere via Hindhead, at first a horse-drawn vehicle which necessitated a trace-horse being stationed at the foot of Longdown Hill to assist in pulling the bus up the hill to Hindhead — later a motor-bus.

In August, 1905, when the Anglo-French Entente was newly made, the French Fleet visited Portsmouth and the officers were taken to London by road. When they were asked whom they would like to see, they chose Admiral Sir John Fisher and Sir Arthur Conan Doyle. On their route from Portsmouth to London at four points on the road there were brass bands, exservicemen resplendent in medals drawn up at attention, and — a nice touch — pretty girls throwing nosegays. With true French gallantry the officers stood up in their car shouting "Magnifique!" They were entertained at Undershaw by Conan Doyle under a banner inscribed "Bienvenue," and had refreshments in a marquee on the lawn. Conan Doyle was described as "a portly man with a Napoleon moustache, informally dressed and wearing a very small straw hat." Ladies all in white with leg-of-mutton sleeves thronged among the guests.

Conan Doyle was also one of the first motorists on Hindhead. In 1902 he bought a 10 h.p. Wolseley, smart in dark green with red wheels, which could carry five people, or seven at a pinch. He accepted delivery in Birmingham and drove it to Hindhead. A large crowd gathered to watch him "sitting high placed and begoggled at the vertical column of the steering wheel as the car chugged along the road amid barking dogs." He mounted the verge of the Undershaw drive but managed to right himself. On a later occasion he was not so lucky. He overturned in the drive and was trapped under the car which weighed nearly a ton. Some soldiers levered it up and released him, apparently unhurt. He was obviously one of the more vivid local personalities for some ten years. In 1906 Lady Conan Doyle died and was buried at St.

Luke's Church, Grayshott, as was his son. A year later he re-married and moved to Crowborough where he died in 1930.

FLORA THOMPSON is one of the less well-known, but nevertheless undoubted masters of English prose writing. She wrote three books which were published — *Lark Rise, Over to Candleford and Candleford Green*. These were subsequently published in one volume as *"Lark Rise to Candleford."* She also left an unpublished book, *Heatherley*. Her books are quiet reminiscences and descriptions of the places where she lived and their people — rather in the vein of George Sturt's writing in *The Wheelwright's Shop."*

In 1966 Margaret Lane published her book, *Purely for Pleasure*. It is a collection of articles written by her, which included one on Flora Thompson which had previously been published in the *Cornhill Magazine*. Flora Thompson was the daughter of a stonemason, one of a large and poor family. She left home at 14 to take a post as assistant postmistress at Fringford. Miss Lane in her essay draws largely upon the unpublished *Heatherley* and from it reconstructed Flora Thompson's arrival at Grayshott as assistant postmistress here:

"So in 1897[†] Flora, at twenty, went to work in the little Surrey (sic) village of Grayshott, where she was to remain for three years. She arrived on foot, dressed in a brown beaver hat decorated with two small ostrich tips set upright in front, like a couple of notes of interrogation. The skirt, cut short just to escape contact with the ground and so needing no holding up except in wet weather was, her dressmaker had assured her, the latest idea for country wear. The hat she had bought on her way through London that morning. It had cost 9s. 11¾d. of the pound she had saved to meet her expenses until her first month's salary was due in her new post, but she did not regret the extravagance — 'a good impression is half the battle,' she had been told as a child. She lived at first with the postmaster's family, then independently in a rented 'little bare room' at 10s. a week. The Postmaster quarrelled with abnormal violence with his wife and prowled about the house at all hours, a prey to suspicions and delusions. Later, the sinister postmaster went out of his mind and murdered his wife and child with a carving-knife — but this was, fortunately, after Flora had left. There too she had her first enthralling glimpses of real writers, for the Surrey highlands had been recently discovered by the intelligentsia, and there being no post office at that time at Hindhead[‡], the celebrities who frequented the neighbourhood bought their stamps and sent their telegrams from Grayshott. Conan Doyle, Grant Allen, Richard le Gallienne and others had taken houses in the neighbourhood, and Bernard Shaw, lately married, had rented a furnished house at Grayshott itself."

Of her writing, Miss Lane quotes Flora's own words: "I used to listen to the conversation of their meeting and greeting each other at my counter,

---

[†] *Margaret Lane actually wrote 1897 here, but in fact Flora arrived in Grayshott in September 1898, aged twenty-one.*

[‡] *There was a post office at Hindhead, but no telegraph facility there until September 1900*

myself as unregarded as a piece of furniture, but noting all. Perhaps these great examples encouraged my desire to express myself in writing, but I cannot remember the time when I did not wish and mean to write. My brother and I used to make up verses and write stories from our earliest years, and I have never left off writing essays. No one sees them, but there was no one likely to be interested."

Flora married John Thompson who became postmaster at Liphook in 1916 and at Dartmouth in 1938†. Her beloved brother was killed in action in 1916.

MR. MAX REESE came to Grayshott in 1952 and has remained here since. He is well-known as an accomplished journalist, reporting not only on local affairs, but also on cricket and football matches for national papers. But his literary and historical interests and work are much wider.

He has published two purely historical books — *The Tudors and Stuarts* (1940) and *The Puritan Impulse* (1975). He has specialist knowledge in Shakespearean studies which resulted in *Shakespeare: His World and his Work* (1953), a pamphlet on *Shakespeare and the Welfare State* (1953), *The Cease of Majesty* (1961), a study of the historical plays, and a short introductory guide, illustrated, to Shakespeare's life and work, published in 1964, the Shakespeare Centenary Year.

Between 1965 and 1974 he had to his credit a great deal of editorial work and many contributions to works of reference. This included editions of four Shakespeare plays (Henry IV, Part 1; As You Like It; Henry V; Midsummer Night's Dream), of Elizabethan Verse Romances and of Gibbon's Autobiography. He was also general editor of a series of collected Documents for History Revision, in which he edited personally volumes on British History 1485 to 1588 and British History 1688 to 1789. In addition, he contributed many articles in Nelson's Dictionary of World History and in the Dictionary of National Biography.

In 1976 a magnificent book on the origin, development and duties of the Master of the Horse, one of the great Officers of the Royal Household, was published, of which Mr. Reese was responsible for writing the text. He is now general editor of a series on the Great Offices of State, of which two volumes are in preparation.

Mr. Reese, in spite of all this volume of literary work, is not a recluse. His is a familiar figure walking in Grayshott and on some of the beautiful footpaths in the neighbourhood. In the fifties he was a founder member of the Grayshott Stagers and for some years was closely connected with them as actor and producer. He was a member of Haslemere Rotary and served as President. For many years he was active in the Hindhead Cricket Club as player, captain, chairman, and now as President.

CANON A. R. WINNETT was Vicar of Grayshott 1959–1970, and is now living in busy retirement.

His *Divorce and Remarriage in Anglicanism* and *The Church and Divorce* were published in 1958 and 1968 respectively. In the latter year his Tercentenary Lecture on Dean Swift appeared as *Jonathan Swift, Churchman*, to be followed in 1974 by *Peter Browne, Provost, Bishop, Metaphysician*. He has written a

---

† *Actually in November 1927.*

history of the Diocese of Guildford for publication in 1977, the fiftieth anniversary of the Diocese. Of more purely local interest was *Fielding Ottley: Sermons with Memoir* (1960) which he edited in remembrance of his immediate predecessor as Vicar of Grayshott. Many Grayshott people will remember Canon Winnett's perceptive and deeply felt address at Canon Ottley's funeral.

Dr. Winnett's published work was recognised by London University in 1976 when it conferred on him the degree of Doctor of Divinity. He, too, like Mr. Reese, was not borne down by his literary work. A brilliant and often humorous conversationalist, he will be remembered with affection by Grayshott people as a friendly, outgoing person, as well as a respected parish priest.

Chapter 7

The Fox and Pelican

That Grayshott had its public house before it had its permanent church or its village hall, and before it became a separate parish, was not due to any well-thought-out scheme of desirable priorities; it was rather the result of historical necessity. The story of its foundation has—quite apart from Shaw's connection with it—an interest in its own right, since it was an early attempt to build and run a public house on reformed lines and under the control of local inhabitants. In 1898 some of the prominent local residents thought it urgently necessary to forestall the ambitions of a firm of Alton brewers to establish an ordinary public house at Grayshott, to be run on purely commercial lines. These residents were, for the most part, precisely those to whom Shaw referred in his letter to *The Herald* of 11th March 1899, and quoted in full in Chapter 5, as those who had "voluntarily assumed feudal duties towards their poorer neighbours."

In 1898 Gerald Hall, brewer of Alton, bought a plot of land in the centre of the village, having a frontage of 150 ft. and a depth of 175 ft. This was part of an allotment of 19 acres to James Lawrence, yeoman farmer, at the time of the enclosure in 1859 for the sum of £130. He had sold some of it in 1893 to John Ward, an estate agent, for £1,625. In May 1898, that part of it which was the plot referred to above was sold to Gerald Hall for £750, and he mortgaged it for the same amount. In 1908 the mortgage was discharged and the title reverted absolutely to Gerald Hall, who re-sold the land to the Ward family for £410 in June 1913. Finally, in September 1913, John Sheldon Ward sold it to Dr. Arnold Lyndon and Thomas Ashley Crook for £430, and in July of the following year they conveyed it to Grayshott Parish Council for the purpose of establishing a Village Green—which it now is.

The Alton brewery of Messrs. Hall was founded by Henry Hall (1814–1899). Born at Ely, where the family already owned a brewery, Henry Hall married a lady of the Archer family of Ely, by whom he had ten children. Having lost most of his wife's money by investing in Welsh slate quarries, he drove across England from Ely into Hampshire, and came to Alton, where he bought a bankrupt brewery belonging to the Hawkins family. He induced the London and South Western Railway to extend its line to Alton and provide a siding for the brewery. He prospered and became a partner in Messrs. Bulpitt and Hall, bankers of Winchester. He installed his sons—Gerald (1844–1940) and Goodwyn (1848–1933)—in the brewery which remained a prosperous family business, acquiring 72 public houses, mostly in Hampshire, but two in Farnham, Surrey and 8 in London. It is significant that one of their houses was the *Holly Bush* at Headley, i.e. in the parish of which Grayshott was then an outlying part. The Hall brothers sold their whole business to the large firm of Messrs. Courage in December, 1903.

The land at Grayshott which Gerald bought in 1898 was his own private property and did not pass to Messrs. Courage in 1903. But its purchase in 1898 alarmed the more public spirited local residents, who feared the establishment of a purely commercial public house. Indeed, in 1898 Messrs. Hall applied at the Licensing Sessions for a licence to build and run a public house on this plot of land. In consequence of this action, a few leading residents, led by Rev. J. M. Jeakes (later first Vicar of Grayshott), Mr. G. V. Cox, Mrs. Charlotte Lyndon, and others, put forward a scheme to provide Grayshott with a public house for the sale of beer and other refreshments "under the reformed methods adopted in other parts of the country." The Archbishop of Canterbury had approved a company, formed into a joint stock company, to provide capital for establishing and running similar businesses. The main idea was that the house was to be under a salaried manager, who received a commission, not upon the sale of intoxicants, but upon the profits arising from the sale of other kinds of refreshment. Thus it was hoped that the manager would not press the sale of beer. In the July 1898 issue of the *Grayshott District Magazine* the following announcement appears:

"There has been a strong feeling in the district for some time past that, owing to the rapid and continued growth of Grayshott, a fully-licensed Public House in the village is a practical certainty at no very distant date.
A scheme has therefore been framed to start a Refreshment House which will supply alcoholic drinks of good and reliable quality, whilst at the same time the villager or the passer-by will be able to procure a good and cheap cup of tea or coffee, a plate of meat, and bread and cheese, or any other refreshments he may require.
It is intended to carry out the scheme on the lines of the People's Refreshment House Association. The necessary land has been secured, and it is hoped that very shortly the scheme will be sufficiently advanced to allow a prospectus to be issued and particulars made public.
Our neighbours, Mr. and Mrs. Nettleship, have most generously offered to allow a piece of ground adjoining the site of the proposed Refreshment House to be used as a Tea-garden, Bowling Green, etc., if there is a general feeling in the village that such a place would be appreciated. That their offer will be accepted there can be very little doubt."

The leading residents referred to above formed themselves into the Grayshott and District Refreshment Association, with Sir Frederick Pollock as Chairman, and Mrs. Lyndon as Secretary. This body issued shares to an upper limit of £2,500 and £2,035 was soon taken up by 68 shareholders. Local builders, Messrs. Chapman and Puttick, had submitted a successful tender of £1,465 for erecting the buildings, and it was estimated that the total cost, including furnishings, would be £2,000. The shares were of £1 each, interest was not guaranteed and would, in any event, be limited to 4%, any profits over that interest rate going to improve the house or to some public cause approved by the shareholders. With regard to the purpose of the founders, the *Grayshott and District Magazine* of January 1899 commented: "What it needs now to give it a good start is the hearty sympathy and intelligent interest of all in the village who are on the side of temperance, whether they are teetotallers or moderate drinkers. For, 'it is,' as one of the pioneers of

Public-House Reform wrote lately, 'an experiment which will be watched *from both sides.*' If our trial here in any way justifies our hopes, it will do something to help on the movement all over the country. And if the movement spreads, it will unite in a strange and unnatural alliance against it those who want to prohibit the sale of alcoholic drink altogether, and those whose personal interest makes them wish to sell as much as they can."

On 14th January 1899, the local paper reported that the Licensing Sessions had granted a full licence to the Grayshott Association. At the hearing the magistrates heard evidence on its behalf from Hon. F. L. Wood about a similar venture in Shropshire and from Major Crauford of the People's Refreshment House Association. At the same Sessions, Messrs. Hall's application for a licence to erect a public house on the adjoining plot had been refused.

The local Association had some difficulty in choosing a name for the inn, but the Chairman resolved the problem, as he described in his book *For My Grandson*:

"Let me mention (since you may well know no more than I tell you about Corpus Christi College and its foundation by that great humanist Bishop Fox of Winchester) that the Pelican 'in her piety' was our Founder's device: whereby hangs the tale of a novel public-house sign. While I was still attached to Corpus in 1898, I was the first chairman of a small company (later taken over by the People's Refreshment House Association) formed to establish and conduct an inn at Grayshott on the borders of Surrey and Hampshire and in the diocese of Winchester. The conjunction of a site in Fox's diocese and the ancient estate of his see with a chairman who was a member of his own foundation was irresistible, and we chose 'The Fox and Pelican.' Walter Crane painted us a might pretty signboard (long since taken indoors to be preserved as a memorial, and replaced by a copy). No questions were asked about it. I suppose most customers took it for an ancient sign. I told Bishop Stubbs and he approved with a hearty laugh. So the sign of the 'Fox and Pelican' at Grayshott has the benefit, I should think unique among signboards, of an episcopal blessing."

Mrs. Winkworth gave the signboard, designed and painted by Walter Crane, R.A. The following description of it was printed in *The Herald* on 7th April 1900:

"Upon the background which is red upon the upper and green upon the lower portion, there is painted a white pelican with outstretched wings guarding a nest where are three of its young [from a fox]. The pelican is pecking her own breast, upon which blood is to be seen, the artist having followed the old fable to the effect that the pelican was accustomed to feed its young from its own breast. The reverse of the sign board has a red background upon which is painted an oak branch with leaves and fruit, and a blue and white scroll with the name of the inn."

The Fox and Pelican was formally opened on 23rd August 1899 by Mrs. Randall Davidson, wife of the Bishop of Winchester who was unable to attend

(Dr. Davidson later became Archbishop of Canterbury). *The Herald* of 26th August reported:

> "An interesting stage in a movement which has excited widespread interest was reached on Wednesday afternoon, when the reform public house, which is to be conducted on the principles of the People's Refreshment House Association, was formally opened in the presence of a large and distinguished company. Grayshott has thus become an unique place, a place which is destined to do its share towards bringing about a change in the methods of supplying intoxicating liquors — a change which all agree is necessary. The causes which led up to the adoption of this experiment … are within the knowledge of all the inhabitants of the district — how the growth of Grayshott necessitated the establishment of a hotel of some sort, and how, bearing in mind the fact that brewers were considering the starting of a public house, and imbued with the idea of the desirability of placing the control of such an establishment in the hands of local people, a number of enterprising residents adopted the scheme of which the new refreshment house is the outcome."

It was stated in the same account that there was a small library of books, "the kind gift of Mr. Bernard Shaw." Shaw purchased shares in the Association. It was natural that Shaw, a bright star in the Fabian firmament, should share the contemporary interest of the Fabian Society in the temperance movement, since he himself was an abstainer. It was equally natural that he shared the Fabian conviction that the great solvent of social and, indeed, political problems was the education of the working class. Later in this Chapter there is a short, but somewhat formidable, list of some of the books which Shaw gave to this inn Library. *The Herald* also noted that the rooms had been furnished under the supervision of Mrs. Macmillan (wife of the publisher) and Mrs. Leon, and that the first manager was Mr. Wallace, late steward of H.M.S. Sanspareil, who was helped by his wife and a small staff.

The opening of the Fox and Pelican attracted considerable national interest. The London *Morning Leader* of 29th August 1899 included — with a line drawing — the following account:

> "The experiment of combining the sale of beer, wines and spirits with what are known as temperance principles was begun yesterday at Grayshott, Haslemere.
> Last September Sir Frederick Pollock and a few friends obtained a full licence for a public-house, the Fox and Pelican, they proposed to erect with this object.
> In 12 months the house has been built, a company has been formed to own and work it under the title of "The Grayshott and District Refreshment Association, Limited," the Bishop of Winchester's blessing has been given to the project, and Mr. Wallace, late of H.M.S. Sanspareil, installed as Manager, with his wife to assist him. He drew his first beer yesterday morning.
> His instructions are to keep the alcoholic drinks out of sight, and only to supply them when asked for. The shelves, on the other hand, are bright

with gingerbeer and lemonade bottles: and spick-and-span pewter and glass make the bar as snug a little place as one would wish to find.

Here, however, are no seats. If you want to rest while you drink there is a large airy room close at hand, with tiled floor, and comfortable chairs and tables; and here some two or three of the Grayshott inhabitants were gathered together yesterday to discuss matters in general.

It could not be said that trade was brisk; indeed, the opening of the new hostelry did not cause nearly so much excitement as the rain—the first thorough downpour the villagers have enjoyed for months.

Though the beer is out of sight it appeared to be the most popular drink sold. The little three-handle beer engine, hidden modestly away behind a curtain, was much more frequently in use than the prominently displayed stores of "minerals" or the barrel of draught ginger-beer. During the half-hour our representative remained he saw only one teetotal drink served, and that, curiously enough, to a cabman.

Landlord Wallace, leaning over the bar, opined that the beer was good. So did the Grayshott people, who are connoisseurs, and the "Leader" representative, who is not.

There is no "four ale." A wholesome, palatable "mild" sells at 2½d. the pint, while bitter ale and stout each fetch 3d. a pint.

The villagers are doubtful about the success of the new venture, though they look on it with friendly eyes.

There is something of the hotel about the establishment, for there are four bedrooms that can be hired by visitors, besides a coffee-room, stables, and a bicycle shed.

Among the backers of the scheme are the parish clergyman, the Rev. J. M. Jeakes, Dr. Arnold Lyndon and his wife, and Mrs. Macmillan, the widow of the great publisher."

On the same day, under the heading "Beer at the Back," and with subheadings, "Grayshott's new Public-House," and "Where Customers Can Have What They Want by Asking for it, but where Temperance Refreshments are Pushed by the Management," the London *Star* gave its own rather more flowery account:

"At the top of a purple Surrey hill, four miles up and up from the nearest railway station, stands the Fox and Pelican, the newest, and perhaps the prettiest, little inn in the world. Yesterday it opened its bar and its coffee-room, its bedrooms and its library, to the thirsty traveller, and thereupon did a trade which kept Mr. Wallace (late steward, R.N.) and his busy wife busier than they have been for many a day.

Late in the afternoon the STAR MAN drove up the long and beautiful Hindhead Hill, past the late Professor Tyndall's somewhat high fence, and thence down the Portsmouth road to Grayshott, where, with a "scrunching" of wheels on the new gravel, the driver pulled up at the Fox and the Pelican.

Ginger Beer Prominent

Spick and span as a new villa, stood the pride and joy of the shareholders in the Grayshott and District Refreshment Association, Limited. High-pitched, red-tiled roof, walls, half rough-plastered and half red-tiled, small-paned windows framed in dark green, and red curtains proclaimed the hand of the modern art-builder.

Entering the open door at the side, the STAR MAN found a square room panelled in green stain and furnished in green stain. Tables and chairs were there, and big pots of ale, and three customers, but at first sight no bar. Off in a side passage stood the bar, very neat and plain, with three beer-handles and a row of shelves, on which ginger beer was the most prominent stock.

Strong Drink at the Back

"You see, sir," said Mr. Wallace, "our instructions are to make as much as we can of the lighter drinks and keep the rest in the background. We are fully licensed, and anyone can have wine or spirits for the asking, but we want to push the refreshment idea."

Then he led the way into the large coffee-room, and upstairs to the bedrooms and a pretty sitting-room.

A Library, Too

And then the STAR MAN found the library which George Bernard Shaw has presented to the new ale-house at Grayshott. Judge of its contents by the following:

Harold Frederic's "Market Place."
"Actors of the Century."
"Plain Talk in Psalm and Parable."
Kipling's "Day's Work."
Tolstoy's "The Gospel in Brief."
"Les Chanteurs de Nurembourg de Richard Wagner."
Du Maurier's "Peter Ibbotson."
Rowntree and Sherwell's "Temperance Problems and Social Reform."

"How do you like it?" asked the STAR MAN when he had got back to the bar-parlour again.

A Grayshott villager looked up from his ale. "It's all right, but there is a sight too much green about," he said.

No Brewers Need Apply

The new venture should do well. A firm of brewers was very anxious to get a license for an adjoining site, but the Refreshment Association won at the Sessions. There is plenty of passing traffic on the Grayshott-rd. Mr. Walter Crane's sign is not up yet, but in its place a painted board with the name and the owners of the license. "I had to put that up," said Mr. Wallace, "I had a policeman in this morning, who wanted to know why we were open before we had the name up."

Much more soberly, *The Spectator* (2nd September 1899) noticed the opening of the Fox and Pelican and linked it up, in noticing an article in the *Contemporary Review* by Charles Booth, with an experiment—not very successful—in reformed management in five public houses in London:

"The *Daily Telegraph* of Tuesday recorded the opening of a new public-house at Grayshott in Hampshire. In itself this is not so unusual an event to justify notice even in the last week of August. What gives it interest is the exceptional character of the house. The 'Fox and Pelican' is a fresh experiment on lines originally suggested by the Bishop of Chester, and already in operation on a small scale under the control of an Association of which he is President. The object of the Association is to turn public-houses into refreshment-rooms, to push the sale of food and of non-intoxicating drinks in comparison with that of alcohol, and to exact from the customers a stricter observance of order and decency. The Association and its kindred houses mean to wage war with drunkenness and rowdyism, while giving decent people, whether workers or wayfarers, all that they can get at the public-house and something more besides. The way in which they mainly hope to secure these ends is by enlisting the interest of the managers on their side. He is charged for alcoholic drinks the full retail price; consequently, on these he makes no profit. But for the non-intoxicating drinks and for food he is charged a price which will enable him to make a profit—20 per cent we believe—on all that he sells. He has a positive inducement, therefore, to push the consumption of the latter, and none at all to push the consumption of the former. Add to this that he is paid a good salary, and is constantly urged by his employers to be very strict in keeping order and in refusing to serve drunken people, and we have the main particulars of the scheme."

Fabian Tract No. 86 (November 1898) had mentioned that the Bishop of Chester had in 1893 introduced a Bill into the Lords "for establishing a system of retail sale of intoxicating liquor by an authorised company." The Bill was defeated on Second Reading. In 1896 the Bishop, together with Major Crauford, had founded the People's Refreshment House Association with the support of Lord Grey, whose object was to promote temperance by acquiring or co-operating with local bodies in acquiring public houses with a view to reformed management.

Writing of the London experiment, Booth said in the *Contemporary Review*:

"The experiment here recorded was in one sense foredoomed to failure. Except as an indication of what, under quite different conditions, might result, it could hardly succeed. Public-houses, of which the entire business basis consists of profits from the sale of alcohol, and in the planning and constitution of which no other idea has been present, are most unlikely to do much in any other line. No doubt they also fill a social function; men frequent public-houses for the sake of company as well as drink; but unless they drank there would be no profit. And it must be alcohol in some form. No one, not even the most ardent teetotaller, spends much money on teetotal drinks.

Thus no great revolution could possibly be effected by the mere giving a bonus to the Manager on non-alcoholic sales, and when the actual figures of these sales are compared with the gross amount of the alcoholic trade done on the premises experimentalized with, it will be seen how small and insignificant they are. Nevertheless, the percentage of increase shown is very noticeable, and may, perhaps, point to a coming or possible change of fashion."

It is, no doubt, significant that the London public-houses which were the subject of the experiment were old-established houses on to which the experiment was grafted, whereas the Fox and Pelican was founded from the start on reform lines.

Shaw, by his support of the Grayshott experiment, showed that he shared Booth's views.

The Spectator article resulted in a letter from Sir Frederick Pollock, printed in the same paper on 16th September 1899:

"It may encourage persons disposed to follow up this matter to know that the "Fox and Pelican" at Grayshott has almost more business than it can cope with, both from passing customers and from staying guests; for it is an inn as well as a refreshment house. In fact, extra help—which will probably become a permanent addition to the staff—has been required ever since the opening. In addition to the features broadly described as an adaptation of the Gothenburg system, the capital of the Association is held by persons resident or interested in the neighbourhood, including local tradesmen and working men, on the Committee. I am not sure that this point is not as important as any. The name commemorates Fox, the great Bishop of Winchester, and his device, a 'pelican in her piety,' which is to this day the crest of his foundation of Corpus Christi, Oxford. It is already public knowledge that the scheme is warmly approved by Fox's present worthy successor. The Association is registered under the Industrial and Provident Societies Act, whereby the divisible profits are limited to 4 per cent, on the capital. It is too early to state any particulars as to the proportionate demands for different kinds of food and drink. Our object, however, is not to dictate to the public, but to ascertain the real natural demand, and to supply it in the best possible manner. Perhaps I may be allowed to give further information through your columns at a future date when we have had more experience."

It is, perhaps, worth noting that *Fabian Tract No. 85* (September 1898) gave an account of the Gothenburg System. It seems that as a result of a Swedish Municipal Reform Act of 1863 a committee set up in Gothenburg arranged that licenses should be handed over to a philanthropic company. The weaknesses were that the system dealt exclusively with spirits and did not deal with beer, and that profits of the company in excess of a permitted maximum were handed over to the public purse of the city of Gothenburg—thus the municipality, and, indeed, the ratepayers, had a direct interest in the sale of spirits.

After these serious accounts and assessments we revert to a more racy account, accompanied with a line drawing, which appeared in *The Clarion* of 28th April 1900:

"When you are in search of a public-house on a blistering hot day in the middle of April, and a local lunatic sends you three miles out of your course, away from the ventricular assuagement, then, I think, you are entitled to sit down and groan in spirit.

I had travelled 40 miles by rail, and had set out on a four miles tramp to find the "Fox and Pelican" at Grayshott, Hants. Instead of which I found myself in the Devil's Punchbowl, which is not a place within the meaning of the Act, but a curious formation of the country in they parts, on the edge of which the late Grant Allen's house and the habitations of other noted literary persons offered but a poor substitute for what I went out to see.

But there were other compensations. I was alone with nature in the midst of a most picturesque and wild piece of Surrey. For miles around me were rugged hills and valleys, black and brown with pine and heather. Here and there the yellow gorse brightened the sober hues, and white ribbons of roads zig-zagged across the swelling hills or skirted their wide waists like a belt. The lark and many strange songsters piped love-songs to their mates, and a soft breeze now and then rippled through the leaves. It was good.

I was just about to make a move which would have taken me still further from my destination when I espied a stone cross on the top of a neighbouring kopje. I rushed the position, and was rewarded by finding a couple of cyclists nooning under a bush, who put me in the right direction for Grayshott. The cross marked the spot of the gibbet on which were hanged the murderers of an unknown sailor, to whom there is also a memorial by the roadside. A beautiful spot for a murder.

Leaving the main road to Portsmouth, a walk of a mile landed me at the Fox and Pelican, in front of which hangs the new sign (not represented in the above picture) painted by Mr. Walter Crane. The name of the house commemorates the great Bishop of Winchester, whose device was a "pelican in her piety." The pelican is represented with outstretched wings protecting her young, and feeding them with blood pecked out of her own breast.

The intelligent reader will have divined that it was not merely to satisfy the customary calls of the body for nutrition that I embarked on this perilous journey to a public-house far from my base. Nevertheless, that was my first business on arriving there.

With remarkable celerity the neat-handed Louie placed before me food and drink sufficient to repair the thefts of the blazing sun and the toilsome walk. Then I asked for the manager.

Mine host of 'The Fox and Pelican' also appeared with remarkable celerity. In respect of the substantial proportions of mine host, the proprietors of this reform public-house have adhered to tradition. Nevertheless, he is brisk, alert, and business-like, and does not appear to have any Dangular proclivities. I asked him to give me the history of 'The Fox and Pelican.'

'The movement was started by Sir Frederick Pollock, who lives in the neighbourhood,' he said. 'Grayshott is only a small village of quite recent growth, and before this house was opened eight months ago there was only an off-license house in the place. It was known that a firm of brewers were going to apply for a license to build a public-house, and Sir Frederick Pollock and his friends, believing that such places should be under the control of the inhabitants, formed the Grayshott and District Refreshment Association, and applied for a license. They were supported by most of the villagers and other people in the district, and were successful, the brewers' application being refused.'

'Is the Association a limited company?'

'Yes. The capital of £2,500 was all subscribed by residents or friends of residents in the district, and has been expended in purchase of land and furnishing the house.'

'What has the effect of your enterprise been so far?'

'We are getting on very well. We have a number of working men in to dinner every day. We give them meat, two vegetables, and bread for sixpence, and we find that, as they are able to get food, they drink less. There is very little trouble or rowdyism. At first there was some opposition—organised, we suspect. Men came with the object of getting drunk and disorderly in order to get the place a disreputable name; but all that has died away. We have a number of books and periodicals, and games are allowed, such as draughts.'

'I understand that there is some arrangement with you by which, you are interested in encouraging the sale of non-intoxicants?'

'Yes. I get a commission on the sale of mineral waters, but not on alcoholic liquors.'

'Have you any staying visitors?'

'Oh, yes. We have six bedrooms, and they are always occupied. I could let forty if we had them. We have a very bracing air, and many people come here for health's sake. Then at week-ends we can always reckon on seeing a large number of cyclists.'

Mine host gave me a tariff, from which I learned that a single bed costs 2s.6d. a night, plain breakfast 1s., a dinner 2s., and afternoon tea 6d. Then I made a tour of the premises. The room on the right in the picture is the parlour of the 'wuk-king man.' The middle door leads into the public bar, and the door on the left into the coffee-room. Everything looks bright and pleasant. All the woodwork is painted dark green and varnished, and the chairs and benches also. The walls are match-boarded threequarters of the way up, the rest is distempered. The floors are laid with wooden bricks. The bedrooms are furnished simply, the wash-hand stands and dressing tables are of dark green wood, and the floor is in its natural nakedness but for a small slip of carpet. There is a small sitting-room for visitors, and a bathroom, soon to be provided with a bath.

One could not desire a pleasanter lodgement, and I could wish the Board would instruct me to watch the progress of this enterprise on the spot. The outside of the house is very striking to the passer-by. The roof is red-tiles, and the curtains are a stunning red. The pillars, and the walls beneath the veranda, and the window frames are white, while the doors are in the grateful and comforting dark green.

The house seems to be a favourite resort of the 'carriage' folk, several parties calling for tea during my stay. The working-class department was rather quiet, and I could not stay late enough to see it fill up. I memorised full particulars of the route back to Haslemere, and promptly lost myself in a gloomy hollow. I was saved by a kindhearted pedestrian, who piloted me all the way to the station. I pumped him about 'The Fox and Pelican.' His ideas about it were very vague. He thought it was a sort of 'Church pub' when it started, but there had been so many rows, that they had given it up to a brewer. O Rumour, Rumour, what a lot you have to answer for."

The cautious estimates made by serious social reformers of the likely success of the 'Fox and Pelican' experiment have to be set against the optimistic and ephemeral accounts of the London daily papers. The fact is that the early years of the new inn were beset with difficulties. It was opened on 23rd August 1899, and within a very short time trouble broke out over its reform character. The local paper reported on 16th September that there was dissension over the Sunday closing time. The manager had announced 8.0 p.m. as the time, whereas the normal Sunday closing time in public-houses was 10.0 p.m. A group of young men went in just before 8.0 p.m. and then refused to leave. They stayed on "quite orderly" until 10.0 p.m. though they were not served. The Committee, who had feared week-end drunkenness, gave way and revised the time to 10.0 p.m. An article in the local paper of 4th October shows that the managing was not easy:

"A very short time proved that the working of the house was not to be at all easy. The very laws framed to prevent drunkenness or anything approaching it proved a stumbling block, as to reconcile them with the intricate requirements of the licensing laws needed very keen management. The hours of closing on Sundays, for instance, caused much comment; but worst of all came the announcement that, on September 12th, a man had been allowed to get drunk and remain on the premises."

The local magistrates fined the manager 10s. for this offence but did not endorse his license. Fairly frequent cases of drunkenness at or near the inn were dealt with by the local Bench.

In a letter to *The Herald* of 9th December 1899, and signed "Not a Shareholder," another side of the picture is shown:

"Considering the adverse criticism lately advanced against the above house, will you in fairness allow me, as a patroniser, to try to remove any antagonistic feelings in the minds of the non-frequenters.
It may not be generally known that the house is now under the management of a gentleman whose experience in catering is recognised in influential circles, and since his advent here insobriety, comparatively speaking, is a thing of the past. Hot dinners are supplied daily for the working class at 6d. a head, and at all hours of the day substantial refreshments may be obtained at nominal cost. Draughts, dominoes, social evenings, and the promise shortly of periodical smokers, provide all to be desired in the way of recreation; and the public here unanimously admit that Mr. Wilshire is the right man in the right place, considering the decrease of rows etc., and the increase of sociability.
The coffee-room is now thrown open, which of course demands that parlour prices should be charged to secure a select company.
Trusting you will kindly state these facts in fairness to the management of the house."

To the above *The Herald* appended its own somewhat tart footnote:

"In fairness to ourselves we must state another fact, and that is that the above letter ought to be charged as advertisement, at 6d. a line. However, out of the love we bear to the house in question and out of our appreciation of the management thereof, we have made up our minds to say nothing of the charge."

Perhaps a trifle illogical, as well as tart.

Another difficulty was frequent changes of managers. The above letter shows that the first, Mr. Wallace, was manager for only a very short time. There were six managers between 1899 and 1904, one of whom sued the company and won his case when he left, the company having to refund his £50 deposit on taking over less £22 which he had spent unauthorised by the committee. Another was fined 10s. for watering the whisky.

That and other difficulties were noted by Joseph Rowntree and Arthur Sherwell in their book *British Gothenburg Experiments and Public House Trusts* (1901). The book summarised the features of the Gothenburg System, contained an account of the People's Refreshment House Association, and also detailed accounts of a few local experiments. The Fox and Pelican occupied the whole of Chapter IV of their book. Much of what they said has already been noted. It may be of interest to quote a few passages:

"The experiment made in 1898 by the Grayshott and District Refreshment Association, Limited, of which Sir Frederick Pollock, Bart., is the president, marked in some respects a new departure in the attempt to apply the principles of the Gothenburg system to the management of the liquor traffic in this country. In all previous attempts a benevolent despotism had been present to assist either in the promotion or the management of the undertaking, the owners of the estate or the local clergyman being responsible for the licence. The Grayshott experiment began on strictly co-operative lines, the villagers themselves taking up many of the shares. It was also the first house in England to receive a new licence for the express purpose of an experiment on Gothenburg lines."

"The proportion of food sold is small, and is much less at the present times than it was under a former manager, who was accustomed to sell as many as twenty sixpenny dinners a day in the tap-room. The sale of non-alcoholic beverages is also comparatively small, although those responsible for the management of the house are clearly eager to encourage the sale of such drinks. It is probable that in these respects the experiment has suffered from the frequent changes in the management, which have prevented strict continuity of policy ... It is also an interesting circumstance that the committee have been able to introduce a lighter beer than that sold in other houses in the district. Indoor games, such as draughts, dominoes, etc., are encouraged, but they are not used to any great extent. A few newspapers are also provided. In connection with this feature of the management it should be pointed out that there is at present no reading-room or social institute in the village; but a Village Hall is about to be built, and this, when ready, will make such provision on the part of the Refreshment House Association as unnecessary as, in the judgement of the present writers, it is undesirable. In view of the efforts needed to break what has become a dangerous and tyrannous national habit, the association of games and other recreations with the sale of intoxicants is surely to be deprecated and discouraged."

"No effort is made to establish bye-laws in advance of the present statutory regulations, although an attempt was originally made to reduce Sunday hours by closing at 8.0 p.m. This effort, however, was resented by a portion of the population, and the new rule was quickly abandoned. Similarly, a tentative experiment was made some time back to establish a "Black List" (i.e. a list of persons of notoriously drunken habits), but it was not found to answer in practice, and was therefore discontinued. There are, however, a few persons whom the manager is instructed not to serve. The general position assumed in reference to these and similar reforms by those responsible for the house is that, where, as in Grayshott, the liquor influence is strong and active, and where everything in the nature of an innovation is eagerly seized upon to arouse prejudice and hostility against the movement, it is risking too much to impose regulations in advance of the licence laws. It is necessary to remember that the Association has not a complete monopoly of the local traffic, but only of the "on" trade. In addition to the Fox and Pelican there is an "off" beerhouse in the village, as well as two grocers' licences, while it is a not unimportant fact that the site adjoining the Fox and Pelican for which a full licence was sought by a firm of brewers at the time the Association was formed, still remains in the possession of the brewers who applied for the licence.

These facts, together with the additional fact that the district appears to contain a somewhat unusual proportion of lawless spirits in its population, must be carefully borne in mind in estimating the success of the Grayshott experiment. That it has not realised all the expectations of its promoters they themselves freely acknowledge. The experiment has been handicapped throughout by a not always scrupulous opposition on the part of the least reputable portion of the inhabitants; and the committee has, moreover, been singularly unfortunate in its managers. But the intention that underlies and governs the experiment is unquestionably single and sincere, and when all limitations and imperfections are allowed for, it is incontrovertible that the interests of temperance in the district are much more securely safeguarded than they could have been if an ordinary public-house had been allowed to be established in the village.

The situation is well expressed in a letter which the Rev. J. M. Jeakes, a member of the committee, addressed to one of the present writers in May 1901. Mr. Jeakes says: 'I am very glad that you have seen the Fox and Pelican. The conditions under which this experiment is made are, I think, exceptionally difficult; but the difficulties we have passed through do not at all alter my conviction that we are, in the main, on the right track, and that we did the best we could do under the circumstances, in view of the great probability of a tied house entirely out of our control.' Looked at from this point of view simply, the efforts of Sir Frederick Pollock and his colleagues are completely justified."

In a review of the book, *The Speaker* probably put its finger upon the main difficulty:

"The writers think that the success of this house would have been greater, if there had not been so many changes in the management. Does this mean that the committee have not been able to find satisfactory managers or that the managers would not stop? Probably the men who are sufficiently disinterested to throw in their lot with novel undertakings of this kind, and also have the qualities which would make the enterprise a success are rare, and able to get more congenial work. At the same time, though the increase of tied houses and houses held by companies has caused an increase in the number of managers of hotels, the experiments noticed in this book are usually on too small a scale to tempt men from lucrative positions."

On the financial side the position fluctuated. In the first year ending on 30th September 1900, the trading profit was over £213, and, after putting aside £100 for initial expenses and depreciation, there was about £114 available for distribution, from which 4% interest was paid to shareholders, leaving a balance forward of about £14. The next year was not so good, a trading profit being made of £123, and after setting aside money for depreciation, only £37 was left for distribution. No dividend was paid. One reason for the poor results had been an expenditure of £300 to install gaslighting. A bank overdraft of that amount was guaranteed by two members of the committee. At the 1901 Annual General Meeting shareholders present included Sir Frederick Pollock, Rev. and Mrs. Jeakes, Dr. Lyndon, Miss James, Major H. J. Crauford, Mr. and Mrs. Bernard Shaw, Mr. E. Nettleship, and Mrs. Charlotte Lyndon (Secretary).

In succeeding years the financial position improved. In the year 1903/1904 general receipts had increased, as had the sale of non-intoxicants and receipts from catering. The bank overdraft had been repaid and there was a profit of £250, so the payment of dividends was resumed and a substantial balance was carried forward.

We have seen that Shaw and his wife attended the 1901 meeting, although by that time they had left the district. Mrs. Shaw purchased some shares in 1904. In 1903 Shaw evinced his continuing interest in the Fox and Pelican in correspondence with Mr. Ingham Whitaker of Grayshott Hall. The Temperance controversy was raging at that time, and Shaw seems to have feared that the Fox and Pelican would be made the subject of attack by extreme temperance reformers, who might well pick on the point that local influential inhabitants had actually started a public house, albeit a reform house, in a district where there had been none before. On 2nd September 1903, he wrote to Mr. Whitaker from Strachur, Argyllshire, though on notepaper with the printed address, 10, Adelphi Terrace, W.C. 1:

"Dear Mr. Whitaker,
    As I shall stay here until the end of this month and then stay a few days in Glasgow to do some political speaking on the fiscal business, I shall not be able to attend the Fox and Pelican meeting. I see that no notice of resolution beyond the adoption of the report is given; so I conclude that the report recommends the maintenance of the status quo. If not, the report should be printed and circulated; so that the absentees may be able to arrange their proxies accordingly. I understand that Mr. Leon has withdrawn, and that there is less friction to be anticipated than formerly. I am a little anxious about the Fox and Pelican, because I foresee that it may be considerably cited in the Temperance controversy; and we may all find

ourselves in the limelight of a blazing publicity. At the foot of the hill, in Barford, you have Gilbert and Lady Mary Murray on the alert and that means Lord Carlisle (not to mention Lady Carlisle!) and the whole Temperance-Liberal press. Lady Mary told me at the beginning of the affair that I had deliberately opened a centre of crime and demoralization in Grayshott; and there is sufficient evidence on her side to induce Frederick Jackson, though he is a shareholder and a violent opponent of Gilbert Murray, to maintain that our clear duty is to resign the license and strongly oppose the granting of a new one to the brewers or anyone else.

Our smaller shareholders do not of course trouble themselves about the public point of view: they have their property and their investment. But we are in a different position; and if a crusade broke out, with Jackson in the *Morning Post* (he can always, it seems, command two columns of it), and Rayner Storr in the local press and the Radical papers, and Lady Mary and her father working the Liberal-Temperance batteries, and Jeakes perhaps unable to support Turner's attitude, it is on you and or Pollock and on me that the guns would be trained. Of course nothing of this may happen; but I am an old campaigner and I see that it is sufficiently possible to make it very important that whatever report we act on in finally disposing of the Fox and Pelican should be one that we can send to the press if necessary. Hence this long letter. You will understand that in pointing out that we may have to face such and such criticisms, I do not put them forward as my own.

Yours faithfully,

George Bernard Shaw."

It should, perhaps, be pointed out that Lady Mary, wife of Gilbert (later Professor) Murray, was a daughter of Lord Carlisle — the Carlisles were protagonists of the extreme temperance position. In mentioning that Lady Mary had "sufficient evidence on her side," Shaw was, no doubt, thinking of the frequent drunkenness and disorders at the Fox and Pelican and the unfortunate difficulties with successive managers. Frederick Jackson of "Tarn Moor," Rayner Storr, and R. Turner were prominent local residents — the latter a supporter of the Fox and Pelican. Rev. J. M. Jeakes, curate of Bramshott and first Vicar of Grayshott, was, as we have seen, prominent in the foundation of the Fox and Pelican. Did Shaw think that his clerical status might prevent him from being a strong protagonist?

Three weeks later Shaw's fears seem to have subsided. On 23rd September, he sent a postcard to Mr. Whitaker:

"Many thanks. I am glad the friction has ceased. I am sorry for the man; but from what I saw myself I am not surprised that the change is inevitable. The same difficulty is always cropping up when pairs are needed. When A is right B is wrong; and vice versa. I wish we could select them independently and insist on their marrying.

G. B. S."

Shaw is evidently referring to one of the frequent changes of manager and to the difficulty of finding a married couple, both of whom were suitable.

The background of Shaw's correspondence is almost certainly the fact that earlier in 1903 the People's Refreshment House Association made an offer to purchase the Fox and Pelican from the local Association. The local paper of 2nd May 1903 reported that the Association had held a Special General Meeting to discuss the offer, and that the requisite majority for a motion to sell was not obtained.

In the event, the Fox and Pelican continued under the management of the Grayshott and District Refreshment Association until 1913, when it was transferred to the People's Refreshment House Association, who held it for many years, until the late 1950s, when it was bought by Messrs. Gales Brewery. Differing social habits had long since taken the sting out of the Temperance Movement. It is worth noting that throughout its existence, and still today, the Fox and Pelican has continued to do a modest hotel and restaurant trade. It is a very orderly house, due in part to the marked decrease in public drunkenness in modern times.

Chapter 8

Grayshott School
and other Schools

The last entry in the first Log Book of Grayshott School, made on 11th May 1883 by the Head Teacher, Mrs. Esther Clark, reads as follows: "This Log Book was commenced in 1873, Greyshott School was opened 4th September 1871, with 7 children. Today there are 51 on the Register."

Like so much else in early Grayshott, the school was founded by the I'Ansons. We have seen in an earlier Chapter that Mr. Edward I'Anson came to Grayshott in 1861 and that ten years later he gave the land on which he built the school, consisting then of one classroom and a lobby. A plaque over the entrance describes it as "Grayshott National School," since it was founded under the auspices of the National Society — or, to give it its full title, The National Society for the Education of the Poor according to the Principles of the Church of England. The Society collected money voluntarily to make grants towards the erection and maintenance of Day Schools and Sunday Schools. As Trevelyan points out in his *English Social History:* "The National or Church Schools became the most usual mode of popular education in the English village." The school was the first public institution which Grayshott had — before the Church, before the Village Hall, and before the public house.

From 1871 to 1886, Mr. I'Anson continued as School Correspondent, when his place was taken by his daughter, Catherine I'Anson, who exercised the office for many years. It was to her that George Bernard Shaw, writing in 1899, made the appreciative reference quoted in Chapter 5. Mr. Edward I'Anson died early in 1888.

That the I'Anson regime was autocratic can be seen clearly from the surviving records; but it was also very benevolent. Miss I'Anson, in particular, envisaged her duty as School Correspondent on very wide lines. She regularly visited the school, often for days on end and for most of the day, not only to inspect the registers and stock, but also to inspect the work of the children, to hear lessons and often to give them, and to act as an unpaid Attendance Officer. An example of this is a Log Book entry by Miss I'Anson in February 1878: "visited Mrs. Carpenter, Mrs. Hibberd, Mrs. Coombes, and Mrs. White to enquire reason of Walter Carpenter's absence, also A. Hibberd's, Annie Coombes,' and Mary White's. Walter Carpenter is kept from school his mother objecting to her son receiving punishment on the 13th of February. Notice of his absence was given to the Churt School Officer on the 1st of March and the matter will receive attention. A. Coombes, M. White and A. Hibberd are ill. C. B. I'Anson." The interview with Mrs. Carpenter may well have been somewhat acrimonious, for on 25th March Miss I'Anson wrote: "Sent word to Mrs. Carpenter that her son was idle, and received a rude reply."

Miss I'Anson also acted as an unofficial inspector, making candid, though often encouraging, comments on the work of the teachers. Perhaps they did not always appreciate her keen interest and scrutiny and may have occasionally breathed a sigh of relief when she departed on a fairly long holiday to the I'Anson house in Clapham or to Switzerland and left them to their own devices, though even then she required children's exercises to be sent to her for inspection and she frequently left her sister, Emma, behind in Grayshott to act as her deputy in visiting the school.

The schoolroom also acted as a Church. From 1873 the Rector of Headley held Sunday Services there, and Mr. I'Anson added a small chancel, still in existence, to the schoolroom in 1878. This event was noted in the Headley Parish Magazine as follows: "The enlargement of Greyshott Schoolroom having become necessary, Mr. I'Anson has added a small chancel which was opened for the first time on September 29th, when the Schoolroom was decorated, and a service was held in Thanksgiving for the Harvest." This arrangement lasted until 1891 when a temporary church was built. The August 1873 issue of that magazine announced that the Grayshott services would commence on 3rd August at 2.30 p.m. "in Mr. I'Anson's Schoolroom, Greyshott." The latter was a common spelling of the name in the 19th century, though clearly "Grayshott" was the correct form derived from the earlier records. From June 1874 Holy Baptism was administered in the schoolroom on the first Sunday in the month as well as the now obsolete Churching of Women service on request.

The school became the social centre of the village. There are frequent notes of entertainments in aid of school funds both at Headley and in the Grayshott Schoolroom. From there was operated the Grayshott end of the Clothing and Shoe Clubs which covered the whole of Headley Parish. The Clothing Club was for people over 60, widows, and families with three or more children under 13. The Shoe Club was for children at school. These clubs, which operated for many years, worked on small weekly subscriptions, and, in the case of the Shoe Club, there was an additional bonus depending on attendance at day and Sunday schools. In 1873 there was distributed £33.18.7., in 1874 £55.4.2., and in 1875 £68.18.0. These social activities in the schoolroom expanded and by the end of 1897 the schedule of meetings included:

Church Lads Brigade	every Monday and Thursday at 7.30 p.m.
Choral Society	every Tuesday at 7.45 p.m.
Orchestral Society	every Wednesday at 7.30 p.m.
Band of Mercy	last Friday in the month at 6.30 p.m.

The first of the regular series of entries in the School Log Book was made on 10th October 1873, two years after the school opened. For the first two years of its existence we have only the annual reports of H.M. Inspectors, who had been established since 1839 to inspect schools receiving grants from the National Society, which itself received a grant from the Committee of the Privy Council on Education. The first report came in June 1873: "The school is in fairly promising condition considering it was opened only 6 months since." Reading and writing were satisfactory but Arithmetic "requires very great attention" — a constantly recurring theme. "Boys and girls are carefully instructed in needlework ... The children are quiet, neat and orderly. The teacher is conscientiously careful and industrious." The report was counter-signed, "C. B. I'Anson." The second report, of July 1873, echoed that of 1872. The only permanent help that the teacher had was an older girl as Monitress of the Infant Class. For some years to come poor Mrs. Clark recorded in the Log Book her struggles to teach arithmetic without much success. This unfortunately delayed for three years the granting of her certificate for which she passed the examination in 1873. There were also annual inspections by the Diocesan Inspector of the religious teaching. These were almost uniformly satisfactory.

As well as members of the I'Anson family the school had for many years to come frequent visitors, many of whom heard, and indeed gave, lessons. Among them was a Miss Woodthorpe of Grayshott House, almost as indefatigable as Miss I'Anson: whenever she came one or more of the classes were required to sing for her. Mr. I'Anson also came and on one occasion in January 1874 "gave a caution to the oldest boys for their disobedience, which, so far, has been effectual." The Rector of Headley, Rev. W. H. Laverty, also made periodic visits, but these seem to have been in the nature of duty visits, since he was devoid either of praise or criticism, two notes of his visits in 1874 and 1876 merely reporting, "he passed no remarks" and "he passed no remarks whatever." The first connection of the Whitaker family came in 1884 when there is the note: "Miss I'Anson and A. Whitaker, Esq." visited – Mr. Whitaker had recently come to Grayshott Hall. Thenceforward for many years the Whitakers showed continuous and benevolent interest. In October 1886, Mr. Apter must have made the following entry with some pride: "Lord Arthur Cecil called at the Grayshott School today to express his satisfaction at the education his tenant's children, James, Margaret and Thomas Mathieson, were receiving. During the two years that they have attended Grayshott Voluntary School he considered they had made good progress."

The notes in the Log Books detailing visitors to the school reads like a roll-call of residents and neighbours of Grayshott prominent in its early develop-ment. Canon Capes, Rector of Bramshott, who visited in 1899 and succeeding years, took over from the Rector of Headley the spiritual care of Grayshott and gave much help and encouragement to the provision of the temporary and later of the permanent parish church. In 1889 Professor and Mrs. Tyndall called at the school. Tyndall's name is indissolubly linked with the development of the Hindhead district. Then in 1890 there was "Mowat, Esq." – the Mr. Mowatt who was connected with the Beveridges and who lived at Hunters Moon, then Kingswood Firs, and whose name persists in one of the roads. In 1890 Dr. Plympton visited. It was in his memory that the Village Hall site was given some years later. In the same year came Sir Frederick Pollock, the jurist, closely identified with the Fox and Pelican. In 1891 a visit of Professor Williamson is mentioned – he lived at Pitfold and was prominent in local life until prevented by ill-health. Mrs. Vertue, who with her husband gave great help to the Roman Catholic community in Grayshott, visited the school in 1892. In the same year we read that "Rev. P. F. Wigan took the Scripture Lesson" – he became the first resident clergyman in the village. Miss Moir paid a visit in 1893 – she founded Lingholt School for girls, which has more recently become The Grove School. These entries illustrate the interest which prominent residents felt they should take in the village school.

Primary education was not free in those days and parents paid fees. These were 2d. a week for the first child, 1d. a week for others in the family. Sometimes, in cases of real poverty, the fees were wholly or partially remitted: "Sarah Harris, Mary Harris and Andrew Harris are allowed to pay one penny each for school pence, instead of two pence for the first child, on account of their mother being a widow." In May 1875 the fees were raised to 3d. a week for all children, but 2d. was to be returned at the end of the school year to children who had made more than 250 attendances. School fees were not completely abolished by law until 1892. Nor was attendance at school compulsory until 1876 and absences were frequent, though Miss I'Anson faithfully pursued the absentees or their parents, demanding to know the reason. The summer months for many years saw mass absenteeism because of local "Club Feasts," rural carnivals of village sickness clubs working on small weekly subscriptions and benefits. The most popular for Grayshott children were held at Churt and Shottermill. The onset of harvest, including whortleberries and hops, led to a mass exodus from school and, as far as possible, the summer holidays were fixed to minimise this trouble. Early entries in the Log Books illustrate this:

29. 5.74: attendance very bad this week on account of the Club Feasts.
17. 6.74: most of the children were absent today to visit a local Club Feast.
24. 7.74: attendances beginning to break off as the harvest approaches.

There are similar entries in 1875 and succeeding years, with frequent references to "herting" (i.e. picking whortleberries). It seems clear that children regularly worked in the local harvest and that sometimes whole families migrated to a more agricultural area for the harvest season — no doubt a way of building up a small reserve of money for the winter ahead.

Again the military summer manoeuvres which took place regularly in this area down to 1914 seem to have been an irresistible magnet for the children. Thus:

31. 7.74: This has been a very broken week on account of the military manoeuvres taking place in this neighbourhood.

In the first week of July 1875 many children were absent for the same reason.

The increasing impetus towards free and compulsory primary education, noted above, had its local impact. In August 1872, a Council for the Management of Education of Children of the Poor was formed in Headley with Mr. I'Anson as Chairman. It decided to levy a voluntary education rate of 4d. (it could not be compulsory until 1876). In 1878 Bye Laws made for the Parish of Headley, including Grayshott, by the School Attendance Committee of the Alton Poor Law Union made attendance of children aged 5 to 13 compulsory, unless for some sufficient reason, or if no primary school was available within 3 miles or, in the case of children 5 to 7, within 2 miles. For children aged 10 to 13 there was exemption if they were certified by the

Inspector as having reached the Fourth Standard. They need only make 150 attendances in the year if they had reached the Third Standard and were "beneficially and necessarily employed." The penalty for parents not causing their children to attend was 5s. and costs for each offence. A School Attendance Officer was appointed to enforce the Act of 1876 and these Bye Laws. Thereafter there are frequent records in the Log Books of visits and correspondence with this Officer. Later in 1878 further Bye Laws restricted the employment of children. Under 10 they could not be employed at all. Over that age they could be employed if either they had passed Standard 2 (extended to Standard 3 in 1879 and to Standard 4 in 1880) or if they had made 250 attendances for 2 years (extended to 3 years in 1879, to 4 years in 1880 and thereafter to 5 years). Further Bye Laws made in 1901 prohibited a child from leaving before the age of 14 unless the Fifth Standard had been passed: prospective employers were required to be satisfied by a certificate to that effect, failing which the employer was liable to a fine. The various Standards mentioned above were specified in the National Educational Code Prescribed by the Committee of the Privy Council and administered by H.M. Inspectors.

The school was financed partly by government grants and partly from voluntary subscriptions and local money-raising efforts. The annual accounts were published in the Headley Parish Magazine and later in the Grayshott Magazine. One example may suffice. In 1896/7, when there were 120 children in the school, the grants totalled £124 and local efforts raised £125. Salaries absorbed £211, books £14 and sundries £5. There are indications in the Log Books that books, writing and other educational materials were often given by the I'Ansons.

Mrs. Esther Clark remained in charge of the school until June 1885. By that time there was an assistant qualified teacher, a Mr. F. E. Child. Mrs. Clark's last entry read: "The present Head Mistress entered on her duties at Grayshott National School September 4th, 1871, when the school was opened for the first time. Her duties terminated today, having received salary for just fourteen years having been engaged the June before commencing duties." Miss I'Anson's entry was laconic: "Mr. F. E. Child and Mrs. Clark relinquished their duties as Assistant and Head Teacher June 25th, 1885."

A selection of entries may illustrate some aspects of the I'Anson regime:

12. 6.74:   "During the absence of the Mistress on Thursday Miss I'Anson very kindly supervised the management of the school."

22. 3.75:   A report by Miss I'Anson: "I attended school for over 3 hours today. The school is in good order, but the attendance is not so good as it ought to be. I spoke to the children and cautioned them about their irregular attendance ... Andrew Harris, Walter Carpenter, Rose Ayling and James Alderton I reproved as I do not consider they have made any progress for the last 3 weeks, the other infants have made progress in reading and arithmetic. The Second Standard children read well this morning. Fair progress is being made in all classes with their arithmetic.

7. 4.78: "Annie Trigg left school on the 3rd instant to go to service with the approbation of Miss I'Anson through whom she obtained her situation."

24.10.75: "The schoolmistress being ill, the school has been managed all week by Miss I'Anson."

14.12.76: "Miss I'Anson visited the school today to bid the teachers and children 'Goodbye' before leaving for Clapham" — a sort of regal departure.

25. 4.78: I (Miss I'Anson) asked Kate Small (monitress) to try and be more energetic in teaching the infants."

9. 7.78: "Mrs. I'Anson requests Kate Small to help her servants every morning, she is to go the first time tomorrow."

31. 7.78: "No meeting this afternoon in consequence of Miss I'Anson giving the children a School Treat."

9.10.78: "Miss I'Anson gave orders that certain portions of History and Geography were to be studied during the next fortnight, upon which she would examine the children when next she visited the school." She duly made her visit and remarked that the work was "not up to the mark."

7. 1.79: "Miss I'Anson gave a note to each child inviting its mother to tea on Friday afternoon."

9. 1.79: "Miss I'Anson gave a practical lesson to the older girls on bread making."

26. 5.79: Mr. Edward I'Anson himself inspected the children's work and noted: "I visited Grayshott School this morning, returning in the afternoon and examined all the children in Standards I, II, III, IV and V, also the Infants. Fair progress has been made by the children in each standard. In Standard I, A. Belton and N. Cover were careless in writing and spelling and N. Cover's reading was indifferent. In Standard II, M. Mansell and P. Rooke are still not as advanced as the children in the same standard. A. and E. Hibberd have improved. A. Budd's reading and spelling require attention. In III Standard, I find the children have made progress, grammar seems well understood, the geography fairly well answered. Standard IV children are careless, but their knowledge is good with the exception of geography. E. Matthews is careless in grammar. M. Small, Edith Cover and E. Belton in V Standard answered well in history and geography, and fairly well in grammar. The Infants have made decided progress, excepting C. Clay who is careless. The school was in very good order. E. B. I'Anson, Treasurer."

24. 4.79: "Miss I'Anson visited after 3 months away in Switzerland. The children decorated the school with flowers in her honour."

The Inspector's Report for 1879 advised that "urinals should be provided for the boys at their offices." The result is noted as follows:

27. 9.80: "All the boys were marched to see the newly erected urinals, its use was plainly explained and the boys cautioned against dirty habits."

24.11.80: "Miss E. B. I'Anson told several children to go to her home for some warm clothing which she was going to give them."

11. 2.81: "20 of the older children went to Headley School Treat." They were invited by Mr. Laverty and this became an annual event.

4. 4.81: An additional member of staff was appointed on the Inspector's recommendation: "Anne May started as Assistant Mistress her duties being to instruct the Infants and children in I and II Standards." Miss I'Anson went to the school to see her and reported: "Have been in school both morning and afternoon to listen to instruction given by A. May and am on the whole satisfied with her style of teaching."

4. 7.81: "No needlework given to any class as the children's hands were so stained with 'hert juice' that they were unfit to touch anything white."

Mrs. Clark could be as magisterial as Miss I'Anson, as is clear from the following note which she sent to a parent: "Mrs. Clark is sorry that A. Dudley is dissatisfied with his son's progress. She also begs to say that no child can be placed in Standard I until he has passed his 7th year, although a child of 8 can pass over Standard II and be placed in Standard III. But Mrs. Clark thinks it unwise to do so, a well-grounded child is more thoroughly educated than one polished off and placed in a high standard. Moreover neither Grayshott School nor Government Rules can be broken to please parents and any parent not appreciating the education of Grayshott School is at liberty to remove his child therefrom. To A. Dudley."

17.12.83: "The poetry for the V Standard was least well said, but it is a piece far too difficult for the children to master words and meanings. Gray's 'Elegy' being the piece selected," we may, perhaps, agree with Miss I'Anson's opinion. The poem had been selected by the Inspector!

14.10.86: In October, Miss I'Anson was going away for some months 'in Africa.' Before leaving she entered the following awesome comment: "I am leaving Grayshott today and may be unable to visit the school for some months. During my absence Mr. N. P. Apter (the Head Master who had succeeded Mrs. Clark) has the responsible position of keeping the school in good working order, giving at the same time attention to the playground and offices, that they are kept properly clean and tidy … Miss Lloyd who is at present replacing Mrs. Apter is a good teacher and well up to her work. Mr. Apter has the school in excellent order and spares no trouble in instructing the children under his care, he is very painstaking and conscientious in his work."

20. 1.90: "Miss I'Anson kindly sent on December 5th Port Wine for children that were attending school, who had been suffering from measles as the above children were very weak."

16. 2.91:   An entry by Miss I'Anson: "The Head Mistress Miss Squire will be absent for one fortnight on account of sickness. During that time I shall superintend work of school in St. II to VII."

4. 1.95:   Before the Spring Term started Miss I'Anson wrote detailed instructions in the Log Book: "All the arithmetic and dictation exercises for Standard III to VI should be on paper and dated.
Example: Dictation, Tuesday, January 5th
             Arithmetic, ditto
Copy Books should be dated on left hand margin ... The writing in Standards IV to VI lacks style, it should be much more uniform in character. During the singing lesson the children should stand. During the singing lesson, except when the time is being beaten, the children should have their hands folded at the back under their shoulder blades.
From January 5th until further notice school will be continued until 3.30. At 3.30 prayers and dismissal will take place. No child shall be kept in school for the purpose of rewriting lessons or doing any school work from the hours of 12 to 1. During that time the windows in the various classrooms should be opened to air the rooms, the fires attended to by the older boys and the rooms dusted by the girls. All children should wash their hands before afternoon school opens ... in cold weather when the lessons are changed, with the exception of the class monitress, the children should stand, clap hands and mark time. Miss I'Anson will examine the school in elementary subjects on January 25th." A grim commentary on the clapping of hands and marking time is given in the temperatures of the classrooms on each day during the first week of February 1895. They varied between the lowest of 24 Fahrenheit at 9.0 a.m. and the lowest of 40 Fahrenheit at 3.30 p.m.

5. 3.97:   Miss I'Anson's summary justice: "William Harris punished for obstinacy. I gave him a box on the ear."

As time went on there were additions to the school premises, provided by Mr. I'Anson. First a second classroom was built which was enlarged in 1895. By 1899 growing numbers again required additional accommodation and in that year the Inspector reported: "The school accommodation is at present inadequate for the average attendance" (the number in the school was 163). "This should be at once remedied or the Grant next year will be endangered (Article 85 (A) of the Code)." In the next year the complaint was repeated. As a result work was started in June 1900, and the new large classroom was opened in October of that year, the summer holiday having to be extended for the completion of the work. This event was celebrated by a tea party for the children and their parents in the "new schoolroom."

The school population had risen slowly in the first 20 years of the school's existence from 7 to something under 70. The last decade of the century saw the beginning of the rapid development of the village. In 1894 the number on roll was 87 and in the next eight years it was more than doubled to 172. School attendance was encouraged by the home visits of Miss I'Anson and the

Attendance Officer and by publishing at first in the Grayshott page of the Headley Parish Magazine, and later, after the separation of the parishes, in the Grayshott Parish Magazine, monthly lists of children with full attendances. Of one of the Attendance Officers Miss I'Anson remarked: "As regards his services at Grayshott they are useless as he never looks up the children" — there can be little doubt that she herself did so. In 1908 Mr. Ward started lantern lectures at the school, admission 1d, but free to children who had attended regularly and punctually in the preceding month—these lectures were partly instructional and partly of entertainment value.

We have seen that Mrs. Clark served as Head Teacher from 1871 to 1885. For most of that time she worked with the assistance of an older girl paid as a monitress. The salary of this assistant was not excessive. In February 1883 a Log Book entry reports: "Mary Young entered on her duties as monitress. Payment until March 15th, 6d. per week, after that date 1/- provided she instructs the infants well." In the later years of Mrs. Clark additional teachers were appointed. In May 1882, a Miss Storer, college trained, was appointed as assistant mistress but stayed only until July. Miss I'Anson remarked in a somewhat peevish tone: "Reason for leaving distance of Grayshott from the church" (i.e. Headley). "Before engaging the assistant mistress she was acquainted by letter that the church was 3½ miles distant and the locality was stated to be dull both by letter and advertisement." In January 1883, the first male assistant teacher, Mr. F. E. Child of Chester Training College, started duty. He resigned in 1885 at the same time as Mrs. Clark. Mrs. Clark's successor was Mr. Henry P. Apter who became Head Teacher in September 1885, with his wife as assistant teacher. An additional assistant was appointed in September 1886.

After Mr. Apter, who resigned in 1888, there came three ladies who in quick succession were Head Teachers: Miss Hannah Jones 1888-90; Miss Sarah Squire 1890-92; and Miss Annie Griffith 1892-93. In April 1893, Mr. James G. Ward was appointed and he remained Head Teacher until 1913. His nickname was "Podgy" for quite obvious reasons. He was a very good schoolmaster and a first-class woodworker and gardener. Unfortunately he had a choleric temperament which caused complaints of the severe corporal punishment which he sometimes meted out, one such complaint leading to his resignation. By 1899 the staff consisted of the Head Teacher, three certificated assistant teachers and a monitress.

We have mentioned that the law permitted children to leave school at the age of 10 under certain circumstances. But it is clear from the Grayshott Log Books that children were sometimes withdrawn for casual work. This can be illustrated by a few typical entries:

23 3.79: "William Boxall absent every morning to mind his father's horses. This makes his progress very slow." His father, Stephen, was the Grayshott carrier.

8.11.82: "36 children present, several boys absent taken by Mr. Phillips (of Grayshott Hall) as beaters."

13.11.83: "William Moorey was sent by Mr. Shepherd to fetch James Belton and Hori Moorey from school to attend him in shooting."

As noted earlier, Bye Laws of 1878 raised the leaving age to 13, but, subject to certain conditions, children could leave earlier. Grayshott parents took advantage of this:

31.10.84: "The parents are in a dissatisfied state at being obliged to send their children to school until they are 13 years of age."

16. 3.98: "7 children were taken by Miss I'Anson in her carriage to Headley School for examination for Labour Certificates."

28. 3.99: "Miss I'Anson took Beatrice Cane and Kate Harris in her carriage to Headley School for examination for Labour Certificates."

4. 5.01: "3 boys taken by Miss I'Anson to Selborne School for examination for Labour Certificates."

The kindly, though autocratic, benevolence of the I'Ansons and later the Whitakers is illustrated by frequent reports in the Log Books and the Headley and Grayshott Magazines. In February 1876 Mr. I'Anson "in a very kind manner advised the children to be strictly obedient after which he left a box of figs to be distributed at the time of dismissal." From the 1890s onwards there are regular reports of the annual school treats, usually in August, at Grayshott Hall—there was sometimes also a treat in the school early in the New Year. There are people who still remember the Grayshott Hall Summer treats— nostalgic memories of the march from the school to Grayshott Hall on a hot afternoon redolent with the smell of newly cut hay, of the popular games and races, of the seeking for cunningly hidden dutch cheeses, of the gifts of new pennies and tea mugs with "Grayshott Hall" and the year inscribed on them. There was sometimes a band, e.g. the Haslemere Band in 1907, to head the march. In a sultry week in June 1900, Miss Hadwen, Miss I'Anson's friend and companion, brought cakes and lemonade for the children daily. In November 1900 a system was started by which Miss Hadwen took charge in one of the classrooms of the children who brought their dinners with them. For many years she and Miss I'Anson daily tied white cloths on the long school desks and made cocoa for these children at a minimal charge. In 1905 the Inspector commented on this arrangement: "by which the children who come from far may eat their mid day meals in a seemly and respectable manner." This work was taken over in 1914 by a School Care Committee including Miss I'Anson, Mrs. Lyndon, Mr. Whitaker and the Vicar. It provided hot cocoa daily at 1d. a week. The Second World War and rationing produced the organisation of school meals for children which is now a permanent feature of school life. School meals actually started at Grayshott School in January 1942, cooked in the wooden canteen which until lately was still in use. There were, as we have seen, pioneers in Grayshott since the beginning of the century.

The Diamond Jubilee had been an occasion for rejoicing—tea and sports for the children and a bonfire on the Gibbet Hill. The coronation of George V in 1911 was commemorated by the planting of trees, on the Children's Recreation Ground by Mrs. Hannah ("Granny") Robinson, and in the Churchyard by Leith Ingham Tomkins Whitaker and Nicolette Simms, daughter of the Vicar: the trees are still there. It was a most inclement day and sports on "Mr. Morgan Brown's football field" (later Philips Green and now the site of the new school) were washed out, but there was a good tea in the schoolroom and a huge bonfire on Hindhead.

In 1902 Balfour's Education Act abolished the School Boards set up in 1876 and handed over the provision and control of primary education to Local Education Authorities, which were the Education Committees of County and County Borough Councils. In consequence voluntary primary schools no longer received a grant direct from the Board of Education but from the Local Authorities, which were to be responsible for the expenses of running the schools including painting of the premises, though these remained the property of the School Managers who were responsible for structural repairs. Thus the control of the voluntary schools became less personal than heretofore, though in the case of Grayshott this was not immediately noticeable. Miss I'Anson continued as School Correspondent with Mr. Ward as Head Teacher, used to the pre-1902 era. So, though the final control was exercised from Winchester, Miss I'Anson's powerful and benevolent influence pervaded the school down to the outbreak of the First World War. Declining health obliged her to give up her work and she died in June 1916.

Down to the First World War the school continued in its usual way, the school year being punctuated by the annual school treat. Mr. Ward was succeeded by Mr. A. E. Bott in 1913. When the war broke out and Kitchener's Army was being raised and trained the school buildings were commandeered for billeting troops and the school used the Wesleyan Church and the Mission Church, the latter on the Portsmouth Road. This arrangement lasted until May 1915.

In the years following the war the school was handicapped by shortage of staff and both Mr. Bott, who resigned in 1919, and Mr. W. T. Varley, his successor, worked under considerable difficulty, having to manage with supply and supplementary teachers for long periods.

Ever since Mr. Ward's appointment the Head Teacher had lived in "Fircroft," a house adjoining the school ground and owned by the I'Anson family who charged a small rent. It is a large house with a good deal of passage room which makes it nearly impossible and highly expensive to heat it adequately. Moreover it has a large garden in which only Mr. Ward took a keen interest. In 1916 the house became the property of Miss Hadwen and continued as the Head Teacher's house. On Miss Hadwen's death in 1930 the property was purchased by Miss Emma I'Anson who conveyed it in memory of her sister, Catherine, for the same purpose as before. The property was vested in the Guildford Diocesan Board of Finance, the administrative trustees being the Vicar and Churchwardens and the School Managers. If at some future time it was not needed for a Head Teacher's house it could be sold or let, the proceeds going to the School Managers' Funds. If the school ceased to be a Church of England Voluntary School and the Body of Managers thereby dissolved, "Fircroft" would revert to the Vicar, Churchwardens and Parochial Church Council to be used for increasing the endowment stipend of St. Luke's Church. Though the school altered its status as a result of Butler's Education Act 1944, it has still remained a Church school. Headmasters continued to live in the house until 1965, but found it difficult to contend with the problems of heating and of care of a large garden. On their side the Managers found it increasingly difficult to cover necessary repairs from the rent charged. This became even more so when the school became Voluntarily

Controlled in 1947, as the Managers then ceased to control any funds with regard to the school. In practice the house became the responsibility of St. Luke's Church, which had frequently to appeal for voluntary contributions.

Mr. Varley retired in July 1938 and there were then three comparatively short headmasterships: Mr. R. E. King, 1937–1946; Mr. E. G. Wardle, 1946–1950; Mr. F. D. Teague, 1950–1957. It was then that Mr. D. H. Roberts, the present headmaster, was appointed.

Whereas the First World War had resulted in the school being commandeered for a time, the Second World War produced the avalanche of evacuees from London and Portsmouth. At one time in 1941 there were 87 evacuees attending the school. This and the increasing numbers of local children in post-war years led to the overspill of classes to the Village Hall and, for a time, to Tudor House.

Butler's Act 1944 reorganised the national system of education. One chief concept was that primary education should provide for the age ranges 5–11, and that all children over the latter age should continue in some form of secondary education. Another feature was a solution of the vexed question of the existence of denominational schools, mainly "Church Schools." In the main these were divided into "Voluntary Aided" and "Voluntary Controlled" schools. In the former group the Local Authority was responsible for all expenses, except repairs to the actual structure of the school buildings. Two-thirds of the Managers were to be "Foundation Managers," one-third were to be "Representative Managers," nominated by the County Council and other local government bodies such as the Parish Council. In the case of the "Voluntary Controlled" schools all expenses without exception were the responsibility of the Local Authority and, in consequence, two-thirds of the Managers were to be Representative Managers, one-third Foundation Managers. In these schools, since the Managers have no financial responsibility, they have no funds and draw their small necessary expenditure from the Local Authority. Their functions are to maintain a lively interest in and close knowledge of the school, to have some say in the appointment of staff, and, perhaps most usefully, to act as a pressure group in seeking from the Local Authority necessary improvements and extensions of buildings and educational equipment. At Grayshott the financial burden of keeping the ageing school premises and "Fircroft" in repair, including the need to re-roof the school, compelled the Managers to seek "controlled" status, which was approved in May, 1947. For many years the Managers regularly elected the Vicar as chairman, until in the interregnum following Canon Ottley's death, Mr. M. B. Hewitt, a Churchwarden, was elected. After Mr. Hewitt's death in 1963, Canon Winnett was chairman for a short time, being succeeded later in the same year by the present writer. The Managers have been fortunate in their School Correspondents who have usually held office for prolonged periods. We remember particularly Mrs. Bazett, Miss Stent, Mrs. Lathbury, Mrs. Durham and now Mrs. Cooper.

Butler's Act also required Local Authorities to formulate in their own areas Development Plans for the future organisation of education. This inevitably took time, but eventually Grayshott School was scheduled for rebuilding on Philips Green, named after Philip I'Anson and given to the Parish Council in 1916 by Miss Catherine I'Anson. The Local Authority bought it from the Parish Council in 1953 for the purpose of a school. In 1961 the Chief Education Officer said that the new school would be started in 1964. It is a sad comment on modern difficulties that it was not in fact started until 1976. Similarly, the school did not finally lose its pupils over 11 until 1956, when they were transferred to a Secondary Modern School at Bordon.

As a pressure group the Managers have had some, but not complete, success. They have been greatly aided by the Parent Teacher Association, a very active body founded as a permanent organisation by Mr. Roberts. It has raised large sums of money for improvements, including the Swimming Pool (1961) and a Library Room (1971) and much equipment and amenities of all kinds. The Association has its own social activities and holds well-attended meetings on matters connected with the children's education and general Welfare.

H.M. Inspectors reported in 1953: "The building is very inconvenient ... every classroom has a defect ... lavatory provision is below requirements." In nearly twenty years since then the Managers have persuaded the Local Authority to provide five temporary and extremely satisfactory classrooms, to convert two classrooms in the old building into a badly needed assembly hall and gymnasium, and to make a small and entirely inadequate start in providing inside toilet accommodation (two lavatories for 260 children!). Those outside in the playground are rather primitive but can be used in normal weather. In severe winter weather, however, they freeze up and there is no means of preventing this. Imagination boggles at the prospect on such occasions of 260 children making use of the two inside lavatories.

In recent years the education of the children has more and more responded to the best of modern methods and has widened considerably. School clubs and societies, swimming, and the many educational visits afford valuable experience. The impression of any visitor to the school must be that it is a purposeful and happy community under the guidance of Mr. Roberts and his staff.

What of the future? A great encouragement is that—at last—after many years of hope deferred, a start was made in 1976 in building the first stage of a new Primary School on the Philips Green site,. which had been acquired for that purpose by the County Council 23 years earlier. We may express the hope and, indeed, the conviction that Grayshott School, in the second century of its existence as in the first, will continue to serve the village well.

The Grove School

The Grove School for girls came to Hindhead in 1928 and settled in the house now known as The Grove on the south-eastern side of the A3 road, just to the east of the junction of that road with the Crossways Road, and in the ecclesiastical, though not the civil, parish of Grayshott. The school had previously been Lingholt School, a private school for "young ladies," which had been owned and conducted by Miss E. Moir, a prominent member of the Grayshott community in the period of its early development.

The Grove School was originally a small private school in Nottingham, founded by Mrs. Lacey, who moved it to Highgate, then almost a country suburb of London. She was succeeded in 1894 by Miss M. R. Lacey who remained Headmistress till 1924. Miss Lacey was a pioneer woman at Oxford, reading a History degree course before women were actually admitted to Oxford degrees. She was also a pioneer in the education of girls. She organised the school not on a Form basis but on individual time-tables, which in a school of 60 girls resulted in 10 major University Scholarships in as many years. Discipline did not depend on a multiplicity of school rules, but to a remarkable extent on self-discipline, based on her principles of "Freedom and Service," which have remained a characteristic of the school.

Miss Lacey was followed by Miss E. M. Fletcher, who was Headmistress for more than thirty years, retiring in 1955. She it was who moved the school to Hindhead owing to the increasing urbanisation of Highgate. There is a lively account in the school magazine of an expedition by charabanc of the girls and staff from Highgate to Hindhead for a preview of their new home. Before her retirement, Hindhead Court was purchased. This and the later acquisition in 1962 of Ardquin, a house in Hazel Grove adjacent to Hindhead Court, completed a school of three houses and some fifty acres of playing fields and lovely grounds. It made possible the organisation of the school into: Hindhead Court as a beautiful boarding house for some 80 boarders; Ardquin as teaching accommodation for the junior school and boarding accommodation for the Sixth Form; The Grove entirely as teaching accommodation.

Today there are some 200 girls at the school, of whom about 100 are boarders. The Junior School caters for the age group 5–11. There is a wide curriculum of academic and cultural subjects, classes are small, and individual teaching is extensively used. The Senior School, 11–18, prepares girls for the Ordinary and Advanced Levels of the Oxford General Certificate of Education, and works in small forms or sets, with each girl having an individual time-table. Some girls prepare for the Certificate of Secondary Education examinations and there is also a secretarial course. In the Sixth Form most girls prepare for University entrance, though for some there is a more general course. Sixth Form pupils do not wear uniform and have an enviable degree of freedom in their own boarding house at Ardquin. They are treated as students.

Since 1906 the school has been inspected and recognised as efficient by the Department of Education and Science and was incorporated as an Independent Public School in 1948 under a Council of Management and Headmistress, at present Mrs. E. N. Bickerdyke. The Grove School is a Church of England foundation, though girls of other faiths and denominations are admitted. Grove School girls frequently form a welcome part of the congregation at St. Luke's Church.

Amesbury School

When Amesbury School came to Hindhead during the first World War it had already had nearly half a century of existence, having been founded in 1870 by Rev. E. Fowle, son of a Vicar of Amesbury—hence the name of the school. It was originally established at Redhill with only one pupil, but, after a year, owing to increasing numbers it moved to Reigate and again, for the same reason, in 1877 to Bickley in the Bromley area of Kent, where its numbers fluctuated between 41 and 28.

The school was bought in 1887 by Mr. E. H. Moore, under whom rising numbers caused a further move to a larger house at Bickley in 1902. A year later Mr. Moore was drowned while bathing, but his widow continued to run the school until 1904 when Mr. E. C. Brown became Headmaster. It was he who, on account of air raids and his desire to have a smaller school with no day boys, moved to Hindhead where he bought Mount Arlington School in Hazel Grove, and in Grayshott ecclesiastical parish. Mount Arlington School had been established for some years, but by 1917 had only one pupil. The Amesbury School magazine in October 1917 remarked, "Hindhead is too well known as a health resort for us to dwell on that point," but the actual move was in February 1918. There were attractions other than those of health, for the Mount Arlington School had a lovely purpose-built Lutyens building. The Amesbury gymnasium was transported, piece by piece, from Highgate to Hindhead where it is still in service in 1977.

Mr. Brown was followed in 1920 by Mr. C. L. Macdonald whom some Grayshott people will certainly remember. Under him Scouting became the corner-stone of school life and remained so for 30 years. Amesbury was a Rugby school and claims that it converted St. Edmund's to the game in 1922.

In 1923 the school secured additional premises by buying Hazelcroft in Hazel Grove which would permit the school to accept more pupils, and this was followed in 1928 by a move from Hazelcroft to Bracklands, a larger house next door with extensive garden and woodland. Mr. Macdonald was joined in 1930 by Mr. J. G. Hill (at Amesbury until 1947) who was as keen on Scouting as Macdonald himself.

In 1931 Mr. L. Queen became a young assistant to the head gardener and succeeded "old Raggett" in that post in 1950, in which he is still going strong in 1977. He is a mine of information and anecdote, particularly of Field Marshal Lord Montgomery's close association with the school.

Montgomery's son, David, was at Amesbury during the Second World War, and in 1943 it was from the small summer house at Amesbury that Montgomery and his staff planned the invasion of Sicily and, from his famous caravan at Amesbury, the later D-Day landings on the Normandy beaches. He himself went direct from Amesbury to the beaches. Mr. Queen remembers that the caravans arrived on a snowy day and that Monty, a staunch teetotaller, forbade the Army personnel responsible for setting up his H.Q. to be served with beer. Another nice touch was Mr. Queen's recollection of Monty judging the boys' boxing competition and giving the loser his wrist watch.

Mr. Macdonald had resigned in 1938 for health reasons, and had been succeeded by Major T. Reynolds, who built the school chapel and was the Headmaster of the Montgomery period.

When Major Reynolds resigned in 1948, two young assistant masters — Messrs. A. G. Peel and J. P. Potter — bought the school in partnership, and on Mr. Potter's resignation Mr. Peel continued as Headmaster. He was a charming, modest man and his resignation in 1970 plunged the school in difficulty, as it was not possible to find a successor. Amesbury was threatened with closure. It was saved, however, by the formation of a charitable educational trust, for which finance was raised by gifts and loans from parents and other friends of the school. It was characteristic of Mr. Peel that he agreed to carry on during the period of uncertainty until the Board of Governors set up under the trust could appoint the present Headmaster, Mr. D. E. W. Spencer, for January 1971. His many friends greatly regretted that Mr. Peel did not enjoy a long retirement.

It was natural, though unfortunate, that the numbers in the school declined in the uncertainty of 1970, but they have increased rapidly since then. The school, through the Common Entrance Examination, sends boys to a wide range of Public Schools. Though in Mr. Peel's time the emphasis was upon Harrow, the field is now much more extensive.

ST. EDMUND'S SCHOOL
104 NOT OUT

In April 1874 the Rev. John Morgan-Brown started a boys' Preparatory School at Hunstanton on the Norfolk coast, and called it Glebe House. It was not until September 1900 that Grayshott saw the first of many young faces in their midst. Mr. Cyril Morgan-Brown, our founder's son, decided to migrate and chose Blencathra, a large Victorian private house on the outskirts of the village of Grayshott, which had been rented in the preceding two years by George Bernard Shaw, after his marriage.

The original house was considerably enlarged, playing fields were laid out, and Mr. Cyril with his colleague and partner, Mr. Ivor Sant, moved in in time for the autumn term. This was five months later than expected, as there were delays in getting things done even in those days. On moving, the name of the school was changed to that of St. Edmund's, after the East Anglian Martyr King.

Since then the school has become part and parcel of the life of the village. The school staff have joined in the many local activities, serving on committees, teaching in Sunday School, and supporting local sport and social functions. Several of the village houses were built in the first instance by staff at the school.

It did not take long for the migrants to feel at home here, and it did not take long either for the local inhabitants to get used to the groups of boys in their midst. The boys revelled in the lovely countryside that surrounded them. Sunday suits and Scout uniform may have given way to track suits and sporting kit, but the spirit is the same. The school was allowed to make use of St. Luke's Church until their own chapel was finished, and there is a mention of the first service they held there, which was the Harvest Festival of 1900, and did in fact take place just before the consecration of the Church. The school choir has sung Evensong in St. Luke's on many occasions since then and have been fortunate in being allowed to use the Church on special memorial occasions, and for their carol services.

St. Edmund's has continued its work of laying foundation stones for life for over one hundred years. More than two thousand boys have passed through the school, and despite two world wars which left sad gaps in the list of Old Boys, and the depression which saw numbers shrink and prophets of doom abound, the school is full — with some one hundred and forty boarders and forty day boys. During its life many scholarships have been won to the public schools, and its Old Boys have made valuable contributions to the life of the country in all its facets.

Cyril Morgan-Brown started our life at Grayshott, but that this start bore fruit has been due to the efforts of many over the years. Ivor Sant, who was his partner for many years, took over when Mr. Cyril died in 1928. In 1934 Ivor Bulley, Mr. Cyril's son-in-law, took up the reins and guided the school through the lean thirties and the war years, until he retired in 1952 — when he was succeeded by Peter Weeks, himself an Old Boy during Mr. Cyril's and

Mr. Sant's reigns. So the line of succession was unbroken and the ethos of the school secure.

One of the features of the teaching staff over the years has been not only the quality of their teaching but also the length of time they stayed here many of them qualifying as honorary Old Boys by more than ten years' service. Peter Weeks has ten such members of his team. Two of them, Tony Pull and John Hardwick, are partners, and Tony Pull is an Old Boy of Glebe House, Hunstanton — so the circle is complete.

No prep. school could function without the presence of the female touch. Miss Mona Morgan-Brown, Miss Winnie Morgan-Brown, and Mrs. Bulley all carried on the family traditions, and Mrs. Weeks has continued these for the last twenty-five years. They have all been supported by a devoted band of matrons, and every generation of boys looks back with gratitude to this motherly help and guidance.

St. Edmund's hopes to be able to continue its contribution to the life of this country for many years to come. In the words of the school motto "Permanendo Vincimus."

St Luke's Church before 1910

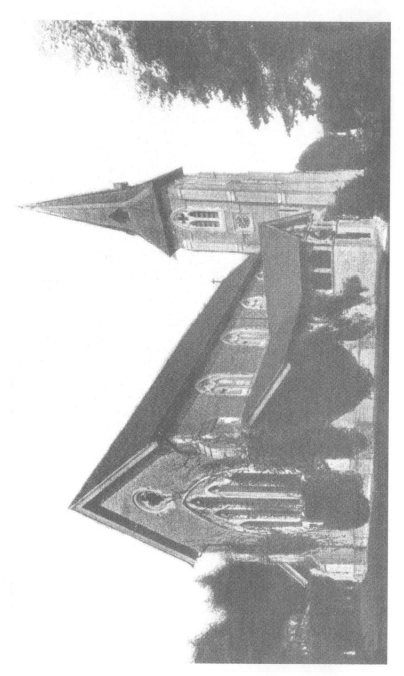

St Luke's Church now

Crossways Road circa 1900

Crossways Road circa 1905

Headley Road circa 1905

Miss Catherine B. I'Anson, died 1916

Mr Alexander Ingham Whitaker, died 1933

Dr Arnold Lyndon, died 1948

Mrs Charlotte Lyndon, died 1936

An old broomsquire, 'Body' Hill and his wife Nancy, circa 1880

A modern broomsquire (Mr Peter Burrows)

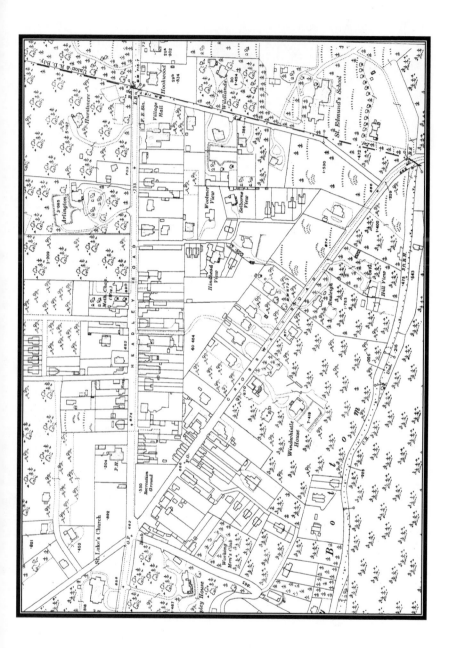

Centre of
Grayshott
circa 1909

112

Chapter 9

Formation of the Parish of St. Luke: The other Churches

We have noted previously that for centuries Grayshott was part of the parish of Headley. An earlier reference to the use of Stephen Boxall's cart as a hearse for burials in Headley Churchyard illustrates the resulting inconvenience. Reference is made in the Chapter on Grayshott School to the Rector of Headley starting regular Anglican services in the schoolroom of Grayshott School in 1873, when the inhabitants of Grayshott numbered about 100. In 1888 the spiritual care of Grayshott passed by agreement from the Rector of Headley to the Rector of Bramshott, though Grayshott still remained part of Headley Parish. Canon Capes would walk from Bramshott to Grayshott via Waggoners Wells or Ludshott Common to hold services in the school or "in the old schoolroom on the Portsmouth Road," which had at one time been a dame school. It was situated at the junction of Kingswood Lane with the Portsmouth Road. The growth of population and the summer influx of visitors to the district had necessitated the erection of a temporary iron church in 1891. One feature of the change of responsibility for church services was that from 1891 the curate of Bramshott resided in Grayshott. The first to do so was Rev. Percy Wigan between 1891 and 1895. He lived at "Grayshott Cottage," later called "Wayside," which was demolished in 1971 to make room for commercial development. His successor was another Bramshott curate, Rev. J. M. Jeakes, who lived at "The Hermitage," an I'Anson house, and whom we have already seen as prominent in the foundation of the Fox and Pelican.

Towards the close of the century the continued increase in population and the early development of the village as a shopping centre, and, to some extent, as a health resort, made the formation of a separate ecclesiastical parish urgently necessary. This had been partially recognised by the addition of a Grayshott section in the Headley Parish Magazine from December 1896, which announced meetings of social, cultural and educational organisations in Grayshott and gave news of Grayshott School. Two years later, when the movement for a permanent church was well under way, a separate Grayshott and District Magazine was started. Miss I'Anson had already given the site for the church and her family and the Whitakers were foremost in the effort.

The Committee which organised the appeal for funds was under the chairmanship of Canon Capes and consisted of Miss C. B. I'Anson, Mr. E. B. I'Anson, Miss James of Westdown, Professor Williamson of High Pitfold, Mr. A. Ingham Whitaker of Grayshott Hall, and Rev. J. M. Jeakes. By February 1898, the Church Fund had reached £4,000 and the building was begun. On 3rd September 1898, the foundation stone was laid by Miss I'Anson: the silver trowel which she used was given to her by Mr. Whitaker and is now in a case at the west end of the church. There appears to have been some indecision as to the dedication of the church. Thomas Wright in his book "Hindhead" (1898) mentioned "a happy suggestion" that the church should be dedicated to St. John the Baptist, "the preacher in the wilderness." Be that as it may, the dedication was to St. Luke. By the end of February 1900, the Fund had reached over £6,200; the cost of the building was £5,161.18.11., and the balance of £1,040 was used to start an endowment fund which was gradually increased over the years. Among the outstanding donations were £250 from Canon Capes, £500 from Miss James, £100 from Mr. Macmillan, the publisher, £725 from the I'Anson family and £1,600 from the Whitaker family. Mr. Edward I'Anson gave his services as honorary architect. Gifts in kind, apart from the land, included the mosaic pavement in the chancel (now covered by a blue carpet) by Miss I'Anson, all the locally quarried Bargate stone and windows by Mr. Whitaker, the carved oak altar by Dr. and Mrs. Lyndon, the oak pulpit (made from beams taken from an old cottage in Headley) by Mrs. Whitaker, the heating apparatus by Mr. I'Anson, the choirstalls by Mr. Haslehurst, Mr. I'Anson's partner, the seats in the nave and aisles by Miss James and Mr. Robert Turner, whom we have seen as connected with the Grayshott and District Refreshment Association, the altar rails and credence table by Mrs. Macmillan, the carved oak lectern by Mr. Robert Foster, who had acted as Clerk of the Works, the organ by Misses C. B. and E. B. I'Anson, the chancel rail and screen by Mr. C. E. Lowry, 150 footstools by Mrs. Whitaker, a lectern Bible and Prayer Book by Grayshott schoolchildren. The font was given by Canon Capes. It had been Bramshott Church font, but an older font had been discovered and re-placed in Bramshott Church, its successor being transferred to St. Luke's.

On 6th August 1898, while the church was being erected, "The Herald" printed the following description:

"The church will contain sittings for 350 people, and will consist of nave, aisles, chancel, organ chamber, and two vestries. The length including chancel will be 102 ft., and the width including aisles 42 ft., and the height of the nave will be 43 ft. The tower and spire will rise to a height of 100 ft. and will be on the south side of the church, but it is not proposed at present to proceed with the spire and upper part of the tower. The style is Early English and the walls will be faced outside with Bargate stone, and on the inside with Headley stone. The nave arcade, the arches of the windows and doors and the tracery of the windows will be in Bath stone. The floor will be laid with wood block flooring and the church will be warmed with hot water."

The new church was first used for services on Sunday, 17th October, 1899, with Communion at 8.0 p.m. and Mattins and Litany at 11.0 a.m., when Canon Capes preached the sermon.

Meanwhile the formalities for the formation of the parish were set on foot. The first was an agreement as to the patronage, completed in 1900 between the Bishop of Winchester, the Patrons of Headley Parish (Queen's College, Oxford) and the Rector of Headley in the following terms:

"Whereas a building has been erected on a piece of land situate at Grayshott ... and the ... land ... and building have been conveyed to the Ecclesiastical Commissioners ... by a Deed Poll ... of 13th May 1899, ... the Bishop ... Patrons ... and Rector agree ... that the perpetual right of patronage and nominating a minister to serve the Church of St. Luke, Grayshott, shall from time to time after the consecration of such Church whenever it shall be required to nominate a minister to serve the same be vested in and for ever after shall be exercised by the ... Bishop for the time being of Winchester."

The next step was the petition for Consecration, which was dated 8th October 1900. It was signed by the Rector (Rev. W. H. Laverty) and Churchwardens (W. T. Phillips and W. B. Ayling) of Headley and it stated that the site contained 3,850 square yards: that there were to be 350 sittings, half to be free: that the land was properly fenced in: and that the Church was to be for "the inhabitants of the District to be assigned thereto."

In November 1900, the Ecclesiastical Commissioners represented to Queen Victoria that there should be established "a consolidated chapelry to be consecrated the Church of St. Luke, Grayshott." The reasons given were that a population had gathered together at the extremities of the parishes of Headley, Shottermill and Churt and that this population was distant from any of these parish churches. A Schedule contained in meticulous detail the boundaries of St. Luke's parish. All that part of it which lies in Hampshire was carved out of Headley, but a considerable area across the Surrey boundary was taken from Shottermill and Churt. It includes Hazel Grove (western side) and High Pitfold on the east, and on the north it takes in Tower Road and land south of the Beacon Hill Road (but not the Royal Huts Hotel) forming the upper end of the Golden Valley.

The last legal formality was the signing of an Order in Council setting up and defining the new parish. This Order in January 1901, was the first Ecclesiastical Order to be signed by the new King, Edward VII. The Church had already been consecrated and dedicated on St. Luke's Day, 1900, by Dr. Davidson, Bishop of Winchester, three years before he became Archbishop of Canterbury. Among the many clergy present were the two most responsible for the establishment of the parish — Canon Capes and Rev. W. H. Laverty.

The Curates of Bramshott in charge at Grayshott were:

1891–1895 Rev. P. Wigan, who married into the I'Anson family.
1895–1901 Rev. J. M. Jeakes.

The Vicars of Grayshott have been:

1901–1907 Rev. J. M. Jeakes.
1908–1926 Rev. A. E. N. Simms, a witty Irishman and a scholar. He had been a curate and friend of Ralph Inge, who later became the "gloomy Dean" of St. Paul's. Mr. Simms was a preacher of learned but very long sermons. In 1921 he was appointed Golden Lecturer. Locally he gave several series of University Extension Lectures, mainly on historical subjects. He was apt to be a trifle absent-minded. On one occasion he

cycled to the Mission Church in the Portsmouth Road to take a Communion Service, but failed to notice that the gates were shut and collided with them, with sad results both to his person and his bicycle. For a short time during his incumbency Grayshott had its only curate, Rev. J. Partridge (1914–1917). He had been a master at Mount Arlington (now Amesbury) School. He married a daughter of Mr. C. E. Lowry of the firm of Chapman, Lowry and Puttick. He later became Vicar of Hale and a Canon of Guildford. Mr. Partridge had followed a resident Church Army Captain, Thomas Wray, who went to Edmonton, Canada, in 1927 where he was ordained and took charge of a large parish. On his return to England in 1935 he had a Yorkshire parish. On leaving Grayshott Mr. Simms became Rector of St. Mary's, Bryanston Square. He died in 1952 after a very prolonged and distressing illness. A memoir of Mr. Simms was written by his nephew, the Archbishop of Dublin.

1927–1942	Rev. E. Garth Ireland, who had a very strong social conscience and did much to organise help for the unemployed of Jarrow in the economic depression of the 'Thirties.
1942–1958	Canon Fielding H.B. Ottley, Canon of Canterbury, Special Preacher to Canterbury Cathedral, Preacher of Grays Inn and also Golden Lecturer. An eminent scholar, he was a saintly and extremely loveable man. A memoir of him and a collection of his sermons were published by Canon Winnett.
1958–1969	Rev. A. R. Winnett, Canon of Guildford (1961). He is a scholar of note, an authority on Samuel Johnson, and an eminent theologian. He and his family were friends to all in Grayshott. He became Rector of Ockham, until his retirement.
1970–	Rev. S. F. Hooper.

Mr. Edward I'Anson had designed a tower for the church, but this was not at first completed. Later he produced a design for a tower and spire. It may be of interest to note that the design provided for a rather squat spire which Mr. I'Anson did not really like when it was built, so he arranged for the present tall spire to be built over and, as it were, superimposed upon the original. A fund was opened in 1907 which by 1910 had reached £1,580, the cost of the work. The tower and spire were completed in that year, together with a clock and three bells for striking the hours and quarters. Mr. I'Anson died late in 1912. He had been the architect and surveyor of St. Bartholomew's Hospital and had served as Master of the Merchant Taylors' Company.

In 1931 five new bells were added and the existing ones were recast at a total cost of £534. Meanwhile in 1916 the pier of the tower which carried the chancel arch was found to be in a dangerous condition, and an additional pier was built. The weight of the bells, totalling about 40 cwts., ranges between the 2 cwts. 3 qrs. and 27 lbs. of the treble bell and the 8 cwts. 1 qr. and 9 lbs. of the tenor. The inscriptions of the bells, including the date of casting or re-casting, are:

Treble:	"E. Garth Ireland, Vicar.
	V. S. Woods, Walter C. Ryde, Churchwardens."
No. 2:	"The Parishioners gave me."
	"Sing, rejoice and give thanks."
Nos. 3 and 4:	These were re-cast bells.
No. 5:	"Kathleen Vance gave me."
	"Come all ye faithful."
No.6:	a re-cast bell.
No. 7:	"Walter C. Ryde and Eleanor Ryde gave me."
	"Lift up your hearts."
Tenor:	"This clock and bell were given in 1910 to the memory of G. S."

In 1932 the original organ was completely re-conditioned and additional stops were added.

The chancel and sanctuary were considerably altered in 1939, the sanctuary being extended into the chancel and furnished with oak linenfold panelling, and a blue carpet was laid from the altar to the chancel steps. At the same time a new altar cross was provided and the carved and coloured reredos was added. The whole scheme was designed by Sir Charles Nicholson and the cost was just under £350: the work was carried out in memory of W. C. Ryde and V. S. Woods, Churchwardens. Later the oak panelling was extended on the south wall of the chancel as a memorial to Rev. E. Garth Ireland.

In 1952 the church had to be re-roofed at a cost of £1,450, which was raised by public subscription between October 1952 and April 1953.

In June 1961, the side altar at the east end of the north aisle was dedicated in memory of Canon Ottley, and the adjacent window was dedicated in memory of Rev. J. M. Jeakes and Rev. A. E. N. Simms by the Archbishop of Dublin, nephew of Mr. Simms.

An interesting gift to the church in July 1967, was a copy dated 1602 of the "Breeches" or Geneva Bible, presented by Captain P. Hicks-Beach in memory of his son.

The stained glass windows in the Church are:

Chancel
　　East Window: placed soon after the first World War: designed by J. Wilson Forster; the symbolism is described by the artist on a framed parchment near the door leading from the south aisle to the tower door: dedicated in memory of Edward B. I'Anson and Catherine B. I'Anson.
　　Small window in South wall: depicts the Resurrection and was placed in memory of Isabella Mary Tomkins née de Pury.
South Aisle: (from East to West): all three-light windows.
　　　　1.　St. Luke flanked by two angels: designed by Jessie Bayes: in memory of Alexander Ingham Whitaker and Berthe Catherine Whitaker, Churchwardens 1900–1928.

2. Rather heavy dark window: depicts sacrifice of Isaac: in memory of 2nd Lt. Arthur Cyril Brickwood, died at Boulogne, aged 18.
3. Plain window.
4. Rather dark window: depicts Adoration of the Shepherds: in memory of Kathleen May Lowry, died 1932.

North Aisle: (from East to West) all three-light windows.
1. St. Peter, Christ and St. Paul: designed by Jessie Bayes: "This window is offered in gratitude for the ministry here of James Malcolm Jeakes (1901–1907) and Albert Ernest Nicholas Simms (1908–1926)."
2. St. Augustine, St. Francis of Assisi, St. Hilda of Whitby: designed by Jessie Bayes: in memory of Marjory Pearman.
3. St. Matthew, St. John the Divine, St. Mark: designed by Jessie Bayes: in memory of Theodora Pearman.
4. St. Clement St. Elizabeth, St. Martin: designed by J. Wilson Forster: in memory of C. E. Corry Lowry (1863–1925).
5. St. Margaret, St. David, St. Patrick: designed by Jessie Bayes: in memory of Robert Crawford Duggan, Churchwarden (1945–1961).

West Window: Plain window: five lights.

It is interesting to note that almost as soon as the parish was formed Mr. Jeakes, supported by Mr. Whitaker and Dr. Lyndon, churchwardens, contemplated establishing an elected Church Council of 10 members, though this was not then—nor for many years after—obligatory in law. The first meeting of the Council took place in April 1901.

In the next year "The Hermitage," where Mr. Jeakes had resided since he took charge of the parish, became the permanent vicarage. The house belonged to Mr. I'Anson who sold it to the churchwardens on generous terms; Miss I'Anson gave two acres of land to form the Vicarage grounds and garden. This building remained the Vicarage until 1971, though the size of the house (and the expense of heating it) and of the garden became an increasing burden on successive incumbents. The land was sold to developers, a small part round the old Vicarage being retained for a new Vicarage and garden. The old building was demolished and a new, comfortable but smaller Vicarage was completed in 1972. On the remainder of the land, dwelling-houses have been erected.

The land for the Churchyard was given by Miss I'Anson: its dedication by the Bishop of Dorking took place in June 1905.

The Church Council decided in July 1905 to abolish pew rents and to make all seating in the church free, except at Sunday Mattins, when they were free "directly the bell stops." In the next year we read in the Parish Magazine of mission services being held at Mr. Deadman's house in Whitmore Bottom, the hymns being led by Mr. Albert Berry with his cornet. There are spasmodic notices of these services for a number of years.

In most years down to the First World War "Rummage Sales" were held at Grayshott Hall for the Church or Endowment Funds: they seldom made less

118

than £50, a notable sum in those days. Another annual event was the singing of carols at Christmas by the choirboys at various houses. These were organised by Miss Monica Morgan-Brown of St. Edmund's School, who drove round in a donkey cart which also carried a piano. Christmas 1906 was very snowy and the Parish Magazine noted: "Mrs. Cane's donkey must be getting used to this work now and safely bore Miss Morgan-Brown and her piano along the perilous ways." The proceeds went to local good causes, e.g. £5.2.8. on that snowy Christmas to Haslemere Cottage Hospital. For the boys, who had consumed numerous mincepies on the way, the best was always yet to come—bowls of hot soup and mugs of sweet cocoa in the St. Edmund's dining hall. The modern equivalent of Miss Morgan-Brown's effort is community carol singing on the Village Green or in the shopping Precinct with collecting tins for a good cause.

After nostalgic memories of Christmas carols we must revert to more prosaic matters. In the summer of 1907 electric lighting was installed throughout the church—a greatly needed improvement.

Over the years there are accounts in the Parish Magazine of church organisations which were founded and which met with varying success, largely depending on the availability of people willing to run them. In the early days of the parish there was a unit of the Church Lads' Brigade which did not last very long and which was to some extent overtaken by the Boy Scout Movement, which has itself waxed and waned over the years. The Girl Guides have had a more continuous existence. A branch of the Girls' Friendly Society was more successful than the Church Lads' Brigade and lasted for a number of years. In Mr. Simms' time a branch of the Church of England Men's Society was formed but died with the First World War. It has been re-founded twice since, and from its last incarnation in Canon Winnett's time in 1961 continued until 1970. A very active branch of the Mothers' Union, founded early in the century, persisted continuously till very recent years. In more modern times church discussion groups and Bible Reading Fellowship have been well supported, but church youth groups have had a more chequered history.

The first choirmaster (or mistress) at St. Luke's was Miss Edwards, who also ran a private school. The organist was Mr. Oliver Chapman, the postmaster and a well-known eccentric character, always attired in a black coat with tails which flapped wildly behind him as he cycled about Grayshott. He was organist for many years. Miss Edwards was succeeded as choirmaster by Dr. Tyler, who was also organist and choirmaster at St. Bartholomew's, Haslemere as well as being Head Teacher of Haslemere Primary School—he also held the post at St. Luke's for many years. After his retirement in 1929 and that of Mr. Chapman in 1932 there were rapid changes in choir-master/organists until Mrs. Hartland took over. Mr. Rowland Owen is the present energetic and very successful organist and choirmaster.

Captain Thomas Wray (Church Army) came to Grayshott in 1911. He revived the week-day evening services at Mr. Deadman's cottage and started a boys' class, a Sunday School, and a Sunday evening service "in the schoolroom by the turning to Kingswood Lane." This endeavour to care for the parishioners who lived at the Bramshott Chase end of Grayshott led in 1912 to the building of a Mission Church on the Portsmouth Road below Bramshott Chase Cottages. This functioned for over twenty years, and the

119

decision to close it in the late 1930s followed several years of rather bitter controversy. It is only fair to say that it had become increasingly difficult to find either the finance or a suitable person in permanent charge of services there, and that Mr. Ireland was convinced that there was a greater need of a Church Room in the village itself.

It was in Mr. Ireland's incumbency that the Guild of God's Acre was formed to maintain and beautify the Churchyard. For many years the Guild provided financial assistance in this work. In more recent years the Parish Council has given annual grants, though not on a permanently continuing basis, after application by the Parochial Church Council, towards the maintenance of the Churchyard.

It is, perhaps, appropriate to mention here that in 1940 Mrs. Alice Woods became Churchwarden in succession to her husband, Mr. V. S. Woods. Her colleague in office was Sir Frank Noyce. She carried out the duties of her office with devoted efficiency and when she retired in 1958 she became Churchwarden Emeritus, a title and office created by Canon Ottley, until her death in 1966. In 1945 Mr. R. C. Duggan became her colleague and remained so until his death in 1961. In the 1960s Mr. W. M. Diamon succeeded Mr. K. Baldock as Churchwarden, and he, Mr. J. G. Pope and Mr. L. Monro covered the greater part of the decade.

In 1960 the first Planned Giving (or Christian Stewardship) scheme for St. Luke's was organised locally and achieved pledges amounting to £1,700 per annum. This scheme was accompanied by a Time and Talents scheme. In 1963 a renewal campaign was run. In 1966 a full Christian Stewardship Campaign was organised under the leadership of Wing Commander Geoffrey Wass of the Guildford Diocesan Stewardship Campaign organisation and resulted in an increase in pledges from £1,900 to over £4,000. A new campaign was undertaken in 1972 under the leadership of Commander Vermuyden. These campaigns have enabled the maintenance of and improvements to St. Luke's, including the provision of the Church Room and the complete re-lighting of the Church, to be accomplished without recourse to special appeals. Perhaps more importantly, the Parochial Church Council has been able to make substantial annual grants, often amounting to some 40% of income, to the missionary and charitable work of the Church at home and abroad, including the annual Diocesan Quota.

The Diamond Jubilee of St. Luke's was celebrated at St. Luke's-tide in 1960 with a number of special services and a Pageant of St. Luke, written and produced by Mr. K. Baldock, one of the Churchwardens, and his wife. It depicted various incidents from the Gospel of St. Luke. On the 50th anniversary there had been a Pageant of the Prayer Book, produced by Mrs. Shirley and Mrs. Meade-King.

Another important development in the work of St. Luke's was the building of the Church Room, the need for which for Church meetings and organisations—as well as for the Sunday School—had been increasingly felt. This need had been only partially met by the renting of a room in the Village Hall. There was some fear that the building of a separate Church Room near the church might lead to a rivalry between it and the Village Hall for lettings, but this was dispelled by a working agreement between the Parochial Church Council and the Village Hall Management Committee, which has proved to be an admirable arrangement. The Church Room was opened by Mrs.

Diamond, whose husband had been closely identified with the project but who had died before it was completed, and dedicated by the Bishop of Guildford in January 1968.

St. Luke's has participated fully in the ecumenical movement. It was one of the founder churches in 1964 of the Haslemere Council of Churches, and in January 1965 the Parish Magazine started an ecumenical section, including notes from the Grayshott Methodist Church, the Presbyterian Church in Tower Road, and the Convent of the Cenacle. In 1968 the Parochial Church Council voted solidly in favour of Anglican-Methodist Union.

In the autumn of 1967 the Parochial Church Council authorised the use of the Series II Communion Service, and some years later the Series III Service was introduced as an alternative to the service in the 1662 Prayer Book.

It would be ungracious to end this account of St. Luke's without grateful acknowledgement of the devoted work over the years of the incumbents and of very large numbers of lay people, of the generous support given on occasions by people of other denominations, and of the strong growth particularly in recent years — of brotherly relations between all the churches in the ecclesiastical parish.

The United Reformed Church (Congregational), Tower Road, Hindhead.

Though the Hindhead Free Church, as it was first called, was not formally constituted until December 1901, there is a record of Congregational activity for a number of years before that happened.

The Rev. Isaac Kettle, Minister at Bowlhead Green, seems to have been the pioneer. In the decade before 1890 he regularly visited houses in Highcombe Bottom, i.e. the Punch Bowl, with tracts and books, and established Sunday Afternoon Cottage Meetings at the homes of well-known and long-established families living there, such as Mr. Boxall, Mrs. Snelling and Mr. Nash. There was an annual tea-party in one or other of the houses, a great social event for the members of the Congregational group. From the early '80s these meetings were kept up chiefly by members of the Haslemere Congregational Church during the Haslemere pastorates of Rev. G. Ramsden and Rev. G. B. Stallworthy. The whole Grayshott/Hindhead area was very inchoate at that time, and we find that Haslemere, Hindhead and Grayshott residents attended the meetings. In Grayshott the regular members included Messrs. Fry, John Rowe and Ernest Chapman, the last of these often presiding over the meeting.

A permanent centre for Congregational worship was provided in Tower Road, Hindhead, by Mr. John Grover, a London builder, who had built himself a country house in that road. In 1895 he started to build the Hindhead Hall to which, by 1901, a Church and a Manse were added. At a slightly later period he also provided Free Churches at Hammer and Beacon Hill.

The designing of these Free Churches is very interesting, for they were certainly designed by Norman Shaw (1831–1912), who has been described as the man who influenced contemporary architecture perhaps more than any other single architect, or, at the very least, in Shaw's office by his chief assistant. An obituary notice on Norman Shaw in 'The Builder' (1912) includes among his works, "Congregational Churches and church buildings at Hindhead, Beacon Hill and Hammer in the XIVth Century domestic manner."

This statement seems not to have attracted any local notice. There was certainly no local tradition linking Shaw's name with the buildings, and the statement in the obituary lay dormant for sixty years until it was questioned recently by a writer who is preparing a biography of Norman Shaw, and who consulted the Rev. F. M. Hodgess Roper, the present Minister.

It was known that John Grover built and gave the Churches. It was also known that Grover had been employed extensively by Norman Shaw in some of his buildings, including New Scotland Yard which Shaw designed and Grover built in 1888–1890. They also collaborated in Chelsea in 1894.

There were no architect's plans among the Church records, but Mr. Hodgess Roper enlisted the willing help of Mr. L. D. Nicholls, Surveyor to the Haslemere Urban District Council, whose archives included the plans submitted at the time of the building in 1895. They were signed by Percy Ginham at 11, Bury Street, Bloomsbury — the address of Shaw's office. By 1895 Ginham was regarded as Shaw's chief assistant, and Shaw's letters refer to him as the man able to deputise for him. It is known that Ginham undertook some of the planning of New Scotland Yard. It is probable that John Grover mentioned to Shaw his intention of building churches in the Hindhead area. It is very likely, therefore, that Norman Shaw provided the plan of the Hindhead Church in general outline, leaving the detailed plans to Ginham.

The Churches are very similar. The Church at Tower Road is built of stone, that at Hammer of brick from the brickworks which were then situated nearby. The Beacon Hill Church is an adaptation of the design by an architect named W. W. Browne. The Manse in Tower Road, built at the same time as the Church, has a stone front to the garden and the road, the rest being brick with tile-hanging.

Services were conducted in the Hall from August, 1896, under the direction of Rev. G. B. Stallworthy, who was then living at Poole. He travelled to Hindhead every month for two or three years and was greatly helped by Rev. Alfred Kluht, formerly Congregational Minister at Billericay, who had come to live at Hindhead for reasons of health. Mr. Stallworthy moved from Poole to come to Hindhead as the first permanent Minister and remained as such until 1909.

From the start the Hindhead Hall was used widely, as explained in the first half-yearly report covering August 1896 to 31st January 1897, "for purposes likely to benefit the neighbourhood, either religiously, educationally or socially." For instance, in that first six months, as well as services there were four lectures on "The South Seas," "Our Troubles in South Africa from the Zulu point of view," "Experiments in Chemistry" and "Legends of the Rhine."

In November 1897, the Hall was lent for an afternoon concert in aid of the fund for building Grayshott Parish Church. It is gratifying to note that at a bazaar held at Mr. Grover's residence, "Heather Bank," Hindhead, in July 1904 to raise funds for furnishing the Free Church, Reading and Club Rooms at Beacon Hill, many leading Anglicans gave willing support. Of a Women's Meeting in January 1898, organised by Mrs. Rayner Storr, it is noted that there was "a laughable original reading by Mr. Conan Doyle."

In Chapter 5, on Bernard Shaw, we noted some meetings in the Congregational Hall in 1899 at which Shaw and Conan Doyle spoke. In April 1899 it was noted that both Mr. and Mrs. Shaw were at a meeting on "Vegetarian Cookery." The same year saw a series of lectures on "The Republic of Plato," arranged by Miss James of Westdown and Mrs. Lyndon of Grayshott.

In December 1901, the Hindhead Free Church was formally constituted as a Church of the Congregational Union. Mr. John Grover had already conveyed the land and buildings to eight trustees, of whom he was one. The others were George Spicer of Enfield, Thomas Ogden of Upper Clapton, Joseph King of Witley, Henry Meadows of Haslemere, Ebenezer Gammon of Godalming, Alfred Kluht of Hindhead and Arthur Grover of St. Martin's Lane. The Trust Deed provided that the Minister must be a Congregationalist, but he was to have power to appoint occasional preachers of other denominations, subject to a veto by a resolution of the Church. The form of trust was the "open trust" as approved by the Congregational Union, i.e. there was no schedule of doctrine included in the deed and there were no required qualifications for membership of the Church. The position was that a congregation of persons worshipping together were forming themselves into a Church. The trustees would permit the buildings to be "used occupied and enjoyed as a place for the public worship of God and for the preaching of the Gospel of Jesus Christ according to the principles and usages for the time being of Protestants of the Congregational denomination commonly being called Independents being paedobaptists under the direction of the Christian Church for the time being assembling for worship therein and for the instruction of children and adults and for the promotion of such other religious or philanthropic purposes as the said Church shall from time to time direct."

In the same document were Proposals for forming the Fellowship (or Church Society). These were very widely drawn and were for that time notably forward-looking. The Fellowship was open to "persons who may be willing to meet together for the help of one another in Christian Character, Christian Thought and Christian Works of Mercy." There were to be no doctrinal tests for membership: "This Church or Society of the Congregational or Independent Order shall be founded, not upon agreement in opinion and belief touching the many matters of theology which form the substance of the creeds and catechisms (most of them being matters respecting which Congregationalists in varying degrees differ), but solely on the recognition by its members of their holy relationship to Jesus Christ, of their Brotherhood and Sisterhood with all, everywhere and in all ages, of like spirit with him and expressly with the Young and the Frail, the Poor, the Sorrowful and Oppressed, the Ignorant and the Tempted, whom he specially declared it his mission to seek and to save."

The Fellowship of the Church was to be open to communicants and non-communicants, to baptised and unbaptised alike, since many did not believe in "outward rites" but relied on "spiritual fellowship with Christ." Nevertheless, provision was to be made at the Church for Communion and Baptism for such as desired them.

In 1901 Mr. Grover installed electric lighting in the buildings. He also provided water heating and the comfortable sofa seats still in use. They were probably designed by Ginham or by one of his friends in the Art Workers' Guild, and recall the decor supplied by Shaw's previous chief assistant, Ernest Newton, at Redcourt, Haslemere, in 1894. In 1904 the present organ was installed in the Church, the American organ previously used being given to the Beacon Hill Free Church. Mr. John Grover, the greatest benefactor of the Congregational Church, died in 1914.

In 1902 Miss Tucker is mentioned as organist, Sunday School Superintendent and Secretary of the Recreation Club which was formed when Mr. Ben Chandler of the Royal Huts Hotel lent his field for a cricket club and boys' and girls' clubs. Miss Tucker resigned her offices in the Church in 1907, on being appointed as the full-time Lady Superintendent of The Hostel (now Mount Alvernia) which had been built at Bramshott Chase by Miss James and Mr. and Mrs. Marshall Bulley of Westdown, to provide periods of rest and relaxation for people in some of the professions, including singers and musicians, actors and actresses, and teachers. Miss Tucker and her friend, Miss Millward, were the founders of the first really organised Dramatic Society in Grayshott, as well as being closely connected with the work of the Congregational Church.

Among other Grayshott people connected with that Church were Mr. Berk, whose name is perpetuated in Berk's Patch, and Mr. Oakley, a member of the first Grayshott Parish Council.

Mr. Stallworthy retired in 1909, and was succeeded by Rev. W. Loosemore until 1913, when Rev. W. K. Burford became Minister and continued for many years. Older residents will remember him as a tall, bewhiskered, rather shambling elderly man who was very short-sighted. He was to be seen ambling along the road with supreme unconcern, his eyes in a book held very close to his face: but the roads were different then. He was a well-known scholar and he claimed that he had gained a reference to himself in George Bernard Shaw's play "Misalliance" (1910), whose scene is placed on Hindhead, as "the Congregational Minister" and as "a nailer at arguing. He likes it." In his own book, "Songs and Sentiments," Mr. Burford commented, "I hardly know whether to take this as a compliment or censure. I am uncertain whether it puts me on a pedestal or in the pillory. Anyhow, I am quite ready either to forgive or to thank Mr. Shaw." There is, however, considerable difficulty with regard to Mr. Burford's claim. "Misalliance" was written and first produced at the Duke of York's Theatre in 1910, but Mr. Burford did not become the Hindhead Minister until 1913. It is at least doubtful whether Shaw knew Burford at the time of writing "Misalliance." On the other hand, it is certain that Shaw, when he lived at Hindhead, knew Rev. G. B. Stallworthy, the Minister at that time and until 1909, and it is also certain that Stallworthy took a prominent part in the intellectual life of the neighbourhood, frequently joining in discussions at public meetings. We have also to remember that Burford published "Songs and Sentiments" as late as 1937. It seems the more likely hypothesis that Burford was mistaken and that Shaw's reference was to Stallworthy. It might be suggested that Shaw had known Burford before the latter came to Hindhead, and that by dramatic licence he imported him as Minister there in 1910. This, however, is very unlikely, since Burford's previous ministries had been at Sheffield and Plymouth until 1911, when for two years he was at Lynton reviving the Presbyterian Church there.

Throughout the years the Hindhead Free Church has faithfully carried on its work in the spirit of those who originally formed themselves into the Fellowship. It is a pleasure to record that its relationship with St. Luke's has always been very friendly, and that in recent years it has entered fully into the growing ecumenical movement during the pastorates of its present Minister, Rev. P. M. Hodgess Roper, and of his predecessor, Rev. Richard Hambly.

On October 5th, 1972, the Hindhead Congregational Church became the United Reformed Church, following upon the union of the Congregational and Presbyterian Churches. By the Act of Parliament regulating the union the words "Congregational − Presbyterian" are for the first five years to be added in brackets to the name of the Church. Thus the Congregationalists and Presbyterians are among the foremost in the cause of Christian unity.

The Methodist Church

As in the case of the United Reformed Church, there was Methodist activity in Grayshott before the Methodist Church was built. Services and a Sunday School were held in the late nineties at the house of Mr. Johnson, a bricklayer who came originally from Haslemere and who lived in The Avenue, Grayshott. He and others had previously had to walk to Haslemere for services.

The Grayshott Methodist Church opened in the summer of 1902 in a galvanised iron portable building which, though intended as a temporary building, has given good service and is still in use. The cost of the building and its erection was £170, as stated in the contract of November 1901, between Messrs. Humphreys Ltd. of Knightsbridge, who evidently specialised in temporary buildings for churches and chapels, and Rev. W. E. Sellers of Farncombe, the Superintendent of the newly-formed Surrey and North Hampshire Mission, which was raising money for a number of churches in that wide area. The actual church measures 40 ft. by 20 ft. with a height of 9 ft. In addition there was a small entrance porch and a lean-to building at the rear of the church. The church was built on a piece of land between Glen Road and the "Rockdale" estate amounting to over 5 acres. Soon after the Headley Inclosure Award this land had been acquired by James Baker of Frensham Hall and he sold it in 1873 to Henry Carter and others. In 1879 they sold it to George Brydon for £120. It again changed hands in 1900 when Henry Mitchell, a well-known Grayshott butcher, bought it for £3,000−an example of the appreciation of land values at Grayshott in the later years of the last century. Mr. Mitchell sold a small part of this land for £275 to the original trustees of the Methodist Church. In 1934 the trustees sold a small piece at the rear of the church for £50. By 1920 the debt on the church had been paid.

The fifteen original trustees in November 1902, came from far afield one from Westminster, another from Bristol, four from Petersfield: Charles Phillips, glass dealer, Charles Rowland, draper, William Burley, Fellow of the Institute of Secretaries, and William Bray, farmer of Nursted. Others were William Nicklen, jeweller of Guildford, Joseph Dyke, draper of Alton, George Kemp, builder of Greatham, and Henry Johnson, farmer of Stedham. Nearer home were Thomas Davies, brickmaker of Shottermill and William May, joiner of Haslemere. The only trustees actually living at Grayshott were John Arthur Welch, ironmonger, and Charles Johnson, bricklayer. This, no doubt, reflects the wide area of the Mission which was undertaking a large programme of building.

The trustees adopted the "Model Deed for Methodist Churches," which had originally been drawn up in 1832 at Skircoat, Halifax, Yorkshire, for "the use of the people called Methodists in the Connexion established by the late Rev. John Wesley." This arrangement continued until 1944 when the trustees changed to "the new Model Deed of the Methodist Church" as set out in the Methodist Church Act of 1929.

The difficulties and devoted efforts of the Methodists are illustrated by the case of Mr. Charles Phillips, one of the Petersfield trustees and a local preacher, who used to catch a train at 8.0 a.m. to come to Haslemere, whence he walked to Grayshott, returning by the same means at night and arriving at Petersfield at 11.0 p.m. — he sometimes walked the whole way back to Petersfield.

During the First World War the Methodist Church served both British and Canadian troops as a canteen and social centre throughout the week.

Over the years there have, of course, been many changes of trustees: Lists of 1902, 1928, 1951 and 1972 have been preserved. We have already noted Mr. John Welch as an original trustee. He and his family are indissolubly linked with the history of Methodism in Grayshott. Mr. Welch was for many years a chapel steward and treasurer of the Church, untiring in his work for it. Among early Grayshott families prominent in the Methodist Church were Mr. and Mrs. Joseph Fry and the Barnes family. The Misses Rogers of Headley Down started their long service as early as 1917, Miss Sylvia Rogers becoming secretary of the trustees and a trustee herself for many years. With these we may bracket Mr. Herbert Obee, builder of Headley Down, who became a trustee at least as early as 1928. Messrs. Welch and Obee and the Misses Rogers were certainly the mainstay of the Church in its earlier years.

Another well-known local family to be identified with the Methodist Church is the Harris family. In the 1951 list of trustees Messrs. D. and R. Harris were described as "new trustees," as was Mr. G. Harris in the 1972 list. In 1950 Mrs. Potter became a trustee. She and the late Mrs. Goodison served their church with outstanding loyalty over many years. Prominent present local members of the Methodist Church include Mr. and Mrs. Scrace.

When thinking of trustees in the Methodist Church it is well to remember that a local congregation in a village like Grayshott may be a small one, which has to a large extent to finance itself, and which is grouped with many similar congregations in a large district under the supervision of a Superintendent Minister. It is against this background that one reads with admiration of the efforts made by local congregations and realises their great need of devoted and wise local leaders.

An impression on entering the Church is one of surprising beauty and calm, the furnishings being of quiet dignity enhanced by their happy placing. Many of them came from the former Methodist Church at Hindhead, include-ing an exquisite tapestry on the wall against which the altar table stands.

The local Methodists — as did the local Anglicans — strongly supported the proposals for Anglican/Methodist union and were grieved that they were not adopted by the General Synod of the Church of England. The relations locally between the two Churches are very happy, and the Methodists have played their part in fostering friendship between all the Churches in the parish.

The Roman Catholic Church

The early history of the Roman Catholic Church in Grayshott centres very largely round Mr. and Mrs. Vertue and Canon Louis Harvey.

Mr. and Mrs. Vertue came to Grayshott in the early 1890s and lived at "The Court," the original I'Anson house. Here there was a private chapel in

126

which services for the local Roman Catholics were held — the first Mass being celebrated in 1891. Mr. Vertue died in 1904 and was survived for many years by his widow, who continued in devoted work for the Roman Catholic community. In 1910 she built St. Joseph's Church and Presbytery, which were opened and consecrated in 1911 by Bishop Cotter of Portsmouth. St. Joseph's is a beautiful and very light church. It is interesting to note that its Lady Chapel Altar was originally the altar of Mrs. Vertue's private chapel. St. Joseph's Parish includes Grayshott, Headley and Headley Down, and is in the Roman Catholic Diocese of Portsmouth. Since 1910 the parish has grown to well over 500 persons. Father Harvey was the Parish Priest.

Louis Harvey was ordained priest in 1906, three months earlier than was usual. This was because he suffered from tuberculosis and the doctors believed that otherwise he would not live to be ordained. He was sent as private chaplain to Mrs. Vertue "to end his days." However, his health improved and he lived for a further 52 years, dying in 1958. He was made Canon in 1952. Father Harvey, as he was always known, was greatly loved and respected in Grayshott by Catholics and non-Catholics alike. His successor as Parish Priest was Rev. P. J. Hartnett, who came in 1959 and is still at St. Joseph's.

When we think of the Roman Catholic Church in Grayshott we think of the Convent of the Cenacle as well as of St. Joseph's. In 1913 Mrs. Vertue moved to another house, "St. Anne's," and gave "The Court" to the Order of Our Lady of the Cenacle. The original house has been greatly extended since 1913. The nuns, apart from following the life of their Order, provide retreats both for Catholics and non-Catholics. These are widely known and greatly esteemed over much of Southern England.

The Convent played its part in both World Wars. From 1914 to 1918 one wing of it was used as a military hospital with 25 beds. The nuns helped with the cooking and work in the wards. In all it treated 835 cases. The hospital was under the general direction of Dr. and Mrs. Lyndon as Medical Superintendent and Lady Superintendent respectively, and of Miss Bewley as Commandant.

In the Second World War the Convent was recognised by the military authorities as an educational centre, where the nuns did valuable work in teaching foreign languages to soldiers of all ranks, and, in some cases, illiterates to read and write.

The Mother Superior and the nuns have worked effectively in promoting friendly relations with and between the various religious denominations in Grayshott.

Chapter 10

Formation of Grayshott Civil Parish

It should first be noted that there were no elected Parish Councils until the District and Parish Councils Act of 1894, civil authority in purely village matters resting with the Churchwardens of the Parish Church and the Overseers of the Poor, elected by the Annual Vestry. The first Parish Council for Headley (including Grayshott) was elected by poll in December 1894. Of the twelve members, three came from Grayshott—A. Ingham Whitaker of Grayshott Hall, Miss Catherine I'Anson, whose father had given the local school, and Oliver Chapman, an expert joiner, of the Chapman building firm. Mr. Whitaker was Vice-Chairman of Headley Parish Council from 1894 to 1904, becoming its Chairman in succession to Sir R. S. Wright in that year and continuing as such until 1908, when he resigned from Headley Parish Council, having become Chairman of the Grayshott Council at its formation in 1902. Thus for four years he combined the two Chairmanships. Mr. Chapman was one of the Headley Overseers of the Poor from 1895 to 1901. Mr. C. E. Lowry of the Grayshott firm of Chapman, Lowry and Puttick succeeded him in 1902—thereafter there were no Headley Overseers from Grayshott. Miss I'Anson served on Headley Parish Council from 1894 to 1904, Mr. Chapman from 1894 to 1901. Mr. Lowry from 1899 to 1901, Mrs. Lyndon from 1899 to 1901, and Mr. Barrett from 1901 to 1903. Thus a number continued on the Headley Council for a short time after Grayshott had its own Council.

It is not difficult to understand the inevitability of Grayshott separating from Headley. It was remote from Headley in the days of complete absence of public transport, and in the last decade of the nineteenth century it was developing rapidly on a residential and shop-keeping basis, whereas Headley remained agricultural: the soil at Grayshott is not suited to agriculture. The people of Grayshott, mostly immigrant and not aboriginal, were anxious about health problems and wanted modern services such as piped water supply, gas, and electricity. Of these their Headley neighbours at that time saw little need and were certainly not willing to supply them for the benefit of Grayshott at the expense of the Headley rates as a whole. The obvious solution was for Grayshott to "go it alone." The final parting of the ways in 1902 came on the question of water supply, but for some years previously there had been strong indications of what would happen.

As early as 1895 Mr. Chapman raised the matter of a polling station at Grayshott, but this does not seem to have materialised.

In 1897 we have the first mention in "The Herald" of Dr. Arnold Lyndon of "Windwhistle." He had recently come to Grayshott with his wife Charlotte, and they were in the forefront of the battle for improvements in Grayshott, both then and for many years after.

In March 1897 Headley Parish Council appointed a sub-committee to "view houses and premises at Grayshott to see whether it is necessary to adopt Bye-Laws and to look at the drainage of the roads and to report generally." We may note that during the next few years there was agitation in Grayshott for the making up of the Headley Road. In April the Council decided to examine new Building Bye-Laws of the Petersfield Rural District Council, which would affect the neighbouring parish of Bramshott. It has, perhaps, some relevance in this connection that Canon Capes of Bramshott had already taken over the spiritual care of Grayshott. In August the local paper, reporting a meeting of the Headley Council, said: "Owing to Grayshott having become so thickly populated and there being so much building going on in that district, in many cases the sanitary arrangements are very bad indeed. It was felt that if these were not improved an epidemic would break out. It was noted, moreover, that some of the buildings in Grayshott were not weatherproof and that, in fact, it was possible to see through them. The Parish Council requested the Alton Rural District Council to prepare sanitary and building bye-laws substantially similar to those in preparation for Bramshott, subject to consideration of details by the Parish Council and to the question how far they should be limited to Grayshott and Stone Hill or other areas."

After some delay the bye-laws were adopted in 1899, in every case the necessary resolutions of Headley Parish Council being proposed by councillors from Grayshott. In October 1898, Dr. Lyndon in the Parish Magazine summarised the bye-laws in their final draft form as follows:

(a)   all new houses to have proper foundations and damp courses.
(b)   every room to have a fireplace or ventilator and a window one third of which must open.
(c)   every privy must be at least 20 ft. from a dwelling.
(d)   every cesspool to be properly bricked, cemented and covered in: to be 50 ft. from any dwelling and 60 ft. from a well, spring or stream used for drinking purposes.
(e)   the District Surveyor to have the right of inspection of all construction work.
(f)   compulsory closing of dwellings unfit for habitation.
(g)   particulars of plans and construction to be sent to the District Council.

Imagination boggles at conditions before the days of sensible and enforceable bye-laws.

Another step forward was the appointment of a resident policeman at Grayshott. We have seen that the district had had an unenviable reputation for lawlessness. In July 1897, Miss I'Anson asked for a village policeman to deal with "a number of rowdies who were in the habit of meeting and engaging in undesirable practices." In October we hear her describing some of the newcomers to the village as "very audacious." The Parish Council decided to write to the Chief Constable asking for a resident Grayshott police officer. The local paper contained accounts which underlined Miss I'Anson's anxiety.

For example, in September 1897, at Alton police court, Fred Adcock or Budd was charged with stealing fowls from Dr. Lyndon, while towards the end of 1898 there was a poaching affray on the Grayshott Hall estate, in which four poachers injured three gamekeepers. Only one, Henry Jackson, or Stanley or Carter, was arrested and sentenced to nine months hard labour. Miss I'Anson succeeded, and by the end of 1898 Grayshott had its first resident constable, P.C. Seaward. The local paper shows, however, that for some years to come he and his successors had their work cut out to make Grayshott a law-abiding community.

At the same time as the bye-laws were under discussion, the questions of water and gas supplies became urgent. In 1898 two Private Bills which affected the district were presented to Parliament. One was the Wey Valley Water Bill, the other the Haslemere District Water and Gas Bill. Headley Parish Council requested Alton Rural District Council to oppose both Bills. The latter Council concurred and reported that it had sealed petitions against both. The Parish Council followed suit and sealed petitions at its meeting in April 1898. A marginal note in the Headley Minute Book states that the Haslemere Bill "is thrown out" and that the Wey Valley Company had agreed to insert in their Bill a clause preventing the exercise of water powers in Headley Parish (including Grayshott) without the consent of the District and Parish Councils. This Bill received the Royal Assent in August 1898. But there remained the hurdle of the local consents required, and in September "The Herald" reported anxiety about the water supply since, in the hot summer, water had to be carted into Grayshott from a local stream outside the parish at a cost of 8/- a day. In August it had commented in a leading article: "We venture to assert that if Grayshott had a Parish Council of its own the supply would have been provided long 'ere this."

Matters moved slowly, however, and in October 1899 a letter from the solicitors of the Wey Valley Company informed the Councils that the Company would not install a standpipe because the employment of a turncock was costly, a penny in the slot system had failed at The Bourne, and a standpipe system at Haslemere "was having miserable results." The Company would, however, meet two points put forward by the District Council, viz. that it would take no water from Hampshire and that it would supply water for public purposes at, say, 1d the gallon. It declined to be put in the position of working up a trade at a loss and then be subject to being bought out at three months' notice "at scrap-iron prices." Mrs. Lyndon and Miss I'Anson proposed that the Company's letter be sent to the District with an intimation that Headley Parish Council considered it could be the basis for reasonable negotiations. A note in "The Herald" in February 1900 made it clear that Headley Parish Council, who feared that the inevitable result of a piped water supply would be a need for public drainage, had proposed to the Water Company that, should drainage be necessary for Headley (including Grayshott), the Company should provide water for flushing at 3d. per 1,000 gallons, and that the Council could at three months' notice take over the drainage system on payment of the cost of the metal in the pipes and the cost of laying them—hence the Company's reference to "scrap-iron prices." Not unnaturally the Company refused these conditions, and further delay was inevitable.

Grayshott people were getting impatient, and one gets the impression that Headley was also getting tired of Grayshott and would be quite willing to lose it. In August 1900, Alton Rural District Council gave an unsympathetic response to the need for the water supply in Grayshott. They, too, feared the consequence of a demand for public drainage.

In March 1901, the Parish Magazine called attention to the need for Grayshott to continue to be well represented on the Parish Council. At present it had four representatives—Mrs. Lyndon, Miss I'Anson, Messrs. Whitaker and Lowry—and it hoped that "Grayshott voters will go to the meeting (the Annual Parish Meeting on March 4th) in good numbers." It also suggested that Mrs. Lyndon should be elected as one of the Headley representatives on Alton Rural District Council. In the next month the Magazine reported the result: "To the Parish Meeting at Headley, on March 4th, we went by carriage, by bicycle and on foot; and, when we got there, we found that we made up the greater part of the meeting. The result was that six candidates from Grayshott were elected on the Parish Council. That is half of the entire Council, a number out of all proportion to our population." In these circumstances a poll was demanded, but the Magazine commented: "We are glad to note that the interest in local self-government was strong enough to take many of us over the three or four miles which separate us from the scene of our civic duty." At the poll four of the Grayshott candidates were elected — Miss I'Anson, Messrs. Whitaker, Lowry and Barrett, while Mrs. Lyndon had been returned unopposed as a member of Alton Rural District Council.

In the second half of 1901 separation became inevitable. The communities were too disparate and remote from one another to remain as one civil parish, and both sides now recognised the fact. In July, Headley Parish Council arranged for a meeting of parish electors in Grayshott Schoolroom on 6th August "to consider whether it is advisable to form Grayshott into a separate parish." It was argued that Grayshott had needs not shared by Headley, for which Headley should not pay, but the meeting adjourned without a decision. A meeting a week later voted unanimously for separation. Much of the discussion centred round the water supply question. From then on Headley— and, indeed, Alton—raised no objection, and in October the Headley Council, on the proposition of Mr. Barrett, seconded by Mr. Whitaker, voted unanimously to approach the County Council to bring this about.

The County Council held an enquiry, reported fully in the local paper, on 4th January 1902, at Headley National School, the Commissioners being four members of the County Council. The majority of Headley Parish Council attended, together with a number of Grayshott inhabitants. The case for separation was put by Mr. A. F. M. Downie, Clerk of the Alton Board of Guardians. He made it clear that members of Headley Parish Council, Alton Rural District Council and Board of Guardians, were present in a position of benevolent neutrality and did not oppose Grayshott's wishes, but that the application could only apply to that part of the newly-formed ecclesiastical parish of Grayshott which lay in Hampshire. He noted that whereas Headley Parish was very scattered, Grayshott was relatively compact. Evidence of Grayshott's recent progress was to be seen in the large number of shops, the possession of a Bank and a public house, the coming of electric light, the number of good boarding houses—Grayshott being in some measure a health resort—and a forthcoming Village Hall which was then in the course of erection. The question of the water supply made an inevitable appearance, Mr. Downie saying that Alton Rural District Council had opposed it for fear that drainage must necessarily follow, and because it was unjust that people should pay for it who would not require to use it. He summed it all up by saying that "very go-ahead people resided there." He recalled that two Grayshott parish meetings had discussed and voted for separation, and that Headley Parish Council, Alton Rural District Council and Board of Guardians had all voted for it. Those bodies thought that, after separation, Headley should have two Rural District councillors and Grayshott one. Mr. Downie also said that it was "an open secret" that Grayshott's ultimate aim was incorporation in Surrey—a remark not then without justification, but curious when we reflect on the bitter opposition in the 1960s and '70s to any such proposals.

It was reported at the enquiry that the population of Grayshott in Hampshire was 666 (1901 census), while in that part of the ecclesiastical parish in Surrey it was 416. A note in the local paper in May 1901 says: "Headley shows a remarkable increase (i.e. over 1891) due to the development of Grayshott. Most of the other villages in the Alton Poor Law Union have decreased." The rateable value of the whole of Headley Parish was £9,900—Grayshott in Hampshire accounting for £2,850.

Mr. Gamblen, Assistant Overseer, told the enquiry of the large amount of building going on at Grayshott—"in recent years the whole aspect of the place has been changed."

Mrs. Lyndon underlined Mr. Downie's points, mentioned that Headley was four miles away, and said the requirements of Headley and Grayshott were fundamentally different—"there were many things which Grayshott people wanted to do which the Headley parishioners would not at all agree to."

Other people of Grayshott spoke in support, including Messrs. Oakley and Cornish, but Mr. Barrett put the whole thing in a nutshell: "Headley was too old-fashioned for Grayshott. They could not govern them with success."

On 12th August 1902, the Order was issued by the County Council establishing Grayshott as a separate civil parish. Elections for the first Grayshott Parish Council were fixed for 15th October. There were fifteen candidates for seven seats. The election was held at Grayshott National School by show of hands, the successful candidates being Miss I'Anson (40 votes), Mr. Cornish (38) grocer and draper, Mr. Oakley (36) builder's foreman, Mr. Mitchell (31) butcher, Mr. Charlwood (26) saddler, Mrs. Lyndon (25), Mr. Chapman (24) builder, Mr. Whitaker was elected as Chairman. This was possible as the Chairman need not be an elected councillor.

There were two residual matters to clear up in 1903. The credit balance of Headley Parish Council in the year 1902/3 amounting to £7.14.2. was divided between the parishes in proportion to their rateable values, Grayshott receiving £2.10.11. The other was the matter of parish allotment land which had been established at the time of the Headley Enclosure Award. Grayshott asked to receive as its share the allotments at Hollywater, and Headley agreed to this "as a final settlement of all claims." In due course the land was legally conveyed to Grayshott Parish Council.

Even after the separation Alton Rural District Council made further delays in allowing the Wey Valley Water Company to supply Grayshott, and the first Vicar of Grayshott, Rev. J. M. Jeakes, invoked the assistance of the Local Government Board, as did Dr. Lyndon who reported that the vicarage well was polluted. Not until December 1903 did the Rural District allow the Water Company to bring the water in.

By the Order of 1902 the union of Grayshott with Headley, which had existed for some 800 years, ceased and Grayshott came into being as a separate parish for all purposes,

Chapter 11

The Village Hall

We have noted previously that the village school was a centre of village social activity and that there was an "Iron Room" in Stoney Bottom. At the end of the century they were becoming inadequate for that purpose, owing to increasing population. A note in the Parish Magazine of June 1900 commented: "Many of us have long felt that the present Iron Room which still serves many useful purposes, has for some time been inadequate to meet the growing needs of the village. But as there seemed no immediate hope of anything more adequate, little has been done about it. However, we announce now, with great pleasure, that a most generous offer of £500 has now been received towards this object, on condition that a suitable site is procured, and the rest of the money raised, so that building may be commenced fairly soon. This is a grand start and we cannot believe that Grayshott will fail to rise to its opportunity."

By September the fund had reached £640 towards the estimated cost of £2,000, and the Magazine of January 1901 recorded that land had been conveyed to the Trustees and a Trust Deed drawn up. In the next month the fund had reached £800, but the estimated cost had risen to £3,500, and in September the foundations were being laid. The site was as to the greater part the gift of Mrs. Plympton Smith, who lived at Hurstmere, in memory of her brother, Dr. Richard Plympton, who had died suddenly in December 1899 at the age of 45, while on duty at the Middlesex Hospital. He was a pioneer in work with X-rays. Mrs. Plympton Smith sold an additional piece of land to the Trustees at the very reasonable price of £100. The land did not include the site of the present Fire Station nor the back car park, that being purchased by the Trustees in 1903. On it, tennis courts and, later, a bowling green were constructed. This was the home for many years of the Grayshott Bowling Club, until in 1960 part of the land, including the bowling green, was sold for £950 to the Hampshire Fire Service.

The Trustees were Mr. S. Marshall Bulley of Westdown, Mr. A. Ingham Whitaker of Grayshott Hall, Mr. John Macmillan of Bramshott Chase, and Mr. Aneurin Williams of Hindhead, and representatives of Hampshire County Council, who would give a grant for the provision of facilities for technical education.

The Hall was officially opened on 23rd May 1902, a day of drizzling rain. The imaginative foresight of its founders was remarkable for, though Grayshott in the area of the present civil parish had only about 700 inhabitants, the Village Hall was constructed on the most generous lines. The buildings opened in 1902 were as they are now, except for the Small Hall (now the Library) which was a later addition, in 1906. They were designed by Messrs. Reid and Macdonald and built by Messrs. Chapman, Lowry and Puttick. A great advantage was the inclusion of accommodation for a resident caretaker who, for many years, was also steward of the Men's Club, which had premises in the Village Hall. The Trustees were able to report that the Hall was free of debt or mortgage. The Village Hall then was, and still is, one of the largest in Hampshire, having regard to the size of the village. In planning it the Trustees had shown the same imagination and faith as had been shown so shortly before by those responsible for building the Parish Church.

When this project was first mooted in 1900 and while the money for it was being collected, Grayshott had not yet been constituted a separate civil parish with its own Parish Council, and the Trustees, two of whom lived outside the boundary of the future parish, looked at a much wider, if rather vague area. Thus they called the buildings the Grayshott and Hindhead Institute and Village Hall, which were to be for "the inhabitants of such portions of the Parishes of Headley (Grayshott was still in Headley Parish), Bramshott, Shottermill, Frensham and Thursley (the latter two in those days had their borders in Hindhead) as can reasonably be construed as being in the district called Hindhead and its immediate neighbourhood." It was to provide "the advantages of an Institute, Association, Library, Club, Village Hall or Coffee House for mutual improvement, social intercourse and amusement, mental and moral culture, literary pursuits, music and physical training," and it was to cater for all: "No person is to be excluded on the grounds of class, party, sex, or creed." The land was—and still is—subject to restrictive covenant in that "no public house, beer shop or tavern may be erected upon it, nor may any band practice or other nuisance be permitted upon it." The last restriction may stem from the fact that a year or two earlier the Grayshott Brass Band had been started, to the foundation of which Bernard Shaw had given a £10 subscription, and it may have been thought that band practice just outside could be inimical to social intercourse and literary pursuits.

The opening ceremony must, according to the account in the local paper, have been an endurance test, for long speeches were delivered by the Vicar and the individual Trustees, and these were followed by a lengthy entertainment in which the Grayshott and Hindhead Choral Society, the Orchestral Society and the Dramatic Society all took part.

For nearly five years the Village Hall was managed by a Committee appointed by the Trustees and financed by the proceeds of lettings, supplemented, no doubt, from the private pockets of the Trustees. From the start it housed the Village Hall Men's Club, which for several years had to run on strictly teetotal lines. This Club continued for about 70 years until changing social habits and increasing competition from similar institutions in the village compelled its closure. The Hall rapidly became the social centre for the area, providing a home for local societies such as an early Dramatic Society, the Hindhead and District Horticultural Society, a Choral Society, the Band of Mercy, First Aid classes, technical and gymnastic classes—and what became a healthy and enjoyable tradition of annual village Social Evenings on New Year's Eve and New Year Night. For many years winter evenings were occupied by courses of University Extension Lectures, often given by the Vicar, Mr. Simms, and generally illustrated with lantern slides.

In April 1907, the Trustees offered to hand over control of the Hall to the Parish Council, if the latter would run it under the terms of the Trust Deed, subject to the approval of a Parish Meeting, which was given unanimously at the Annual Parish Meeting in May. Mr. Whitaker, Chairman of the Parish Council, reported that the land, buildings and furniture were valued at £5,500, and that there was a village library of 1,100 books, which was run by Mrs. Marshall Bulley. The Vicar, Mr. Jeakes, referred to the gift by the Trustees as a "unique opportunity of a small parish receiving such a splendid gift." In August 1907, the conveyance was signed and a Management Committee appointed, consisting of all the Parish Councillors "for the present," one representative from each of the Higher Education Committee, the Entertainments Committee, and the Friendly Societies (who had made it their meeting place, and who were the Manchester Unity of Oddfellows and the Tunbridge Wells Equitable Society), and two representatives from the Village Hall Men's Club. In addition, the Hampshire Education Committee for many years rented the Technical Room (now the Common Room) for one afternoon each week for the instruction in woodwork of boys from the village school.

This constitution continued until 1938 when it was altered in accordance with the Local Government Act, 1933, which provided that such committees must be composed, as to at least two-thirds of their number, of members of the Local Authority. The revised constitution resulted in a Management Committee of all members of the Parish Council, together with one representative of each of the Village Hall Men's Club and the Oddfellows Friendly Society. In the previous year, owing no doubt to the Local Government developments and increasing populations in the surrounding areas, the connection with Hindhead in the name of the Village Hall was dropped, and since then it has been simply Grayshott Village Hall.

That the Village Hall possessed large solidly-built premises was certainly an asset, but this also raised over the years a serious and continuing problem of raising enough income from lettings and money-raising events to provide for the day-to-day cost of running the premises and for their adequate upkeep and maintenance. That it never failed to fulfil its functions is a testimonial to the hard work of its Management Committee and to the public spirit of the village. From time to time the financial position seemed desperate and, in the absence of any substantial endowment fund, it existed for quite long periods on a hand-to-mouth basis. The Committee partly for social reasons, were always reluctant to increase letting charges and, in any event, were fearful lest doing so should prove counter-productive. Nevertheless the Hall survived and continued to fulfil its purpose.

When the Hall was conveyed to the Parish Council there was a provision in the Trust Deed that no alcohol could be sold or consumed on the premises before January 1911, nor after that date unless the Management Committee consented. The Men's Club requested in March 1912 that the ban be lifted. The Parish Council complied to the extent of permitting it to supply beer to its members "on condition that it be consumed only in the Club Room." Not until 1925 was this concession extended to the sale of spirits.

In October 1914, the Parish Council anticipated that the Village Hall might be taken over for billeting troops and, indeed, the King's Royal Rifle Brigade entered into occupation in the November of all the buildings, and also erected tents on the tennis courts. The Management Committee had to provide heating and lighting, and received a payment of nine pence a head per night for men sleeping on the premises. These troops were succeeded by a battalion of the Black Watch. The military occupation continued until the summer of 1915, i.e. during the recruitment and hasty training of Kitchener's Army.

It would be tedious to try to deal in detail with the financial anxiety as it recurred over the years. The Minute Books of the Management Committee and of the Parish Council abound with references to it. As early as 1922 the latter body discussed the finances against the background of the need to undertake exterior painting and to renew the heating apparatus, when there was no reserve fund to meet these costs, and also of the increasing day-to-day expenses of running the Hall. Without "voluntary assistance" the year would end with a heavy deficit. In 1928 the Management Committee asked the Parish Council to hold on its behalf securities to form an Endowment Fund. The Parish Council agreed to this, but, alas, no really substantial endowment was ever accumulated. During the Second World War and a few years after it the caretaker, William Levett, and his wife Norah organised dances at the Hall, the profits of which, amounting to a total of £780, were added to the funds of the Management Committee. This was a very considerable amount in those days and, no doubt, eased the financial position for some time. But by 1953 Mr. F. L. H. Harris, Chairman of the Management Committee, reported that income from ordinary lettings only covered half the expenses, the remainder coming from two major regular lettings, that since the War between £1,500 and £2,000 had been provided out of revenue for maintenance and improvements, and that in 1953 a further £400 was needed for roof repairs. In the January of that year Mr. Harris consulted the Hampshire Council of Social Service who considered that the Parish Council was bearing too great a responsibility as Trustees and advised the formation of a Trust under the Charity Commissioners, as this would make it easier to get grants and loans towards necessary expenditure. In 1954 the Parish Council took over the cost of insuring the Hall and its contents. By this time, too, it was possible to make modest grants from legacies left in trust for the Parish by Dr. Lyndon and his wife, Charlotte.

A financial crisis was precipitated when it became necessary in 1955 to put in a new and improved drainage system and consequent alterations to the cloakrooms and caretaker's cottage, at a cost of nearly £800, which was followed less than two years later by the cessation of auction sales at the Hall which had been held by Messrs. Cubitt and West for about ten years, the letting fees for which amounted to one-quarter of the revenue of the Hall. As a result, the Management Committee feared an annual deficit of about £250. They requested the Parish Council to consider ways of dealing with the situation and put forward several suggestions: an annual rate grant from the Parish Council: or the Parish Council to take over full responsibility for maintenance, repairs and decorations: or an annual grant from the Lyndon Trust Funds: or an investigation into the possibility of selling or leasing the Small Hall to the Hampshire Fire Service for a new Fire Station. It was believed that the County Fire Service would consider this. The Parish Council considered the matter carefully, chose the last suggestion, and decided to discuss the matter informally with the County Fire Officer. By March 1957, the basis of an agreement on a lease basis had been informally agreed.

The approval of a Parish Meeting was necessary before the matter could proceed further. This was held in March 1957, when about 50 local government electors showed their interest by attending. Mr. Harris outlined the financial position and said that a 25 years' lease to the Fire Service would reduce expenditure on the Halls, would bring in some steady revenue, and would ensure an efficient Fire Service for 25 years. He said it was not possible for the Parish Council to submit a detailed proposition at that meeting, but a further Parish Meeting would be called to consider any recommendation on the matter. Mr. Max Reese made a powerful speech against any suggestion of abandoning either of the Halls which had been given to the public. He put forward the idea of forming a Social Committee to organise functions at the Halls to raise money. The present writer seized on this suggestion, supporting Mr. Reese and suggesting that the financial position could be remedied partly by rate support and partly by the efforts of a Social Committee. He seconded Mr. Reese's motion "That a Social Committee be created forthwith to redeem the deficit of £250 per annum in order to save the Halls." This was carried by 27 votes to 12, and Mr. Reese agreed to organise such a committee, subject to the Management Committee lifting some restrictions — particularly on the sale of alcohol. The Social Committee carried on for some three years on the basis of a Village Hall Social Club having monthly meetings at which there was a licensed bar and organised entertainment of the cabaret type. Eventually it came to an end owing to difficulties about the bar and arranging organised entertainment at frequent intervals. In the course of its existence it raised substantially more than the £250 per annum which it had undertaken to provide.

Meanwhile, the Parish Council, seeing the strength of the opposition, decided in May 1957 to drop the scheme of leasing the Small Hall to the Fire Service and to enter into negotiations with that Service for the sale of some of the Village Hall land as a site for a new, larger, modern Fire Station. This land was sold in 1960 for £950, the proceeds being invested to provide a small annual revenue for the Village Hall. Unfortunately it involved the demise of the Bowling Club.

In fairness it should be said that the sale was not prompted solely by the financial state of the Village Halls, but also because it had become apparent that the Hampshire Fire Service were not prepared to continue providing a Fire Brigade at Grayshott with inadequate premises and equipment.

Though the immediate crisis of 1957 had been averted, some anxiety remained, largely because of the dire need of external decorations which in 1959 had last been done twelve years previously. The Parish Council came to the rescue by obtaining the consent of the Annual Parish Meeting of that year to make from the Parish Rate an annual grant of £100 towards external decorations and small external repairs, but not towards any major structural repairs. Accumulation of these annual grants enables the Management Committee to deal with this important item of upkeep without undue anxiety. In recent years male members of that Committee have made a public-spirited contribution by themselves doing some of the internal decorating.

Happily it has also been possible to raise additional revenue. Grants have been obtained from central and local government sources for specific improvements such as surfacing the forecourt, installing more modern lighting, and providing and equipping a fine kitchen. Income from lettings has also improved, partly from an increase in fees and lettings and partly by leasing the Small Hall. to the County Library Committee, thus providing a permanent Village Library. Apart from the traditional use of the Village Hall by many local societies and organisations, which provides valuable income, the Further Education Classes provide not only income but also a real social and cultural asset.

Extremely valuable service has been given over the years by the Management Committee, particularly its officers. Dr. Arnold Lyndon was Chairman and Miss Mildred Paine Secretary for many years before the Second World War. In the 1950s and 1960s great service was given by Mr. and Mrs. R. E. B. Meade-King. In more recent years Miss A. M. Littlejohn has been a valued and energetic Chairman, and has been loyally supported by Secretaries such as Mr. W. M. Diamond, Mrs. Griffiths, Mr. J. J. T. Gavin, Dr. Ray Campbell, Mrs. Donaldson, and now Dr. Field. Since the War there were times when there were too frequent changes of caretakers, but for some years now the Halls have enjoyed the efficient and willing services of Mr. and Mrs. Mowinski. Mr. Mowinski (or "Bruno" as he is more often called) came to Britain as a result of the Second World War. Born in Poland, he was still at school when the Germans overran that country in the brief campaign of 1939. In 1942 he was drafted by the German authorities into a Labour Corps and was sent first to Denmark and then in 1944 to France. Here he, with a few companions, seized a chance of escape during fighting in the Ardennes. In the see-saw of the military operations they found themselves on the bank of a river, the opposite side of which was in American occupation. They stripped and, in Bruno's words, "went for a swim," thus passing from enemy to Allied territory. He was sent to Scotland where he joined the Polish Army and in 1946 married Janet, his Scots wife. At that time he had no idea of what had befallen his family in Poland, and it was some years before—with the help of the Red Cross—he was able to trace them, but in 1947 he had the satisfaction of going to Poland to visit them. He became a naturalised British citizen in 1976 and is waiting, perhaps a trifle impatiently, for the opportunity of exercising his citizenship in a General Election.

What was started in faith as an ambitious project in 1902 has continued for more than 70 years as a social centre for the village and has, in later years, considerably extended its provision in that respect. This has been made possible only by the selfless work of many people throughout its existence.

Chapter 12

The Grayshott Murders

There have been two macabre murders at Grayshott, which exhibit similar characteristics. In both cases there was no doubt as to the fact that the accused committed the murder; in both cases the defence was a plea of insanity and in both this plea succeeded — in one case at the trial, in the other subsequently.

In its issue of 3rd August 1901, the local paper, under the heading "Shocking Tragedy at Grayshott," reported:

> "The good people of the quiet little village of Grayshott were considerably startled on Monday morning (29th July) by the report that an awful tragedy had been committed in their midst. The news, at first regarded as incredible and impossible, unfortunately proved to be only too true, and great excitement broke out in the village."

Village gossip had noted that for a considerable time past the postmaster, Walter Gilman Chapman, and his wife had had a far from happy relationship. They had fairly recently been separated for about three months but were living together again. On that Monday morning, while Mrs. Chapman — who had recently given birth to her fifth child — was bathing one of the children, her husband stabbed her to death.

Attracted by her screams, a young man, Gilbert Winchester, apprentice to Walter Chapman, carpenter and joiner, was almost immediately on the scene and rushed for help. Dr. Arnold Lyndon was called and found that Mrs. Chapman was dead. The local constable, P.C. Merritt, who was also present, arrested Mr. Chapman on the charge of murdering his wife and got in touch with police headquarters at Whitehill. Later in the same day the accused was conveyed to the police station at Alton.

On the Tuesday morning there was a preliminary hearing before the Magistrate, Mr. J. Gathorne Wood, the accused — who was 45 — being brought from the police station to the Magistrates' Clerk's office "in a four-wheeled conveyance of which the blinds were closely drawn," from which there emerged "a middle-aged, thin, respectably-dressed man, fairly tidy except about the feet, and looking like anything but a murderer." The Whitehill Police Sergeant gave evidence of examining the body with Dr. Lyndon and of arresting the prisoner, who declined to ask any questions of the Police Sergeant. The police then applied for a remand which was granted for a week, and the prisoner was transferred to Winchester.

At the inquest at Grayshott on the next day the prisoner did not attend, though he had been informed that he could do so. The Coroner offered to adjourn the inquest, but the solicitor for the accused was content to proceed.

The first witness, Annie Harding, in Mrs. Chapman's domestic service, described how she prepared and took breakfast with Mr. and Mrs. Chapman on the Monday morning. After breakfast Mrs. Chapman sent her upstairs to fetch clothes for the baby, and as she went up she passed Mr. Chapman coming down. Just afterwards she heard the children crying, so she ran downstairs again to the breakfast room where she found the baby on the floor and Mr. and Mrs. Chapman struggling. "She (Mrs. Chapman) was sitting in the chair and the man was just behind her. She had some blood on her clothes, and she noticed that Mr. Chapman had something in his hand, though she could not say what it was. Witness did not see him strike her, nor did she hear them speak to one another, but he was holding the weapon over her with uplifted arm." Witness, being frightened, picked up the baby and left the room. Just outside the house she met Gilbert Winchester coming towards the back door. Annie Symonds, assistant at the post office, came into the post office for about five minutes, leaving at about 9 o'clock. Mr. Chapman came into the office soon afterwards but stayed only a few minutes and then went into the living-room. The accused reappeared about twenty minutes to ten, stayed for three or four minutes and then returned to the living-room. A few minutes later the witness heard several screams" and being frightened as to the cause she ran to the front door and called for help."

Edith Henrietta Smith, another assistant in the post office, said Mr. Chapman came into the office a few minutes before ten and served a customer and then went into the living-room. "There did not appear to be anything unusual the matter with him." She noticed nothing further until she heard the screams. She said that when she first went to the office, about nine months ago, "there was considerable unpleasantness between Mr. and Mrs. Chapman, but that had abated of late."

The next witness was Gilbert Winchester, who described hearing children's screams. He could not make out where they were coming from and ran first out of the back of the shop and then immediately along the outside passage leading to the road where he met Annie Harding at the back door. She spoke to him and seemed very frightened. The living-room door was open and he looked in and saw accused holding Mrs. Chapman in his right arm. He did not notice any struggling, nor see any blow or anything in accused's hand, but there was blood on Mrs. Chapman's clothing. Mr. Chapman did not speak to him, and, being frightened, he ran for help and called Mr. Ernest Chapman.

Ernest Chapman's evidence was perhaps the most vivid, and it is worth quoting part of "The Herald" report verbatim.

"They (i.e. Mr. and Mrs. Chapman) had been married about eight years. At times there had been real unpleasantness, and Mr. Chapman had before threatened her. Witness went in one day about five or six months ago, when Mr. and Mrs. Chapman were having a terrible row, and of course he was quarrelling with everything. He was accusing his wife of infidelity and was very excited. Witness was called in and tried to calm him, and told him he was suffering under a delusion, and that he had no right to treat his wife like that. He told him if what he said was true he had no right to have such rows like that for it might lead to something bad. They should separate. He told him he had no right to revenge himself upon his wife, even were what he said true, for they read, witness reminded him, that "Vengeance is mine. I will repay, saith the Lord," and Mr. Chapman then said to his wife, "It is that text which saved you from having a bullet through you." Soon afterwards she ran away from her husband and took her four children, and he refused to have her back. About two months ago he took her back, and a reconciliation took place, and they had been getting on wonderfully well together, so far as he knew. He had not seen any quarrelling, though statements had been made to him by the wife. Witness was going to the office on Monday morning last, and was just getting off his bicycle when Gilbert Winchester beckoned to him, and told him something. The time was about a quarter to ten. Witness rushed into the sitting-room of the deceased and there he saw the deceased lying by the corner of the table, huddled up. He saw no blood at first, but he went to her, knelt down on the floor, and took her up in his arms, and then he noticed a small pool of blood on the floor. The deceased was not dead then, for she groaned a few times. She was not able to speak, for witness spoke to her, and she made no reply. He saw no knife or anything like that about then. Witness subsequently saw his brother, who was upstairs, when some little time afterwards he was brought down by the constable. Witness spoke to him and said, "O brother, what did you do this for? You had no business to send her into Eternity like that. Why did you not go away, or send her away?" Chapman said to witness, "Don't think too bad of me," but that was before witness spoke to him. Witness said to him, "There's nothing but the blood of Jesus can wash away your crime." He made no reply to that. Witness said further to him, "Brother, if you had lived in the love of God, you would never have done this; this is what your atheism has brought you to." He did not reply. Witness believed deceased was 38 years of age."

Dr. Arnold Lyndon, "who affirmed after the Scotch manner of making an oath," gave very precise medical evidence as follows:

"He stated that at ten minutes to ten on Monday morning, the 29th July, he was called to the residence of the deceased. He went into the sitting-room and found the deceased upon the floor supported by Mr. Ernest Chapman, the last witness. He examined her and found that she was dead. She was fully dressed, but her dress was disordered and open in front, and the chest and clothing were covered with blood. Witness could see several punctured wounds on the chest, which must have been caused by a sharp instrument. It might have been caused by the carving tool (produced). He did not notice any weapon about. Subsequently he found the shank of the instrument firmly embedded in the deceased's back, for he had to remove it with a pair of pincers. Great force must have been used to drive it in, for the part in the body measured four inches. The instrument fitted a handle subsequently found in the room. Shortly after he had arrived the policeman came and he told him to go upstairs to see to Mr. Chapman. He saw Mr. Chapman, but he did not speak to him, nor did he make any observation to witness. He had made a post mortem examination of the deceased. The body was that of a fairly healthy woman. Witness had attended her for some time, but although she was not a robust woman, she was not afflicted with any mortal or deadly disease. On the left hand there were slight cuts on the third and fourth fingers and also upon the palm of the left hand. There were two punctured wounds in the front of the left fore-arm, three punctured wounds over the left elbow, and one on the outer side of the left arm above the elbow. There was a punctured wound on the outer side of the left thigh. There was an incised wound two and a half inches long over the front of the left knee. There were six punctured wounds over the left breast and two over the breast-bone, and four over the right breast. Then there was the deep punctured wound in which the instrument was found at the back. Several of the wounds in the front of the chest must have been made with great violence, and inside the chest he found a punctured wound into the left lung, and there were two wounds in the heart which were the fatal wounds. All the wounds were such as might have been caused by that instrument. Undoubtedly the cause of death was the injuries to the heart."

After evidence of arrest the Coroner summed up by stating that the facts seemed clear and instructed the jury that they were only concerned with the cause: "whether there was any justification or whether the perpetrator of the deed was in his right mind were not questions for them that day. They had to say by what reasons, in their opinion, the deceased came by her death, did she or did she not come by her death in consequence of the wounds and injuries which she undoubtedly received. If they believed that that was so, then they had to say whether they were inflicted deliberately and intentionally."

The jury, without retiring, unanimously found a verdict of wilful murder against Walter Gilman Chapman, and he was remanded to the next Winchester Assizes.

At the Assize Trial in November the accused said: "I plead guilty to manslaughter," but on the request of his Counsel a plea of "Not guilty" was entered. The prosecuting Counsel recited the facts of the case and stated that careful investigation had been made into the prisoner's antecedents and previous conduct, and into the conduct of the murdered woman. He said that "some years back" the accused had shown signs of insanity, and that "three or four years ago and again recently before the commission of the deed, prisoner had suffered from delusions with regard to his wife's morality, for which there was no foundation. He had also been under the impression that he was being shadowed by detectives wherever he went. There again was no foundation for the delusion. Medical evidence would show that there was a very strong indication of insanity." Prosecuting Counsel told the jury that if they found the accused guilty they would have to consider the state of his mind at the time.

The evidence on what actually happened on the day of the murder differed not at all from that given at the inquest, except that Mr. Ernest Chapman produced a letter which the prisoner had given to him in May in a sealed envelope marked "to be opened in case of my death." Witness had opened it after the murder had occurred. Defending Counsel read from the contents. It mentioned the names of several people whose names were not made public, and referred to an indecent letter. In another part of the letter purporting to be the accused's will, he left whatever he had for his children till they were 21 years of age. Thereafter his estate was to pass to his brother and sister, leaving the children without anything.

The defence relied solely on the plea of insanity. Under cross-examination Dr. Lyndon said that the brutal nature of the murder suggested insanity and that he had been anxious about the prisoner's mental state since November 1898, when he had made accusations to him of his wife's immorality and had referred to being shadowed. Dr. Lyndon had been so concerned that he made a note of his strange behaviour at that time, but since then had not obtained sufficient evidence to certify him as insane. He had no doubt that he was insane at the time of the murder to such an extent as not to be responsible for his actions. Then came questions and answers between the judge and defence Counsel and Dr. Lyndon:

His Lordship: Do you think he knew right from wrong?

Dr. Lyndon: I think many insane people know right from wrong. I am not prepared to say he did not.

Mr. Matthews (Defence Counsel): Do you mean he was not capable of appreciating the quality of the act?

Dr. Lyndon: I think the insane delusion led to the murder.

Mr. Matthews: At the time he committed the murder was he responsible in the sense that he appreciated what he was doing?

Dr. Lyndon: I am not quite prepared to answer that. I believe he was absolutely insane.

His Lordship remarked that insanity was a disease. The question was what stage the disease was in.

Dr. Lyndon: I don't think he realised the enormity of the crime. I think that undoubtedly he knew he was murdering his wife. I believe it was due to an impulse which he was unable to control owing to mental defect.

Dr. Worthington, medical superintendent of Hampshire County Asylum, had examined the prisoner on the instructions of the Treasury, and had reported that "in his opinion prisoner was insane on July 29th. He believed that at the time he was under an uncontrollable influence, and did not know what he was doing." The medical officer of Winchester Prison corroborated that opinion.

The judge gave a brief direction on the question of insanity to the jury, who at once, after a trial which had lasted for less than two hours, returned a verdict of guilty but not responsible at law for his action. The judge ordered the prisoner to be detained during His Majesty's pleasure.

The Second Grayshott Murder

The First World War incidentally furnished Grayshott with its second murder which, though not of Grayshott, occurred in Grayshott at a house then named "Arundel" (now "Rathellen")[†] in Crossways Road, which had for some years past been conducted by a Mrs. Knopp as an unpretentious but comfortable boarding house. Mrs. Knopp left Grayshott for London and her house was taken by Canadian military officers at Bramshott Camp who were expecting their wives to join them from Canada. Bramshott Camp had been

---

[†] *Originally, and currently, 'Hindhead Chase'*

constructed in 1915 and was used as a training camp for the Canadian Forces, the maple trees which now form an avenue along the A3 road across Bramshott Common being a permanent reminder of their occupation.

The "Hindhead Herald" reported the case very fully at all its stages of inquest, trial and appeal. Perhaps the outstanding features were the sheer brutality of the murder, the fact that there was never any doubt that the accused had committed the murder – indeed, the defence made no attempt to argue otherwise – and that the defence was a plea of insanity.

Both the victim and the accused, Sergeant Henry Ozanne and Lieutenant George Codere respectively, were serving in the 9th Canadian Mounted Rifles, who had arrived at Bramshott Camp only a very short time before the murder. At "Arundel" there were residing the Lieutenant-Colonel, the Major, and Lieutenant Codere, the Assistant Adjutant, together with their batmen – the wives not having yet arrived.

The bare facts are that early in the evening of 8th December 1915, having lured Ozanne to "Arundel," Codere battered him on the head with a trench stick and dragged him down into a cellar as far as the bottom step of the stairs, where, according to the medical evidence, Ozanne – though unconscious – was probably still alive. Codere then mutilated him savagely, forty-five slashes with a carving-knife being found on the body, and cut his throat "from ear to ear," almost completely severing the head. As a next step Codere ordered Corporal Keller, batman to the Major, to burn the trench stick broken in the onslaught on Ozanne, to clean up the bloodstains in the room where the first blows were struck, to bind the body with wire inside two blankets, and to carry it out into the stable at the rear of the house. Codere then ordered Keller to remove his trousers, which were stained with blood. Codere took them away and Keller never saw them again. Keller and Corporal Desjardines, another batman, who was present after the attack and saw the body in the cellar, gave their reasons for not reporting these ghastly events immediately as their fear of Codere and the fact that they were used to obeying him as an officer. They did report the matter to the Major the next morning, when Codere was placed under arrest and handed over to the civil police.

After the usual inquest on the murdered man and a preliminary hearing in the magistrates' court at Whitehill, the trial, presided over by Mr. Justice Darling, occupied two days at the Winchester Assizes in February 1916.

Evidence was given that Codere's own bank account, which he had opened in November 1915 with the Bank of Montreal in London, was overdrawn; that on 4th December Sergeant Ozanne, who was the secretary of the regimental canteen fund, handed him the Canadian currency which had been spent by the troops on the voyage from Canada, and which the accused had offered to change into English currency at Cooks & Sons in London; that on the same day Codere had cashed two cheques totalling £150 at the Bramshott Camp Branch of the Capital and Counties Bank, the cashier paying him the money on his promise to call later with dollar currency to cover the amount, and that on 6th December Codere exchanged the Canadian dollars into £360 of English currency. The cheques for £150 were dishonoured by the Bank on 7th December, and the cashier reported the matter to a senior officer who interviewed Codere. The latter handed over to him £150 in English £5 notes which he paid into the Bank on Codere's behalf. This transaction left Codere unable to refund to Ozanne the full proceeds of the exchange.

Meanwhile in the days preceding the murder Codere had curious conversations with a Major Bouchard, a Lieutenant Morin and a Sergeant Martin. During the conversation with Major Bouchard "a few days before the murder" Codere produced a trench stick and asked, "Is this good enough to kill a man?" He received the reply, "Surely. If you let it drop on anyone's head it would not do him any good." On the train journey on 6th December to London to change the currency, Lieut. Morin travelled with Codere, who asked him if he would like to make some money, and told him that he was holding some money belonging to Ozanne, which he would pretend to pay to him in a vacant room in the Officers' Mess. Codere would get a receipt signed by Ozanne, whom he would kill while Morin was checking the amount of English currency. Codere further stated that he had arranged with Sgt. Martin for the disposal of the body. On the same day Codere met Sgt. Martin at the Savoy Hotel and made some remarks about "making a man disappear," offering the Sgt. 500 dollars if he would assist in this project. Subsequently, on the evening of 8th December, Codere asked Martin to take a large box to "Arundel" in which he wanted "a thing" placed. In cross-examination Martin said that on 9th December he took a large box big enough to put two bodies in.

Unfortunately none of these men took Codere seriously—he was always referred to in the regiment as "fou Codere."

After his arrest Codere wrote a letter to Corporal Keller in an attempt to fasten the murder upon him.

The defence made no attempt to rebut the evidence as to facts, but concentrated on trying to set up the defence of insanity. Senior officers stated that Codere was not a good officer, his rank as Assistant Adjutant carried no real duties, and that it had been decided not to take him with the regiment to France as "he was not balanced enough in his mind to have the lives of 60 men in his charge." Fellow officers spoke of his fits of meaningless violence, such as breaking chairs in the Mess, and loss of temper; "all that he does is a great farce." He was known throughout the regiment as "fou Codere." All through the macabre happenings and the legal processes Codere had seemed at ease, almost nonchalant, unconcerned about either the deed or his own danger. There was evidence that Codere had suffered from asthma from childhood, and that there was a history of insanity in his family. He was only twenty-two. He had twice been reported to the Colonel for striking soldiers on parade, and there was a curious story of his attacking a civilian who was watching a parade of the regiment through a town. As usual, there was a conflict of expert evidence as to the state of his mind.

Mr. Justice Darling summed up very carefully, taking it as self-evident that Codere had killed Ozanne, but advising the jury to concentrate on the law with regard to a defence of insanity. He said, "In every case where this defence was set up, that every man was presumed to be sane and possessed of sufficient reason to be responsible for his crime, until the reverse was proved, and it must be clearly proved that at the time that he committed the act the accused was labouring from such a deficiency of reason as not to appreciate either the nature or the quality of the act he was doing, and that he did not know at the time he was doing what was wrong." His Lordship drew attention both to Codere's pre-murder conversations and his post-murder attempt to attribute to Corporal Keller the responsibility for the crime.

The jury retired for only twenty minutes. They had three possible verdicts: not guilty — but this was ruled out by the defence's tacit admission of the actual facts of the case: guilty but insane: guilty, i.e. without accepting the plea of insanity. On their return they gave the verdict of "Guilty." The judge asked, "Guilty, simply?" and received an affirmative reply. The death sentence was then passed.

The defence lodged an appeal which was heard before the Lord Chief Justice and Mr. Justice Atkin. The former thought Mr. Justice Darling's summing-up at the Assize trial to have been quite unobjectionable, that the jury had reached a verdict after having all the evidence put clearly to them, and he gave a learned exposition of the McNaughton Rules on a defence of insanity. The appeal was dismissed, but the Lord Chief Justice added to his judgement a significant reminder that the Home Secretary had discretion to make further investigation, particularly with regard to information which could not be open to the Assize Court or to the Appeal Court, and he stated that anything said in the Appeal Court was not intended to prejudice the Home Secretary's exercise of this discretion. The Lord Chief Justice was obviously referring to the fact that the family of Codere had been under the impression that their evidence, as to state of mind, could be given under commission, since that was possible in the Canadian Courts, though not in the English Courts.

In fact Codere was not hanged. The discretion was exercised in his favour and he was transferred to a Canadian prison for the insane.

It is curious that the two trials for murder in Grayshott hinged upon a defence of insanity, and that in both cases that defence prevailed.

147

Chapter 13

The New Parish: The First Decades

We have already traced the formation of the ecclesiastical parish in 1901, and the Civil parish in the following year, and have noted that the former — which included parts of Surrey — was larger than the latter, which was confined to Hampshire.

At the turn of the century there still lingered some of the lawlessness and sometimes violence for which the neighbourhood had a reputation. In April 1900, Samuel Bungay was charged with being drunk and disorderly at Grayshott while on private property. P.C. Kenrick ejected him onto the highway where he became abusive and wanted to fight. He was fined 4s. with 11s. costs. In December 1901, Luke White, a Grayshott labourer, was charged with stealing 15 live tame fowls, the property of James Muir of Shottermill. It appeared that he had hidden the fowls in a sack under a large holly tree on the common, and was arrested while retrieving the sack. His defence was that on his way home he had noticed the sack under the tree, and merely went to see what was in it. He was sentenced to four months in prison. On 27th December 1902, Percy Read, a young painter, was drunk and disorderly. P.C. Young gave evidence that at about 7.15 p.m. he was on duty at Hindhead Place, Grayshott, when he heard Read shouting about the policeman and using very abusive language. At length he was taken away by some friends singing "The Soldier's Farewell". He was fined 15s. Perhaps he had been celebrating Christmas too wholeheartedly. On 23rd December 1902, Henry Envis was found carrying a gun without a licence. Constable Young, on duty on the Grayshott Road near Grayshott House, saw Envis come from the direction of his house towards Waggoners Wells road. He took from one pocket the barrel of a muzzle-loading gun, and from the other the stock. He went to the hedge side and looked over into Mr. Whitaker's plantation and was about to fire when the constable spoke to him. Alas, he was prevented from acquiring a Christmas dinner: instead he was fined £1 at the next Court.

Next, two unusual cases. The first, in May 1900, concerned Dr. Coleclough, who seems to have lived in Stoney Bottom. He was summoned by James Belton, who certainly lived in Stoney Bottom, for "being on enclosed premises with the unlawful intent of laying poison to take life." Several dogs had died swiftly and mysteriously within half-a-mile of the doctor's house, and Belton had found bits of meat lying about. He and his brother, Henry, decided to hide at night and keep watch over their own favourite collie dog. At about midnight Dr. Coleclough came over the hedge and approached the kennel, when James rose from behind some gooseberry bushes, seized him and took a bit of meat from his hand. The Doctor said he only wanted to see what dog was barking. But a vet at Haslemere found enough strychnine on the meat to poison several dogs. The Doctor was fined £10 and £5 costs.

Perhaps it is no coincidence that "The Herald" of 15th September 1900 reported that Dr. Coleclough had left the district.

The second unusual case occurred on 26th December 1902. Frederick Collins, a young man of Grayshott, was charged with wearing the uniform of the Hampshire Regiment on that date in such a manner as to bring contempt on that said uniform. Superintendent James said that he met a party of mummers on the road leading from Headley to Grayshott, defendant among them. He was dressed in a field service cap, regulation serge with the white cuffs of the Hampshire Regiment, a pair of infantry leggings and a pair of trousers with red stripes, and a white cloth sash across the shoulder. The Superintendent stopped him and asked, "Are you a soldier?" He replied, "No," and was told he would be reported for wearing the King's uniform in such a manner, to which he replied, "I did not know I was doing wrong." The uniform belonged to his brother who was home on working furlough. In Court he pleaded ignorance of the law and said, "We were only out for Christmas play." He was let off with a 5s. fine and 9s. costs.

Now for two early motoring incidents. In April 1900 "The Herald" printed the following account:

"One day in last week the team and waggon belonging to Mr. E. R. Oliver of Shottermill was passing up the Portsmouth Road, and when opposite the Hotel Moorlands, a motor car passed them at full speed. The horses became frightened and bolted and the driver was thrown out. One of the horses was captured near the Royal Huts Hotel and a second in the Punchbowl, but the last of the three caused considerable trouble before it was caught. An unpleasant circumstance about the whole affair was that the driver of the motor car did not attempt to stop and enquire what was the matter. Although the driver was incapacitated from work for some time we do not believe that he sustained any serious injuries."

The second motoring incident took place in May 1903. Edwin Slade of Shaftesbury Avenue, London, was charged with driving a motor car at excessive speed at Grayshott. Constable Young said that he was on duty at Grayshott Cross at 3.0 p.m. when he saw a large white motor car coming from the direction of Hindhead down the Headley Road. He timed it from Cox's and Well's shop (this should have read Coxhead and Welch's shop). 220 yds towards Grayshott Cross below the Fox and Pelican, the distance being covered in 17 seconds which was at the rate of 26 miles an hour. The distance had been measured previously. There were five cross roads just below where he was standing in full uniform and in view of the driver all the way down the road. There were no vehicles in the road at the time. This looks like a deliberate speed trap. In Court the defendant objected that a stop-watch had not been used, that the distance had been measured previously, and that the constable was not in the road but came out of a hedge surrounded by a crowd of boys. He said he could not have turned the corner if he had been going so fast. However, the Bench said that if he had been going at only half the speed stated it was beyond the statutory speed limit. Slade was fined £1 and 12s. costs.

Even when Grayshott men were in the right, or supposed themselves so to be, they could take fairly extreme measures. In January 1902, Sir Archibald

Macdonald endeavoured to close ancient paths across his land past Waggoners Wells from Grayshott to Bramshott. The Petersfield Rural District Council and Bramshott Parish Council had appointed a committee to collect evidence of rights of way, and a recently-formed Commons Preservation Committee was interested. But Grayshott men could not wait for these deliberations. On Sunday 2nd February, large numbers of Grayshott and Bramshott men converged on Waggoners Wells and forcibly removed Sir Archibald's barriers. The right of way was vindicated.

A little later in the same year, however, a rather similar demonstration failed. Some Grayshott men thought there was a right of way across the Grange Estate belonging to Mr. Frederick Jackson, i.e. between the Grange and Beacon Hill, and they assembled with billhooks to cut a path—and in fact did so. However, Mr. Jackson took them to court, seeking to establish that they had been trespassing on private property and that there was no right of way. The defendants in the resulting Court of Chancery case were well-known Grayshott men. They were Edgar Read, Peter Robinson, Amos Winchester, James Pook, James Moore, Thomas Boxall, James Belton, Henry Belton, George Read, Edward Garner, Harry Stevens, Fred Ayling, Abraham Light, Harry Jackson, Thomas Madgwick and Percy Read. This was not a criminal prosecution. Mr. Jackson won his case and the defendants had to pay his costs.

It is pleasant to look back in retrospect for seventy years at a few of the personalities of the time. We have said much of Miss Catherine Blakeway I'Anson and of what she did for the village. Her appearance never seemed to change. She always wore a black velvet bonnet with jet trimmings and a long black ankle-length coat, and always carried an umbrella. For many years she ran the Sunday School and sat with the Sunday School children at the back of the Church at matins. She was perhaps rather frightening to young children. Whether in School or Church she had a disconcerting habit of poking the umbrella into the ribs of any child observed to be inattentive or naughty. But behind the rather forbidding exterior there was a warm heart, as many of the villagers could testify.

Mrs. Charlotte Lyndon was unpaid Clerk to the Parish Council from 1902 to 1928, and then its Chairman until her death in 1936. She was also a Justice of the Peace, represented Grayshott for many years on the Alton Board of Guardians and Alton Rural District Council, and for a time the Headley Division on the Hampshire County Council. Robertson Glasgow included a short but vivid description of her in his book, "46 Not Out," in which he drew from memories of his schooldays at St. Edmund's School, 1908–1914: "Mrs. Lyndon seemed always to be bicycling against the wind and giving out a preoccupied smile. But she was a great hand, it is said, at parochial matters, at meditation on the bicycle between meetings and enquiries, and at speaking up for the accused as a magistrate at petty sessions." A shy woman, she did many acts of personal generosity by stealth.

Mr. Oliver Chapman was the Grayshott postmaster and St. Luke's Church organist for a very long period. He was also a highly-skilled cabinet maker. As in the case of Mrs. Lyndon, his means of propulsion was a bicycle and, as he always wore a swallow-tailed coat, his progress when delivering telegrams or going to Grayshott Hall to court the lady who became his second wife was certainly striking, especially in a high wind, with his coat-tails streaming behind him. He had a habit of talking to himself and repeating what he said. One joyous memory is of the Sunday Evensong when the electric organ blower ceased to function. His organist's uniform consisted only of a white surplice, and the effect was strikingly comic when he gathered his music and, with what was reminiscent of a rather short nightshirt flapping about his legs, strode from the organ keyboard to the piano in the body of the Church repeating loudly, "No wind, no wind."

Then there was a lady who, in the summer, always decorated her hat with cut roses from her garden. The choirboys stared down the Church, waiting in delighted anticipation for the petals to drop, which they seldom failed to do.

Miss Marion Menzies, a huge Scotswoman, had come with St. Edmund's School from Hunstanton to Grayshott. When she retired as school cook, she set up a china and sweet shop at Edinburgh House, now part of the premises of Messrs. Gould & Chapman, where she also took paying guests. She was "Aunt Marion" to a number of Grayshott children, who revelled in her children's parties at Christmas, when the diversions always included bobbing for apples and toffee-pulling—resulting in a delightful state of dampness and stickiness. In her heyday she topped eighteen stones. One summer morning she was unpacking a crate of china just outside her gate in Jubilee Road. Being near the bottom of the crate she was bending further and further over the edge. A young man passing by could not resist the temptation of such a target as might never present itself again, and crying, "Now I've caught you bending!" delivered a sharp blow which resulted in the swift appearance of an angry face, which soon dissolved in laughter as she realised the humour of the situation. "Aunt Marion" was a curious mixture of generosity and sharp practice. During the First World War, Canadians occupied the camp on Bramshott Common. A mess sergeant came into her shop to buy large meat dishes for the turkeys for the men's Christmas dinner. The writer was impounded to help by taking out the dishes from a shelf under the counter. They were clearly marked on the back at some trifling sum, such as sixpence. She bent down -and whispered, "Rub the prices off," and promptly charged a uniform price of half-a-crown each for stock she had taken over from her predecessor more than ten years before. She had her own satisfactory explanation, "They get plenty of pay—far more than our laddies." Yet this same Miss Menzies stood in the doorway of her shop with tears streaming down her face and, as the Rifle Brigade—who had been billeted in the village—marched out, stripped her shop of sweets, chocolates and biscuits to give to the men.

Another well-known character was Jim Moorey, a member of a family of broomsquires in Stoney Bottom. He was reputed to sleep out in the woods during the summer, and was untidy and rough, and had no regular jobs. He did not mind being called Jim by small boys, but had a fixed antipathy to "Mr. Moorey" or, worse still, "Professor Moorey." If one said, "Good morning, Jim," one got quite a cheerful reply. It was fearsomely delightful to say, "Good morning, Mr. Moorey"—from a reasonably safe distance—and to wait for the bloodcurdling threats and picturesque language which resulted.

A prominent resident was Lady Agatha Russell, who lived at Rozeldenes. She was a daughter of Earl Russell who, as Lord John Russell, had been a mid-Victorian Prime Minister, and was often visited at Hindhead by her brilliant nephew, Bertrand Russell, the mathematician-philosopher. Lady

Agatha is buried in St. Luke's Churchyard. The writer had the social—but undoubtedly tearful—distinction of being rescued by this lady. He had wandered away at the age of three and was utterly lost at the upper end of Headley Road, where Lady Agatha, passing in her carriage, found him in distress and brought him home.

We may finally note Miss Agnes Weston, who lived at "Ensleigh" in Crossways Road. She devoted much of her life to work among sailors, especially Royal Navy men. A prominent feature of her care for them was the foundation of "Sailors' Rests," first at Portsmouth and later elsewhere. They were forerunners of the Union Jack Club for Service men. Here sailors on shore leave could find food and lodging at reasonable prices, and escape the temptations of public houses and worse. A few years ago a penknife with a bone handle engraved "H.M.S. Hood" was unearthed in the garden of "Ensleigh"—lost, no doubt, by one of the many sailors who had visited her there. For a number of years at the beginning of this century Miss Weston, or "Aunt Aggie" as she was affectionately called in the Service, used to arrange for parties of sailors from Portsmouth to give concerts at Grayshott. The local paper published annual statistics of the Sailors' Rest at Portsmouth of which the two following are examples:

For 1903: "128,000 sleepers, 42,000 baths, 500 eggs per day, 2¼ tons of butter, 3,871 gallons of bread, 116 sheep, 28½ bullocks, 1,300 lbs of pork assuage Jack's hunger."

For 1905: "sleeping 363,708, baths 79,610, meals 677,137, receipts £31,000. Meat 100,008 lbs, tea 6,704 lbs., eggs 374,000, milk 20,090 gallons."
In that year the Sailors' Rest had helped to entertain the French Fleet.

In the early years of the new Parish a valuable and deservedly popular institution, the Fire Brigade, was founded. For some years there had been anxiety about the exceptional danger of fire damage to life and property in an area where common land, and common fires, abounded. Shaw made a reference to it in a letter which he wrote to the local paper in March 1899. The first step was taken in March 1904, when the Parish Council asked Alton Rural District Council to install fire hydrants and to put them on the water main "which is now laid through the village." But the District Council declined. A sub-committee of the Parish Council recommended 12 hydrants, each to cost £3.10s., a hose cart, 300 yards of hose and "requisite appliances." On these latter the advice of the Haslemere Fire Brigade was that the cost of the cart, hose and standpipe would be between £70 and £80. An appeal for voluntary subscriptions had produced £78 by July 1905. By a year later £106 had been collected, 9 fire hydrants had been installed, other requirements had been ordered, and volunteers to man the Brigade were asked for. In January 1907, the Parish Council appointed Dr. R. Gray as Chief Officer.

Rules drawn up gave it the name of Grayshott and Hindhead Fire Brigade, and provided for 12 volunteer firemen who were to receive free uniforms. They were to be paid for attending fires at the rate of 1s. an hour, subject to a minimum charge of 5s., and there was to be an additional charge for out-of-pocket expenses for horses, callers and assistants, and for damage to any of the equipment. If the services of the Brigade were found not to be necessary, the charge per man was fixed at 2s.6d. The brigade was not to operate outside the Civil Parish of Grayshott and the Hindhead District except at the discretion of the Officers, when an additional charge of £2.2.0. would be made. A wooden Fire Station was erected on Village Hall land, on a site facing the Headley Road, directly in front of the Small Hall. Early in 1909 electric fire bells were fitted at the Firemen's houses. The statement of accounts, as published in January 1907, is as follows:

Receipts	£	s	d	Expenditure	£	s	d
Grayshott Dramatic Society,				Hose, hose cart and			
May, 1905.	5	6	0	fittings	66	17	10
Donations (59)	110	13	0	Shed	17	19	0
"Social Evenings,"				Fire bells and			
January, 1907.	6	10	0	fixing same	6	3	6
Interest allowed by Bank	1	16	5	Nine hydrants	36	0	0
Grant from Parish Council	5	0	0	Small items		9	0
				Balance in hand	1	16	1
	129	5	5		129	5	5

Meanwhile, on the wild night of 19th February 1908, the new Brigade, with its rudimentary equipment, had its first fire call. "Tarn Moor," the residence of Mr. Frederick Jackson, was on fire, and Mr. Mitchell, seizing the bell of his butcher's shop, rang it in Headley Road, shouting "Fire, fire!" The Parish Magazine reported as follows: "Our newly-formed Fire Brigade did its utmost but with the scanty means at its disposal success was impossible—it was too late when the Haslemere Fire Brigade arrived." The local paper reported that the Grayshott fire hose was too short, and that when the Haslemere Brigade arrived and rectified that difficulty, the water pressure proved insufficient. In the event the building was totally destroyed, though the Grayshott and Haslemere firemen managed to save much of the furniture.

By October 1914, Dr. Gray and two of the firemen were on military service, and although the latter were soon replaced, Dr. Gray did not return until 1916. In that year a motor hose cart was bought and the shortage of personnel was being helped by men from Hindhead. In 1919 the extent of the Grayshott Brigade district was accurately defined because Hindhead had been transferred to the Farnham Joint Brigade area. An agreement with Farnham left Hindhead as far as the Golf Club to be served by Grayshott additional aid, if needed, to be sought from the Farnham Brigade. The definition of districts was necessary because of differential charges as between fires inside and outside a Brigade's area, and the Brigades themselves were very hostile to attempts to poach within their areas.

We have already described the development of social life in the last decade of the 19th century. It continued unabated in the early years of the new century.

A Village Cricket Club had been formed at least as early as 1897, for in that year Grayshott is recorded in the local paper as having beaten Churt by 101 runs to 47: and in 1899 as having won five and lost nine matches. The Club held its first annual dinner at the Fox and Pelican in December 1900. What gave an immense and permanent impetus to cricket, not only in

153

Grayshott, but also in the villages around, was the inauguration by Mr. Edward I'Anson in 1901 of the I'Anson Cup Competition. In the first year of the Competition the result was a tie between Grayshott and Linchmere, neither side having been defeated during the season: but in a final play-off for the cup Grayshott was defeated. In the next year Linchmere again won the cup, but Grayshott brought it home in 1903. In the early years home matches were played on "Mr. Whitaker's Cricket Ground" at Grayshott Hall, in whose hospitable coach-house the players were lavishly entertained. Among prominent local cricketers of early days were such men as Arthur Conan Doyle, John Macmillan (much later Bishop of Guildford), Ingham Whitaker, L. Sant (a master at St. Edmund's), Oliver Chapman, Bert Chapman, Bob Petter and, a little later, Fred Puttick, Percy Burrage, Ernie Johnson, "young" Bob Potter, and P.C. Messenger.

A Football Club was started in 1898 but did not survive. It was refounded in 1902 and has been in existence more or less continuously ever since.

Quite early, an annual Sports Day was organised by a committee of local tradesmen, and combined with the Band of Mercy Show of horses and ponies, gentlemen's carriages and tradesmen's turnouts, and an exhibition of pets. It was held at Grayshott Hall. There was always a local band, and children's sports and dancing took place in the evening.

The annual Boxing Day Meet of the Chiddingfold Hunt at the Royal Huts Hotel was a great event, if the weather was fine. The hounds usually moved off from the edge of the Punch Bowl, where the car park now is, and it was a great sight for hundreds of spectators to see them and the Hunt gradually making their way down the slope. If you were very lucky they might raise a fox soon after they started, of which you might even catch a glimpse — as well as of the hounds streaming behind, and of the scarlet huntsmen following to the sound of the huntsman's horn. There was great drinking of beer in the local pubs on that day.

Cultural activity also flourished. At the Village Hall were classes, usually organised by the County Education Committee, for adults and children in subjects such as gymnastics, gardening, woodwork, poultry keeping, dress-making, cookery, First Aid (taught by the local doctors), and dancing. In the period 1901–1904 there was an Orchestral Society under Miss Edwards, who ran a small private school in Boundary Road: and throughout there was an active Choral Society whose successive conductors were Miss Hecht, Miss Edwards, Mr. S. Marshall Bulley and Mr. W. E. Muir. Among works performed were "Hiawatha," "The Ballad of the Revenge," "Ode on St. Cecilia's Day," "Acis and Galatea" and "Sir Patrick Spens."

There had been a dramatic group in the village before the end of the century, but it seems to have been somewhat spasmodic. Its most fruitful period was when Miss Florence Millward was its producer. This lady was the great friend of Miss Tucker, whom we have noticed previously in connection with the United Reformed Church. The Dramatic Society was a real village society, acting, making all scenery and costumes, and including in its acting ranks gardeners, carpenters, painters, chauffeurs, domestic servants and teachers. It usually did one production, a three-act play, a year and filled the Village Hall to capacity. It regularly gave its small profit to some local cause, e.g. the new Fire Brigade, Haslemere Cottage Hospital. It built up no fund and started each year from scratch.

There was also a Grayshott and Hindhead Horticultural Society from an early date. From 1901 it held an annual Flower Show.

Among the social developments in this period we may note the appointment in 1911 of Grayshott's first District Nurse (Nurse Kidd) and the foundation in 1912 by Captain Molyneux, who lived at Downleas, of the first village Scout Group. In 1908 the Grayshott Aid Committee was founded by the Grayshott Churches with a representative Committee. This has continued to the present, though now called the Nursing Association. We read of the formation in 1910 of a local Coal and Clothing Club, though this was a revival of an earlier similar club. One odd advertisement appeared over a brief period of the: "Hindhead Grammar School: Day and Boarding: Mr. Peter Ferguson, M.A., B.Sc. (Inter): English subjects, Classics, Mathematics, Modern Languages, Science, Drawing, Music, Physical Drill, etc: Pupils prepared for all public examinations: Selborne View, The Avenue, Grayshott." Evidently an ambitious enterprise which never really got off the ground.

The First World War put a temporary stop to most of these activities, when units of Kitchener's Army were billeted in Grayshott and the neighbouring district. Considerable efforts were exerted by the local inhabitants to make the men billeted on them as much at home as possible. The first units to arrive were the 7th Royal Rifle Corps and the 8th Rifle Brigade. They went to France in 1915 and were decimated on the Somme in one of the first German gas attacks. The 8th Rifle Brigade alone got 2 Victoria Crosses, 2 D.S.O.s, 2 M.C.s, and 7 D.C.M.s. Even across the years it is pathetic, and at the same time a cause for pride, to recall letters written from the front to the Rev. A. E. N. Simms and Dr. Lyndon:

From Colonel Maclachlan, 8th Rifle Brigade:

"We had only gone into those trenches that night, and for the next twenty-four hours were fighting for our lives. Practically all the officers are gone; Sheepshanks, Govell-Barnes and myself represent the remnants, and we lost in killed and wounded about two-thirds of the men. We cannot trace a large number of them, I fear, as the Germans got the front trenches thanks to using those devilish gases! I am so awfully proud of them all, but it is hard to start afresh. The officers were a very happy family, and we often used to discuss our jolly billets at Grayshott, and recall the hospitality shown to not only the officers but the men as well."

"The remnants of the 8th Battalion, Rifle Brigade, are greatly touched by your sympathetic letter, and we are most grateful to all at Grayshott for their kindly remembrance of the battalion. Everyone in the battalion fought right well, and I've never in my life felt so proud of them. The companies in which the heaviest losses were are A Company, billeted in the village, and C Company at the Hall. They were both in the front line and were simply enveloped in this flaming liquid. Curiously enough both Mr. McAfee and Mr. Scrimgeour survived the first attack but both were killed in the afternoon at the head of their men, gallantly leading a counter-attack across the open ground against simply murderous machine gun attack. I hope to get many of the wounded back later on, but I fear nearly all those reported missing were killed fighting in their trenches. I want to add that every officer, N.C.O. and man of the battalion looked back on their time at Grayshott with the happiest recollections, and it was a very frequent topic of conversation in the trenches, and the hospitality of all has never been forgotten."

From Colonel Rennie, 7th King's Royal Rifle Corps:

"The fight of the 30th was a horrible affair, but the Battalion fought splendidly and there were many acts of individual heroism although, when all did well, it is difficult to specialise."

In the early months of the war Bramshott Camp was being built on Bramshott Common for the reception and training of Canadian troops. Grayshott made itself responsible for manning one of the Y.M.C.A. huts with volunteers, and the Village Hall, Mission Church and Wesleyan Church were for a time opened as recreation centres for the men.

Throughout the period with which we are dealing the infant Parish Council was presided over by Mr. A. Ingham Whitaker and guided by its Clerk, Mrs. Lyndon. It exercised vigorously its function as a pressure group upon the superior Councils at Alton and Winchester, but its finances were simple in the extreme. It was fortunate in being able to rely for many things upon the voluntary financial support of its residents. It started off boldly in 1902 by precepting for a £20 rate for Parish purposes, but does not seem to have precepted again until 1904, when it did so for £10. In July, 1906, the annual precept was increased to £76 (a 3d. rate), but this was to meet the forthcoming cost of appealing against the high valuation for rating purposes of properties in Grayshott. Thereafter only on one occasion did the precept exceed £20, and indeed in 1918 the Council minuted: "No precept was drawn, expenditure being very small." The total expenditure of the Parish Council in 1911–1912 was £11.13s., and in the next year £10.18s.2d.

For three years, 1906–1909, a battle raged about the Grayshott assessments of properties for rating. Indeed, as early as 1903 Mr. George Cornish had proposed that Grayshott should ask to be incorporated in the Farnham Rural District because rates were lower in the parish of Frensham, and because the roads would be kept in better repair. It is amusing to compare this with the utmost opposition when, some 60 years later, Haslemere Urban District Council proposed that Grayshott should be transferred to its area and, in consequence, to Surrey. In the early years the rateable values were determined by Overseers of the Poor, elected at Triennial Parish meetings. In April 1906, the Grayshott Overseers received a "severely worded request" from Alton Rural District Council to review the parish assessments. The Annual Parish Meeting asked the Parish Council to appeal to Quarter Sessions against the revaluations "on the grounds that the new assessments are unfair compared with other parishes in the Alton Poor Law Union" and to seek legal advice. The Council decided, as a first step, to appeal to Quarter Sessions "to get all the Parishes in the Alton Union re-assessed in order to lessen the rates, if possible, at Grayshott." Legal advice was that appeal was possible under an Act of 1862, but that "very heavy expenditure might be incurred." This was an obvious cause for alarm, and a solicitor was employed to draft, as an initial step, a letter to the Assessment Committee of the Alton Guardians pointing out that only Grayshott had been re-assessed and that "as a matter of justice the other Parishes should also be revalued," and adding a veiled threat "that Grayshott Parish Council had power to raise the question of under-assessment of other parishes, but that they were loath to resort to a course which would involve the whole Union in considerable trouble and expense." Meanwhile some information was collected on the assessment of comparable properties in Grayshott and other parishes. Mrs. Lyndon, the Grayshott representative on the Board of Guardians, proposed to that body that the whole Union should be revalued so that "representations of Grayshott Parish Council should receive proper consideration." She had to report in August 1907 that her resolution had been defeated, though all Overseers had been instructed to go through their valuations and submit supplementary lists by October 31st, in default of which the Assessment Committee would appoint a valuer to re-assess their parish. This produced no result, and it was decided to proceed to appeal. On legal advice the Parish Council appointed a profess-sional valuer to value certain Grayshott properties against whose valuation it was proposed to appeal, and to compare his assessments with those of similar properties in Binsted, Bentley, Kingsley and Selborne. An appeal to Quarter Sessions was lodged. Alarmed at this, the Board of Guardians consented to employ a valuer to re-assess the whole Union. Thus the purpose of the Parish Council had been attained at considerable cost, but they did not formally withdraw the appeal. There were further negotiations as to payment of costs which had amounted to over £120: the Board of Guardians agreed to make a contribution of £50, the remainder falling on Grayshott. Finally it was reported in March 1909 that the revaluation of the Union had resulted in an increase of £34,000; in some parishes valuations increased by 70 to 80 per cent; and the result had been beneficial to Grayshott.

The Parish Council constantly complained of the unsatisfactory state of the two main roads in the village, and, at its third meeting in November 1902, called the attention of the local Surveyor to this matter. In 1905, the Council complained to Alton Rural District Council about the use of unsuitable stone for repair work and got redress. In the next year the District Council offered to install drainpipes and gullies in Headley Road if the property owners would pay for the pipes, but this suggestion was robustly rejected. The position obviously did not improve, for in 1910 the Annual Parish Meeting "draws the attention of the Rural District Council to the bad state of the chief roads in the village of Grayshott and the unsatisfactory condition of the footpaths on the sides of the roads and requests the Rural District Council to take steps to have the roads and footpaths put in a better state of repair." A little later the Parish Council suggested the use of tarmac and the District Council agreed to use it on an experimental length. Complaints recur regularly at Annual Parish Meetings about the state of the roads, and the criticisms of 70 years ago have a familiar ring today.

The Parish Council also tried to get the County and District Councils to take responsibility for repairing two of the ancient roads — Waggoners Wells Road and Stoney Bottom. Both cases were resolved after public enquiries by a committee of the County Council. On each occasion Mrs. Lyndon led the case for the Parish Council.

The Waggoners Wells Road enquiry in 1905 was technically on a com-plaint by the Parish Council of inaction by the District in regard to repairs.

Mrs. Lyndon quoted correspondence and complained, "The Rural District Council generally allowed the letters to lie on the table." She maintained that the road was a highway before the Enclosure Award of 1855. The County Council did not question that it was a road commonly used for going to Petersfield Market, and said that it was not necessary for the County to prove previous repair by the parish. It was stated in evidence by elderly inhabitants, collected by Mrs. Lyndon, that for 70 years past a large amount of vehicular traffic, mainly horses and carts, passed along it between Grayshott and Liphook and Petersfield, "but now it is nearly impossible to go up and down." The Petersfield Surveyor had said the road was scheduled as a public road, but there was no record of repairs. The Alton Rural District Council asserted that the road was now used mainly for picnic parties, and added "that, of course, was an attraction to the parish of Grayshott, but this was no reason why the expense of repairing a road for picnic parties to use should be put upon the ratepayers of the whole district." The Alton Surveyor estimated the cost of putting the road into reasonable repair at "something under £20." The difficulty was that if the District Council once did this, it would remain their responsibility. Grayshott won its case: the County Council requested the District Council "to make it reasonably passable for ordinary traffic at all seasons of the year." In her letter of thanks to the County Council Mrs. Lyndon "trusted that they would see that their request to the District Council was carried out."

The enquiry on Stoney Bottom Road in 1914 had a different result. There had been much correspondence between the Parish and District Councils, the latter refusing to take any responsibility except to try to stop storm water rushing down the Headley Road into Hill Road and then into Stoney Bottom. It was clear that from time to time property owners had either singly or acting together done some elementary repair work and moved major obstructions. A difficulty which had also cropped up in the Waggoners Wells Road case was that responsibility for repairs could not be placed on the District Council unless it could be shown that the road was repairable by the Highway Board before 1833. The District did not question that Stoney Bottom was a right of way. Again Mrs. Lyndon tried to marshal witnesses who would say much the same as had been said in 1905, but, unfortunately, of the four then called, three had since died, and the other was in the workhouse infirmary. However, Mrs. Jane Pook, aged 84, who was born at Waggoners Wells — there were then two or three old cottages near the Waggoners Wells end of Kingswood Lane, of which there is now no trace — gave evidence that "cows went that way to water and ponies went that way on to Ludshott Common" and "the broomsquires used to bring their carts down to fetch their things away," and John Heather remembered his father taking timber in 1864 over it from Kingswood Firs to Liphook Station, "in a waggon drawn by four horses." There was, however, evidence that the lower end of the road at Waggoners Wells had been blocked by a well-house built across it at least 50 years before. The enquiry reported that, although the road might be an ancient highway, the Parish Council had not succeeded in establishing the fact, but further action could be taken if additional evidence could be found. This Mrs. Lyndon sought hard but unsuccessfully, and so the Parish Council case lapsed. The upper part of Stoney Bottom is now listed as a road to be adopted by the District Council at some future time.

Early in its life the Parish Council had to consider traffic hazards on the roads. We have already mentioned an early case of excessive speed in Headley Road. In October 1903, consequent upon the passing of the Motor Car Act, Alton Rural District Council asked the Parish Council if there were places in the village where reduction of speed would be desirable under County Council Regulations. Mrs. Lyndon had consulted "some gentlemen who had personal experience of driving motor cars" and, as a result, informed the District Council that there was no special need in Grayshott for speed limits "beyond any general restrictions that the County Council may make for driving through villages." Again in 1904 she informed the County Council that "nothing need be done at present" with regard to erecting sign posts at dangerous places. Four years later the Parish Council changed its opinion and asked the County to erect warning signs to motorists at the Crossways Corner, in order to protect children. In 1912 it reiterated this request, but to the Automobile Association. That body offered two signs, provided that the cost of erection was met locally. This cost the Chairman 2s.6d., since the Parish Council had no power to meet the cost. In March 1914 the Council discussed the danger at Crossways Corner arising from buses, cars and cyclists: and, in consultation with the Road Surveyor, the corner at the junction of Headley and Crossways Roads was rounded off.

At its second meeting, in September 1902, the Parish Council opened the question of street lighting and asked the Clerk to obtain estimates for erecting and running electric lamps. The Hindhead Electric Light Company quoted £3.13s. as the cost of each lamp, but if six or more 12 ft. standards were installed and lighted from dusk till 10.30 p.m. the total cost would be £3.10s. per lamp per annum. At the Annual Parish Meeting of 1903 the idea was defeated on grounds of cost. It was resurrected at the end of 1912 when estimates were obtained from the Haslemere Gas Company and the Hindhead Electric Light Company. The matter was put to the well-attended Parish Meeting of 1913, in the form of a resolution to adopt the Lighting and Watching Act, 1833. The cost of installing and lighting seven street lamps would be about £20 a year (less than a ¾d. rate). Objections were made as to the expense and also because the scheme would only light the two main roads, and the residents in other roads would not benefit. Dr. Lyndon replied that the latter argument was always used when improvements were suggested in a village, and that the increasing rateable value would in a few years make it possible to put lamps at dangerous corners on other roads for the same rate. Although a majority voted for the resolution, the two-thirds majority necessary for decisions on parish expenditure was not forthcoming. Dr. Lyndon demanded a parish poll, which cost £1.8s. for two Polling Booths, and which produced a total of 64 in favour, 37 against. This again was insufficient, as in a parish poll it was necessary that a clear majority of Parochial Electors should have voted. Dr. Lyndon was not completely beaten. In March 1914, he told the Annual Parish Meeting that Haslemere Gas Company, of which he was a Director, had agreed to put a standard at Crossways with a 350 candle power lamp, for one year, "practically as an advertisement" and the small charge would be met privately.

There were certain inconveniences from which Grayshott suffered, but not quietly. The postal facilities were one. One gets the impression that Grayshott people wanted as many daily deliveries as possible, and that they seethed in a frenzy of frustration if the deliveries were late. In 1903 the G.P.O. arranged for Grayshott mail to be brought direct by mail cart from Haslemere and delivered by postmen starting from Grayshott Post Office. In 1905 the Council was badgering the postal authorities for an evening delivery, which they must have got, for in October 1910 they asked that the third daily delivery of letters should be extended "throughout the Parish," as the Post Office was crowded by those calling for their letters in the evening. The Council returned to the charge on this matter three times in 1911, and won its point in January 1912. The quarrel in the next three years arose from the decision of the G.P.O. to close the Grayshott Office on Wednesday afternoon "except for telephone and telegraph services at the side door." The Council protested that this would cause "very serious inconvenience to the public." In January 1914 the G.P.O. closed the correspondence with a magisterial statement that "they did not consider the circumstances justified an exception to the general policy of the Post Office." The Council complained in 1915 that some so-called improvements had only made things worse, to which the Portsmouth P.O. Surveyor replied counselling patience as "full improvements from recent changes could not be obtained at present owing to partial dislocation of Services." This was not unlikely in war time. War with the Post Office was renewed in 1919, when the G.P.O. gave notice of closing the Post Office daily between 1 p.m. and 2 p.m., to which the Council replied that this had not been necessary in war time, and they could not see why it was necessary now. Later in the same year the grievance was that the latest collection of mail was too early, for "London letters, posted by country mail were frequently not delivered till the afternoon." The G.P.O. Surveyor somewhat weakly promised improvements.

Another bone of contention was the registration of births and deaths, for which purposes Grayshott people had to go Headley—an undertaking of considerable difficulty in the absence of public transport. In January 1903, the Parish Council asked the Alton Board of Guardians, who were responsible for registration arrangements, to open an office at Grayshott. This was turned down as the Registrar considered it unnecessary, since he was bound to attend at the house of any person for a fee of one shilling. The matter was re-opened in 1908, when the Parish Council asked that the Registrar and Relieving Officer should attend at Grayshott once a fortnight, free of charge. In 1909 the Council appealed direct to the Registrar General, only to receive the reply that "on account of the (local) Registrar's age he cannot well insist on his going to Grayshott, but he would consider the matter again when a vacancy occurs in the Registrarship." The Registrar General was thanked with a somewhat tart request "that he will keep his promise in mind." The opportunity did not occur until 1913, when the aged Registrar retired and an arrangement was made, after further correspondence, that the Registrar and Relieving Officer—one and the same person—should attend at Grayshott Village Hall each Monday afternoon.

A rather similar grievance was that there was no polling station at Grayshott for local and Parliamentary elections. This was achieved earlier than the registration solution, an Order being made in 1905 establishing Grayshott as a separate Polling District.

An early tidying operation was the provision of parish allotment land. We have already seen that at the separation from Headley the Hollywater Allotment Land was conveyed to Grayshott Parish Council. It was obviously too remote to be of any practical use. In 1905 a special Parish Meeting author-ised the Council to sell the Hollywater land and to purchase some allotment ground at Grayshott. The Hollywater ground fetched £350, of which £295 was used for the purchase of the Stoney Bottom allotments and for certain expense for fencing it in. The resultant 13 allotments were to be hired at 3d. per rod per annum, and they were all taken in 1906. Six years later there were more applicants than allotments. Mr. Whitaker came to the rescue by giving half an acre of a field in Headley Road — now the Playing Fields — at a nominal rent of 10s. a year. This provided 7 plots, each of 10 rods, for which, after the first year, each allotment holder would pay a rent of 2s.6d. a year. In the summer of 1920 Mr. Whitaker made a gift of 2½ acres of land adjoining the Playing Fields, to be used as allotments.

A recurring cause of complaint was an "offensive smell" emanating from what Bernard Shaw had described as "a stinking pond" (see Chapter 5) when he resided at "Blencathra" in Boundary Road, to which St. Edmund's School had moved from Hunstanton in 1900. This stagnant pool, on the east side of the dip at Pooks Hill, was in truth seepage and overflow from septic tanks serving the school. It was first mentioned at the Parish Council in November 1902. Since the pool was just in Surrey the Alton Rural District Council could do nothing about it. Mrs. Lyndon was instructed to ask the Headmaster of St. Edmund's — Mr. Cyril Morgan-Brown — to remedy the nuisance. Mrs. Lyndon reported his assurance that he would do everything possible to make the septic tanks effective, but "two members of the Council mentioned that the smell had recently been particularly offensive." All was quiet until 1906, when "after lengthy discussion" it was resolved "That the residents of Grayshott be asked to sign a memorial to the Farnham Rural District Council to take immediate steps to remedy the offensive condition of the pond adjoining the boundary of the Parish of Grayshott." We have no record of any result, but in October 1915 the Council again complained, and in March 1916 it was reported "very bad" and to have caused soldiers at Camp (Canadians at Bramshott Camp) to complain. The Council reported this to the Farnham Council but "did not wish to put any unfair burdens on the owners of the septic tanks." At the Annual Parish Meeting of 1918, complaint was made from the floor, but a little later the smell had abated. This improvement did not last, and in July 1920 the Parish Council wrote again to Farnham, whose Surveyor visited the spot and could not detect the nuisance. The last word was with the Parish Council: "In the opinion of Grayshott people it un-doubtedly exists."

The Coronation of King George V was celebrated in 1911 on the traditional formula of Church services, children's sports and tea. There was a large communal bonfire on the Gibbet Hill in a heavy downpour of rain. Yew trees were planted in the Churchyard by Tommy Whitaker and Nicolette Simms, and in the Children's Recreation Ground by Mrs. Hannah Robinson, one of the oldest inhabitants, who kept her little general store in Crossways Road. A small balance of the fund which had been collected was used for a drinking fountain and trough for men, horses and dogs, at the corner of Hill Road and Headley Road. It has long since been removed.

In the closing years of the period we are considering, council housing began to be discussed. In 1913 the Medical Officer of Health asked about the provision of houses for the working class. Was there a deficiency or any overcrowding? The Council replied that there was no serious shortage "for those employed in the parish, but that if 20 cottages, rented at about 6s. to 7s. a week, were built, they would be used by labourers who live at some distance from their work." When similar questions were asked in 1917, the Clerk had given particulars and had suggested 12 council houses for Grayshott. Early in 1919 Mr. Whitaker said that as a result of correspondence with the District Council he had suggested suitable sites, and the matter was brought up at the Annual Parish Meeting in that year, the attention of the District Council being drawn to "the very urgent and immediate need for more cottages in Grayshott." The Meeting also resolved that ¼ acre of land should be allowed for each cottage, whereas the Local Government Board suggested half that amount. In April 1919 Mr. Whitaker offered a site bordering Headley Road and School Road on which the District Council architect hoped to build 12 houses. By July the site and its purchase price had been approved and plans for 12 cottages, each with ¼ acre of land, had been passed. There were some delays, but by March 1921 some of the houses were completed. The Parish Council pressed for a reduction of the proposed rent of £1 a week, including rates. After lengthy correspondence between the Councils the rent was fixed at 18s. a week, inclusive of rates.

A fortunate but characteristic development came in the early years of the new parish — fortunate in that it secured for the village an attractive village centre and an extensive playing field, and characteristic because it came from splendid and imaginative gifts by its prominent residents.

In January 1904, the Parish accepted the gift of the triangle of land at the junction of Headley and Crossways Roads, to be used as a recreation ground for children. Under the terms of the gift the land was never to be built upon, and bye-laws were to be framed for the safety of young children. The anonymous donors promised to lay out the ground with paths, seats and flowering shrubs before handing it over. The "Grayshott Sanitary Association" promised to pick up bits of paper and other rubbish free of charge for three months. Would that there were such a body in recent times! To add to its attractions the Grayshott Brass Band were permitted to play there, if they so wished, not more than two evenings in any week. In July 1908 permission was given to Father Hopkins, a noted evangelist, to hold a Sunday afternoon meeting there, provided that "six men should be arranged for to keep order and prevent damage." There is no record that they were needed. The village school was also allowed to use the ground on Empire Day. This became for some time an annual event of saluting the flag, singing the National Anthem, "Land of Hope and Glory," and other patriotic songs, and displays of physical drill.

We have mentioned in the Chapter on the Fox and Pelican an unkempt, frowsy little piece of rough grass and much litter, enclosed in high and gloomy hedges, which was owned by the Hall family, prominent brewers of Alton, and which could possibly become in the future the site of a tied public house in rivalry to the Fox and Pelican. As it was, it was sometimes used by small travelling fairs and "cheapjacks," — and, as it was private property, the Parish Council could do nothing to prevent this. Partly for that reason, Dr. Lyndon, Mr. Whitaker and Mr. Ashley Crook (of Apley House) purchased the land in September 1913 from an estate agent who had bought it from Mr. Gerald Hall. These three gentlemen now offered it to the Parish Council as a

Village Green, subject to certain sensible conditions. They had it cleared and turfed, and promised to provide several seats. At the outbreak of war in 1914 it was used as a training ground for the Civil Guard two evenings a week, "provided it did not seriously damage the grass."

In January 1914, Miss I'Anson gave the 2¼ acres, named after Philip I'Anson, as Philips Green. She died before the conveyance was completed, but her sister, Emma I'Anson, actually gave it in October 1916 and their great friend, Miss Edith Hadwen, paid for fencing it in. During the war years it was used as war allotments. Then it reverted to its purpose as a recreation ground mainly for games for children. The Chapter on Grayshott School related how it was sold by the Parish Council to the County Council, as a site for a new primary school, the first phase of which was not started until June 1976.

Finally, at the Annual Parish Meeting in March 1919, Mr. Whitaker announced his magnificent gift of the 10-acre field which is now the Village Playing Field.

Few villages can have been as fortunate in their formative years in securing in so short a period such generous provision of adequate land for recreational purposes.

The last years of the 19th century and the first two decades of the present one had seen immense progress in laying the foundations of the new parish. By 1921 its population had nearly doubled in 20 years (666 at the 1901 census, 1,230 in that of 1921). In the first three years (1899 to 1902) the basic provisions had been made of a village inn, a large Parish Church, a Wesleyan Church and a Village Hall. By 1920 the Roman Catholic Church and the Convent of the Cenacle had been added. Public utilities had been brought into the village: electricity (Hindhead Electric Light Company, 1901), mains water (Wey Valley Water Company, 1904), gas (Haslemere Gas Company, 1909), and a start had been made in street lighting (1914). Land had been given which formed a very pleasant village centre and gave large and beautifully placed playing fields. Grayshott had also received its first council houses. By any standards this is an impressive list and a striking testimony to the foresight and the spirit of public responsibility of prominent residents in its early years.

Chapter 14

Between the Wars

After the First World War a local committee, representative of the Parish Council and of village organisations, was formed to consider suitable War and Peace Memorials, and to collect funds to provide them. It was decided to erect, at a cost of about £400, a Memorial Cross on the Village Green, to be designed by the Surveyor of Hereford Cathedral on the basis of the ancient Clearwell Cross in Gloucestershire" in York stone, on which the names of men of the ecclesiastical parish who fell in the War were to be inscribed. Some of these were of men over the border in Surrey. In this connection it is interesting to read that at a Special Parish Meeting in 1932, which authorised the re-siting of the Cross, Mrs. Lyndon remarked that it was unfortunate that, technically, Grayshott (i.e. the civil parish) was entirely in Hampshire, although for all practical purposes there was a Surrey side that really belonged to the village.

There was some controversy as to the Peace Memorial, some led by Dr. Lyndon advocating a Cottage Hospital: while others, feeling this too ambitious, particularly as there was a good Cottage Hospital at Haslemere, suggested the erection of a Nurse's Cottage, to include a Maternity Room and possibly a School Clinic. Several public meetings were held and the final decision was for the latter.

The Memorial Cross was unveiled and handed over to the Parish Council on 17th July 1921, and the Nurse's Cottage in School Road was built on land given by Mr. Whitaker, and was in use before the end of the same year. A School Clinic was built on the same site.

The Village Green did not prove to be the final resting-place of the Memorial Cross, which was on a site peculiarly liable to litter. In July 1932, Major Wessel, speaking on behalf of the British Legion, the Grayshott Branch of which had been recently formed, proposed that the Cross should be moved to the Children's Recreation Ground and placed at the western end of it, at the junction of the Headley and Crossways Roads. This was felt to be a suitable site on which it would be more practicable to look after it. The British Legion offered to level and prepare the ground, to arrange for the removal and re-erection, to supply and erect iron railings to form an enclosure, and to assume responsibility for maintaining the hedges and grass—a promise which they have kept faithfully. They would raise the estimated cost of £100 by voluntary subscriptions. At a Special Parish Meeting in August the resolution for removal was moved by Major Wessel. He described the Cross on its existing site as "just a dark Cross in the middle of a field surrounded by scraps of paper, cigarette boxes and other refuse," and the proposed site as "more fitting and worthy where the beauty and dignity of the monument could be seen." He did not believe that satisfactory improvements could be made on the existing site. Dr. Lyndon objected to the taking of any part of the

Children's Recreation Ground and hinted darkly at the reversionary rights of Guy's Hospital if the Children's Recreation Ground were used for other than its original purpose. He much preferred some improvements on the existing site, which the Parish Council had discussed in 1931. Major Wessel replied and said he thought he had answered all Dr. Lyndon's criticisms, but proved to be over-optimistic — for the latter characteristically replied, "But you have not convinced me." The motion was carried, 40–2. 'The Herald', commented: "A decision which must be rare in the annals of this district was made by a Parish Meeting on Tuesday last week when a resolution was adopted authorising the removal of the War Memorial from the village green to the corner of the children's playground." When the centre of the village is seen some 40 years later, there can be little doubt that the decision taken in 1932 was a wise one.

In the inter-war years the parish boundaries were extended to the present position. The first alteration, in 1921, was really a tidying-up of the boundary between Grayshott and Headley from Whitmore Vale on the north to Headley Road on the south. As a result of an Inquiry the adjustment was authorised, thereby adding 35 acres of land, mainly on the Land of Nod Estate, to Grayshott.

In the minutes of the Annual Parish Meeting of 1921 there is the following interesting note: "The Clerk (Mrs. Lyndon) asked that mention should be made in the Minutes of the old apple tree which for generations had been mentioned as the boundary point where three parishes and the Districts of Alton, Petersfield and Farnham meet. In the perambulation this is described as the "Wagners' (sic) Wells Bottom head, at the corner of the hedge by the apple tree. The old tree died during the Great War and in February this year Mrs. Mowatt had had it dug out, after being photographed, and a young apple tree planted on the exact spot. A piece of the trunk of the old tree having been sent to Kew Gardens, the experts there stated they believed the tree to have been some 300 years old." The three parishes that met at this spot were Grayshott (formerly Headley), Bramshott and Shottermill, and Wagner's Wells Bottom head was the eastern end of Stoney Bottom at Pooks Hill. Alas, there seems to be no trace of the successor to the old tree.

The second extension of boundary, to include the Kingswood Firs Estate, added considerably more land and ensured that the future building estate there would be part of Grayshott, instead of an outlying part of Bramshott Parish. The alteration was effective from April 1932.

There were persistent rumours early in 1936 that the Hampshire, Surrey and West Sussex County Councils were negotiating for the rationalisation in this area of their respective boundaries. Dr. Lyndon referred at the Annual Parish Meeting to a rumour that "one of their neighbouring authorities wished to grab Grayshott," and, to applause, declared, "I do not wish to be grabbed. I would rather remain in Hampshire than go into Surrey." Mrs. Lyndon said that the Hampshire County Clerk had assured her that "Hampshire County Council are not going to sell Grayshott to Haslemere or anybody else," and she referred to the first Annual Parish Meeting in 1903, when a resolution for such a transfer, made by a few ratepayers, had been defeated by a large majority. Now, in 1936, the Parish Meeting unanimously resolved, "That this Grayshott Annual Parish Meeting wishes to affirm that it strongly disapproves of any suggestion that the parish of Grayshott should be transferred from Hampshire to Surrey." There were no further developments at this time, but the problem arose again more acutely some 30 years later.

Down to the Second World War there were periodic perambulations of the parish boundaries, usually in company with representatives of the neighbouring parishes.

Throughout the greater part of this period the Parish Council continued to be elected by show of hands at Annual Parish Meetings—at which, if a resolution was carried with the requisite majority, a poll could be demanded. At the Annual Parish Meeting in 1931 there were 11 candidates for 8 seats, and a poll was demanded. This, however, became unnecessary when immediately after the Meeting a sufficient number of candidates withdrew. This kind of thing was obviously open to objection. In 1937 the Parish Council declared themselves to be in favour of election by poll and requested the County Council to make the necessary Order. This was made without delay—in fact Grayshott was the first parish in Hampshire to take this course. When War broke out in 1939 the Government suspended Local Government Elections, which were not resumed until 1946. In the earliest part of the inter-War period Grayshott elected one representative to the Alton Rural District Council, always Mrs. Lyndon, but later an additional representative was allowed.

Mrs. Lyndon and Mr. Whitaker served continuously as Clerk and Chairman respectively of the Parish Council. In 1928 Mr. Whitaker left Grayshott and Mrs. Lyndon succeeded him as Chairman, being herself succeeded by Mr. C. Gordon Macpherson of the well-known Hindhead firm of solicitors. This skilled professional advice has been of great benefit to the Parish Council, and hence to the parish, as has been abundantly shown by more than 25 years of invaluable service as Clerk by Mr. Macpherson's successor, Mr. D. P. Lawson. Mr. Whitaker, perhaps Grayshott's greatest benefactor in gifts and service, died in Belgium in 1933. Mrs. Lyndon died suddenly in 1936 while on holiday at Shrewsbury. She and her husband had been founders of village life and institutions at Grayshott. In her last address at an Annual Parish Meeting, in 1936, the expression of her views was characteristic. After mentioning the enormous increase in the work of local government, she regretted that so much had to be left to officials and not enough left to voluntary workers—especially in the fields of public assistance, care of the blind and feeble-minded, infant welfare, recreational facilities and care of village halls. If more reliance was placed on voluntary work there would be a saving in rates and an increase in sympathy and understanding. One of the wreaths at her funeral bore this testimony: "She lit a candle in many a dark room."

Mrs. Lyndon was succeeded as Chairman by Mr. R. C. Duggan (1936–1937), a beloved Churchwarden and Bank Manager. He was followed by Major P. T. Wessel (1937–1944), who retired from the Chair owing to ill-health and Mr. Duggan again took over until 1946, to be followed again by Major Wessel (1946–1947).

While we are following in some detail Parish Council affairs, it is worth mentioning that in July 1926 the Council considered joining the National Association of Parish Councils, subject to the payment of the annual subscription being a legitimate charge upon the rate fund. This was cleared satisfactorily and the Parish Council joined the national body in 1927. Over the years membership of this body has proved very valuable. The National Association works through County and District Associations of Parish Councils, The National Association keeps close watch and, if necessary, makes representations upon legislation affecting parish matters and the functions of Parish Councils. It has been of vital importance that the democratic control of many local matters, particularly at the grass roots at parish level, should be not only preserved but even enhanced. It is only at this level that electors and elected representatives are in daily contact, and that the representatives cannot evade the electorate. In all the stages of the Local Government Reform of the seventies the individual parishes and their own Association fought a hard, and, to a great extent, successful struggle to preserve and extend the role of this lowest tier of democratic government.

The main expenditure of the Parish Council was upon the maintenance of parish properties and street lighting: down to 1930 the annual parish precept for these purposes did not exceed £45. In the thirties it averaged about £65 but had increased to £180 by the middle of the next decade.

We have seen that Philips Green was used for War allotments in the First World War. In 1924 there was a suggestion that village tennis courts might be sited there, but an alternative site was found which is, in fact, their present site: and Philips Green continued to be used almost exclusively as an addition to the adjoining village school playground, and a footpath was opened from it to School Road. For a few years a cricket pitch was provided on Philips Green for scouts and cubs. Once more in the Second World War it was used for growing vegetables.

The Children's Recreation Ground was—and still is—subject to a bye-law prohibiting cycling thereon. Mrs. Lyndon secured the prosecution, after warnings, of one juvenile offender, but it must be confessed that the Parish Council was fighting a losing battle on this matter. The western corner of this green was improved when the War Memorial was moved there. The scattering of litter on these greens, particularly round the War Memorial while it remained on its original site, was a constant problem, and the Annual Parish Meeting of March 1925 resolved to ask Alton Rural District Council to provide a house-to-house collection of dry household refuse, the Vicar (Mr. Simms) pointing to the importance of making the village attractive "owing to our partial dependence on visitors." This request was granted and the Ministry of Health by Order made Grayshott a Contributory Place, so that the cost of this dry scavenging fell upon the parish rate. The Alton Council applied for an Order to allow expenditure on collection of street litter, and in March 1929 it was reported that the dry scavenging was effective. But again it must be confessed that no permanent or complete solution has been found.

In 1927 the Parish Council formally constituted a Management Committee to administer the new Playing Fields, consisting of three members of the Council and representatives of each constituent club of the Grayshott Recreation Club, but the Charity Commissioners made some difficulties which were finally resolved in 1930. Mrs. Lyndon bequeathed two cottages in Beech Hanger to the Parish Council with a hope that one of them would be let to the caretaker of the Playing Field, and the adjacent Tennis Courts, and this has been done ever since, to the mutual benefit of caretaker and the user clubs.

There was some agitation just before the Second World War to build a permanent Boys' Club on the field, but there was a strong feeling that this was unnecessary, since there was a perfectly good boys' club in premises next to the Village Hall which are now the British Legion Headquarters. In any event the outbreak of War brought an end to the idea. For a few years after the War a Cadet Unit and a Rifle Club used part of the Playing Fields.

In the early 'twenties the Fire Brigade ran into difficulties over the appointment of the Chief Officer. Dr. Gray, who had held the post from the start, wished to resign but carried on until a suitable successor could be found. There were also financial troubles, the account being overdrawn in January 1922, at a time when more hose was needed and when Shottermill, which had made an annual contribution in return for coverage of part of that parish, had decided to contribute to the Haslemere Brigade. The Annual Parish Meeting of that year was faced with three possibilities: to close down the Brigade, to finance it from the rates, or to make adequate provision through voluntary financial efforts. The Meeting resolved to encourage the Brigade to continue on a voluntary basis. In January 1923 Captain Shaw succeeded Dr. Gray who, having moved to Hazel Grove, insisted on resigning. A little later a new schedule of charges, that of the National Fire Brigade Association, was adopted. This, somewhat ironically, reduced the pay of firemen from 3s.6d. to 2s.6d. an hour. Unfortunately Captain Shaw was frequently absent from the district for lengthy periods, and it was not easy to find a suitable Second Officer. Captain P. J. White was appointed Chief Officer in October 1925. Early in 1927 he reported that the Ford hose tender and the fire escape ladders needed replacing, and that the Manual Engine of 1908 "no longer met the needs of the district." The Parish Council decided to launch a special appeal and, if need be, to raise a loan to finance the replacements and to purchase a Dennis turbine trailer engine. The total cost would be about £700, towards which many donations had been received by March. A new hose tender with a fire engine had arrived, and the Dennis turbine Trailer pump had been ordered. Silver National Fire Brigade medals for 20 years' service were presented in 1927 to Superintendent W. J. Read, Senior Fireman W. Hicks and Fireman W. A. Levett. In 1928 the Alton Rural District Council commenced an annual grant of £10, the only condition being that the Brigade would serve the parish of Grayshott. In 1929 Alexander Wilson was appointed Second Officer, an office which had been vacant for some years.

In 1929 and 1930 there were negotiations with Frensham who paid an annual retaining fee of £105 to Farnham "but nearly all fires in the Parish are attended by Grayshott Brigade." Frensham wished to transfer their contrib.-ution "wholly or in part" to Grayshott Brigade. After some legal doubts had been resolved an agreement was made with Frensham Parish Council for an annual contribution of £45 in return for which the Grayshott Brigade would serve the whole of Hindhead and an adjoining part of Churt. The Fire Brigade Committee was enlarged to include representatives of Alton Rural District Council and Frensham and Shottermill Parish Councils. At the same time the charges were revised to 5s. a man for attendance, 3s.6d. a man per hour of attendance, falling to 2s.6d. after 5 hours.

Captain White left the district in 1929 and there was an interregnum in the post of Chief Officer until the appointment of Major Wessel in April 1932.

Two years later he referred to the insufficiency of voluntary contributions, especially as Frensham Parish and Haslemere Urban District Councils were ceasing their contributions. In consequence, the service of the local Brigade was restricted to the civil parish of Grayshott and any properties covered by private arrangements. At the same time the title of the Brigade was altered to "Grayshott Fire Brigade." In 1936 Mr. Wilson became Chief Officer and Superintendent Read was appointed as Second Officer for a short time until his retirement, on completing 30 years of service. Mr. B. White became Superintendent in 1938.

Early in 1939, when the possibility of War became acute, fire protection became the responsibility of the District Council. In March of that year the Parish Council placed on record "That the Brigade is not a Parish Brigade and that the property does not belong to the Parish Council. This decision was made in view of the facts that the Brigade has never been rate-aided and its accounts had never been audited by the District Auditor, and moreover four-fifths of its income during the past 32 years has been from a large number of small subscriptions." The Fire Brigade contracted off the Brigade to the Rural District Council for one year, which continued during the War; but its personnel remained the same and it continued in the same premises. When the air raids began and the local brigade was often on call, and was frequently called out quite far afield — e.g. Portsmouth — the men were allowed the sole use of the Library in the Village Hall as a rest room, and in 1942 the National Fire Service built a hut on a site adjoining the then bowling green, which provided sleeping accommodation, showers and facilities for cooking and recreation.

The state of the village roads and roadside footpaths was a cause of complaint and representations to the senior local authorities throughout the period. By 1924 a number of houses had been built along the occupation road running from Glen Road to Whitmore Vale Road, and this caused some confusion, particularly for postal services, since the road had no official name. Now the Parish Council asked the District Council to agree to name it "Church Lane." Two years later the Parish Council informed the District Surveyor that a white line at Crossways Corner was necessary, but that "the one there now is both useless and dangerous, as it is impossible for a large vehicle coming down the hill to turn the corner to keep within the line." This was altered satisfactorily.

In March 1928 the Council was complaining to the District Council about Whitmore Vale Road, describing its condition as "quite dangerous," and asking for proper repair: but in June the District replied, "This by-lane is sufficiently good for the amount of traffic which may reasonably be expected to use it." The Parish held on to the subject, and in October asked the District to roll the upper part of the road "owing to its extreme roughness and to the increasing amount of traffic." The Annual Parish Meeting of 1929 resolved "That the Rural District Council be urged to do something as soon as practicable to remedy the bad state of Whitmoor (sic) Road." The Council reiterated this request in October 1931. The Surveyor promised some remedial work. Presumably this was done, for the complaints of the Parish Council subsided — at least for a time.

There were also complaints of storm water from the Headley Road damaging Hill Road, which was not a District road, and the 1930 Annual

Parish Meeting drew the attention of the District Council to the dangerous condition of the road "caused to a great extent by water coming from the District Road." Reference was also made to motor cars trying to use Hill Road as an access to Waggoners Wells, and the road notice was to be amended to include "Impossible for motors." But little help was given by the District Council, since Hill Road was not an adopted road.

In 1930 the County Council took over maintenance of classified roads and almost immediately received complaints from Grayshott of uneven road surfaces, non-clearance of drain gratings after storms, and heaps of rubbish near Crossways Corner. In the next year trouble arose over the kerbing which was being installed in Headley Road, and a petition signed by 91 inhabitants was presented to the Annual Parish Meeting, calling on the County to stop what they were doing and to amend it "in such a way as to meet with the requirements of the traffic and safety and convenience of the inhabitants." Mrs. Lyndon said the County had not consulted either the Parish or District Councils, but presumed the County were trying to implement the provisions of the Road Traffic Act, 1930. Apparently the main cause of the Grayshott complaint was that the County efforts were, in fact, narrowing the pavements.

There was clearly increasing anxiety over hazards, particularly to pedestrians owing partly to inadequate street lighting, but mainly to the absence of roadside footpaths. In April 1934 the attention of the County Council was drawn to the need of a footpath in the place of the ditch on the north side of Headley Road between St. Luke's Church and the Playing Field as "the present position owing to increased motor traffic is actually very dangerous." The Parish Council did not favour a kerbed path but wanted the ditch filled in. This was apparently done, as in 1938 it was reported that the County would continue the footpath on the north side of the road and would pipe the ditch on the south side for about 50 yards. They had been asked in the previous year to fill in the ditch on the south side and make footpaths on both sides as there had been accidents in the dark. That there was a real danger is illustrated by a Parish Council Minute in January 1938, reporting that five women returning from Christmas Eve Midnight Mass at St. Joseph's Church had fallen into the ditch on the south side, with the result of three sprained ankles, and Major Wessel had had to drive them home. The County replied in 1939 that it was not yet possible to accede to the Parish Council's request, but "it would be kept in mind" by the County.

In the 'thirties two small but important improvements were made to the lay-out of the roads at Crossways Corner. When the War Memorial was moved, a small length of kerbed footpath was constructed to form a seemly entrance to the memorial enclosure. The other improvement was to round off the corner of the churchyard at the junction at Headley and Whitmore Vale Roads, where the churchyard then ran out to a sharp point enclosed by banks surmounted by holly hedges. This prevented a sight line at that dangerous corner. Major Wessel suggested in March 1934 the removal of the hedges or the widening of the corner, and the County Surveyor was consulted. The Vicar, Rev. E. G. Ireland, wrote that the Church authorities would do their best to help. The County Council agreed to carry out the work if the land were provided free, except for the cost of the necessary Faculty and the provision of a new boundary hedge. The Church Council agreed and the County negotiated with the Church Commissioners on that basis. The improvement had been completed by April 1935; the land at the corner was dedicated for a highway but remained the property of St. Luke's Church. Not only was this change a safety measure, it also enhanced the appearance of the Crossways Corner.

Another danger spot on the village roads was the dip in the Crossways Road at the bend at the bottom of Pooks Hill, which in those days was devoid of adequate footpaths. In January 1939, Mr. F. L. H. Harris, who had come on to the Parish Council two years earlier, gave notice of a motion which was discussed in March. One main difficulty was that, while the northern slope of Pooks Hill was in Grayshott and the Alton Rural District, the southern slope was in the Haslemere Urban District: so that a decent job would require the co-operation of the two District Councils. Mr. Harris' reasoned motion, which was carried, regretted Haslemere's decision not to improve their section in view of the great danger to public safety at that point. His motion set out the reasons: the existing path on the east side of the road was useless to pedestrians, including many schoolchildren and women with perambulators, because it was too narrow and they were forced into the road; the Petersfield buses frequently crossed at that point; the bend in the hill made it impossible to see oncoming traffic, and was in any case difficult for motor traffic to negotiate; and there had been a considerable recent increase in traffic owing to new building. The resolution concluded: "In view of the foregoing and that Crossways Road is one of the main roads to Grayshott, the reconsideration of the matter by Haslemere Urban District Council is earnestly asked for and any reversal of their previous decision will be appreciated by this Council." In July it was reported that the Alton Council were seeking Haslemere's co-operation. The War came along and put a stop to this project for the time being.

We may conclude this section on roads by mentioning that whenever Grayshott was the victim of heavy snowfalls there were complaints of the inadequate and tardy clearance of snow by the authorities. On one such occasion the Minutes of the Annual Parish Meeting in March 1927 record: "Mrs. Kirkness said her housemaid went out on her bicycle and had to be brought back on a lorry."

The question of speed restrictions came up from time to time. As early as 1928 Mr. Beere complained of excessive speed of motor vehicles, especially motor bicycles and small buses. Thirty-mile speed limit signs appeared, and in 1945 the Parish Council wanted the one near the Vicarage moved to the Headley side of School Road, and the one at Church Lane to a point opposite Philips Green. The County Council approved these recommendations and applied to the Ministry of Transport for sanction—but nothing was done.

The spirited guerrilla warfare which the Parish Council had waged with the Post Office continued unabated. In 1923 the Council complained that the last mail was despatched at 5.45 p.m., whereas the afternoon delivery did not reach many houses until 4 p.m.—obviously no time to answer by return of post. The Council won this round and noted improvement at their next meeting. In 1926, owing to sorting of the mail being done at Haslemere, "there being insufficient accommodation at Grayshott," it was impossible to post letters at Grayshott addressed to Grayshott for the next delivery, except at early hours when the box was cleared for general mails. It seems that Grayshott people had a passion for writing urgent letters to their neighbours.

However, we won, for the Haslemere Postmaster arranged for collections at Grayshott at 5.55 a.m. and 2.15 p.m., to connect with Grayshott morning and afternoon deliveries.

In 1929 the Parish Council actually thanked the Haslemere Postmaster for an extra daily collection, but at the same time complained of Wednesday afternoon closure of Grayshott Post Office and of the lateness of the first delivery in Headley Road. They were promised an earlier delivery.

In 1930 there was a three-pronged attack: "That the Post Office be urgently requested to arrange for the collections of letters at Grayshott on Sundays at a later hour, as the 3.45 p.m. collection is inadequate: That attention be drawn to the very insufficient second delivery on Saturdays in particular, parcels posted in London on Friday afternoon are often not delivered until Monday morning and the punctual receipt of letters from any district cannot be relied on: That the Post Office be asked to provide a machine for the sale of stamps outside Grayshott Post Office." Honours were perhaps even: a Sunday collection was arranged for 5.30 p.m. and the public were informed that they could collect parcels and letters at Hindhead Post Office on Saturday afternoons, but unfortunately the stamp machine was not possible as the owner of the premises would not agree. Undeterred, the Parish Council pressed on. They again demanded the stamp machine and enquired whether there were to be two Sunday afternoon collections. The answer to the latter was in the affirmative, and a little later the stamp machine was promised. It was certainly installed, for the Parish Council courteously thanked the Postmaster in July, 1932.

All was quiet until March 1938 when, although the Postmaster was thanked for slightly later collections and a larger letter-box, dissatisfaction was expressed over "present deliveries" and a request was made for earlier delivery of letters and parcels by the first post, and for a second delivery "about mid-day." One member of the Council considered there should be a third delivery, that the Post Office should remain open on Wednesday afternoons, and that an extra postman should be employed, if necessary. A month later the Council fired a broadside: "While this Council appreciates the arrangements for the despatch of letters from Grayshott which on the whole are satisfactory, they would call the attention of the postal authorities to the very serious inadequacy of the delivery of letters and parcels in the district. The morning delivery of letters in several parts is as late as 9.30 a.m. and parcels 10.30: letters posted in good time in the West and North of England, and even in Essex, are not delivered here until 4 o'clock in the afternoon and often later. On Saturdays the parcel delivery and the second delivery of letters are most unsatisfactory; the important Indian and Australian Mails are not received by residents until the Monday morning.

The service compares very unfavourably with that in force nearly twenty years ago and the Council requests earlier and more frequent deliveries of the mails." Nothing seems to have been done, for in July the Council notified the Haslemere Postmaster of their disappointment at the long delay, but in October they felt that the morning delivery was better, and the Postmaster had written that "a larger scheme under consideration would further accelerate that delivery."

When, in the summer of 1937, the Postmaster proposed to suspend the 4.15 p.m. delivery on Wednesdays, so that postmen could have a half-holiday, the Council objected strongly and suggested that the Post Office should employ sufficient relief staff "to enable the postmen to have a half-holiday per week and that it should not be done at the inconvenience of a public service." We may be very glad, for their peace of mind, that the Parish Council were not gifted with prescience — at any rate in the matter of postal services.

After the First World War the Parish Council renewed its efforts to install street lighting, but continued to meet with rate-payer resistance. At the 1923 Annual Parish Meeting the Council submitted a resolution to adopt the Lighting and Watching Act, 1833, under which the necessary powers could be acquired. They stated that six gas lamps could be lighted for six months in the year for £18, less than a ½d rate. Mr. Lowry, the Vicar (Mr. Simms), and Dr. Lyndon supported the resolution, but opposition came from Messrs. Barnes and Peter Robinson, who said distant houses would not benefit, and from Captain Parker who argued that "inadequate lighting was more dangerous to the motorists than dark roads." He did not mention the interests of pedestrians. Though the resolution was passed, the necessary two-thirds majority was not obtained and Mr. Lowry demanded a poll which resulted in 214 valid votes being cast, of which 190 were for and 21 against. This was unfortunately less than a majority of the total number of electors entitled to vote and so, under the law as it then was, the matter fell.

In 1925 Mrs. Lyndon said street lighting could more readily be installed through the District Council obtaining urban powers for the Parish Council than through the antiquated Lighting and Watching Act. By December 1925 she, on her own responsibility, asked the District Council to do this, and the Ministry of Health had given sanction. The District Council had constituted a Grayshott Parochial Lighting Committee consisting of the members of the Parish Council and the Grayshott representatives on the District Council. Thus the constitutional machinery for street lighting had been set up. By October 1926 there were 8 street lamps. Thereafter the main features were requests for more lamps and determination of their sites. By the autumn of 1935 there were 14 lamps, at an annual cost of £39. By 1938 there were 27. The village streets were dark during the War, except for three shielded lamps, but in January 1945 the Gas Company were asked to make provisional arrangements for full lighting "as soon as it becomes possible."

Mr. Whitaker left Grayshott in 1927, having sold the Grayshott Hall Estate. This caused considerable repercussions, principally in the matter of footpaths and land development. A Mr. Horace Wright bought much of the land, and concern was expressed about "paths of long usage into Whitmore Vale" if the land was sold for development. The Parish Council set up a new Committee, the Footpaths and Rights of Way Committee, to safeguard the position. This committee became the permanent Footpaths Committee of the Parish Council. There were protracted and sometimes difficult negotiations, but in 1928 Footpath No. 7, along the top of Whitmore Hanger, was dedicated. Great care had been taken to preserve the fine clump of beech trees through which the path enters from the east.

Later on there was some doubt as to the correct course of Footpath No. 8, running northwards from Headley Road near Bede Cottage to cross Footpath No. 7. There had been an old barn a little way along, long since derelict, of which some remnants of foundations remained until quite recently. In 1936 the Parish Council informed the District Council "that the footpath by the old

Barn as shown on the Ordnance Map has been obstructed, the attention of the owner having been called to it some time ago, but nothing has been done." The Parish Council eventually lost patience and instructed its groundsman "to remake the path along the right of the barn according to its old course as set out in the old Ordnance Survey Map," but later decided, instead, to approach the County Council. The matter was settled early in 1939. It cropped up again, however, about 30 years later when the Waggoners Wells Estate was being developed.

The change of ownership of the Grayshott Hall Estate opened up prospects of considerable housing development in the north-western part of the parish, particularly the undeveloped land lying to the north of Headley Road opposite Grayshott Hall and Park, and to the west of Bull's Farm (now Grayshott Hall Farm). On 12th December 1927 a special Parish Meeting was requisitioned by two Parish Councillors to consider the matter. Dr. Lyndon said that about half the acreage of the parish was about to change hands, and Mr. Horace Wright, the new owner, was going to sell much of the land for building. He was offering plots for sale with no mention of conditions. In these circumstances, said Dr. Lyndon, Grayshott should consider the preservation of its amenities. Mr. George Whitfield, Chairman of the West Surrey Joint Planning Committee and of Haslemere Urban District Council, attended the meeting by invitation and advised the Parish Council to adopt the Town Planning Act of 1925, and apply it to Grayshott. The meeting passed without any dissentient vote two resolutions:

"That this Parish Meeting, called to consider the effects of the development of the Grayshott Hall Estate for building, strongly urges the Alton Rural District Council to pass a resolution without delay to prepare or adopt a Scheme under the Town Planning Act 1925 for the Parish of Grayshott or any part thereof."
"That this meeting asks the Parish Council to do anything possible to further the above resolution and, if it should seem desirable, to approach the Ministry of Health. It further suggests that, if any preliminary expenditure, such as obtaining professional advice, appears desirable, the Parish Council or persons authorised by the Council should accept voluntary contributions to meet such expenditure."

With surprising speed the District Council passed the necessary resolution and arrangements had been made for Mrs. Lyndon and Mr. Guy Ellis of the Parish Council and the Chairman and Clerk of the District Council to meet an officer of the Ministry of Health. At the Annual Parish Meeting of 1928 a resolution was passed thanking the District Council for this and urging it to take immediate steps to prepare the Scheme, since "the present owner of the Grayshott Hall Estate has laid it out for building plots and is selling a number of plots." In June it was reported that the District Council was proceeding with a scheme for part of the parish, a draft of which had been informally approved by the Ministry of Health. The worst fears as to the development of the Grayshott Hall Estate were not realised, the development being confined to the Kiln Way and Fir Way area in the extreme west of the parish.

The addition to the parish of the Kingswood Firs Estate, then undeveloped, in 1932 raised another suggestion of large-scale development, and in the

April of that year the Parish Council asked the District Council to prepare a scheme for the estate. In the event, however, the development of this area did not take place until much later.

The fears and reactions of those years about large developments marked the first stage of the consistent policy of the Parish Council, backed by the parish, to preserve as far as possible the pleasant rural surroundings of Grayshott and to preserve it as a genuine village in a country setting.

We have seen that the first 12 Council cottages were occupied at reasonable rents by the autumn of 1922. Mrs. Lyndon thought that more were required, and in 1923 she was urging the District Council to take advantage of the Government subsidy then available to build more. The Parish Council backed her in a resolution expressing the need and hoping that the District would carry through a scheme for additional cottages "at an early date" and that this would make possible "the much-needed reduction in the rents of all the District Council cottages." The District Council refused, owing to a probable loss placing a burden on the rates, and, instead, sought approval from the Ministry of Health to sell some of their vacant land at Beech Hanger for cottage building. But no satisfactory offer was forthcoming owing to the price fixed by the District Valuer. The Parish Council therefore asked in 1924 for a reduction in rents which "were much in excess of what the class for whom they were built could afford to pay." Mrs. Lyndon promised to explain to the District Council the position of many of the tenants. Nothing seems to have been done at the time, but a reduction to 16s. a week came in 1928.

In March 1936 there was a reference to the "newly-formed Utility Society" which proposed to build small houses at Whitmore Bottom. This was, in fact, a reference to the Grayshott and District Housing Association, founded in the previous year. Major Wessel suggested the Beech Allotments as a suitable site for council cottages, and it was agreed to approach the Ministries of Health and Agriculture. A representative of the latter visited this suggested site with Mrs. Lyndon and the Clerk. He did not seem to favour the site, though no official letter had been received. The Ministry of Health had written asking a number of questions, including one as to whether it was proposed to sell the land to the Grayshott Housing Society. It transpired that that body was negotiating for the six acre field to the west of the Playing Field. The Ministry had informed the District Council that they doubted the suitability of the site in Whitmore Bottom, and the District Council had asked the Parish Council whether there was a need for cottages at Grayshott which could not be met by private enterprise, to which the latter replied "that the provision of at least 10 to 12 working class dwellings" (i.e. council houses) "at a rental not exceeding 12s. a week is still badly needed." There the matter rested until after the War.

The Grayshott and District Housing Association referred to above, a very useful but little-known Grayshott organisation, was founded in November, 1935. The initiative was taken by Mrs. Lyndon, and the background was the need of cottages at rents which could be paid by weekly wage-earners, and which the District Council was tardy in supplying. Mrs. Lyndon gathered a provisional committee of a few local residents interested in alleviating this problem, whose idea was to issue 3½% Loan Stock and also £1 shares to purchase suitable land on which to erect and let "working-class cottages." Mrs. Lyndon was the first Chairman until her death in 1936, when Dr. Lyndon succeeded her. The Association joined the National Federation of

Building Societies, and its Rules are as approved by the Federation. The Committee is not representative—vacancies on it are filled by election by the Committee. Miss L. Chilton Thomas is the sole member of the Committee who has served continuously since 1935. As it did not prove possible to find a site, the Association in 1936 bought 12 suitable cottages in Beech Lane and Glen Road, for a total of £4,260, to which a substantial sum had to be added for essential repairs. These cottages were rescued from probable purchase by Investment Companies, which would have resulted in the position of the existing occupiers not being protected, and a considerable increase in the rents. They remain the property of the Association. Since, in the late 'thirties, it seemed that the District Council would build more council cottages, the Association did not pursue its original policy, and this was confirmed when 16 additional council houses were built after the War. To the 12 cottages purchased in 1936 have been added 14 more properties given to the Association by generous donors—Mrs. Disney-Rosbuck and Miss D. Pearman. These include 7 purpose-planned flats for elderly people. Dr. Lyndon continued as Chairman until his death in 1946. Subsequent successors have been Messrs. R. C. Duggan (1946–50), D. P. Eccott (1950–59), R. E. B. Meade-King (1959–72) and J. H. Smith (1972–). In recent years the Association has spent a lot of money on maintenance and modernisation of its properties, and has the common problem of inflation. It has been forced to increase the rents, although they remain low in comparison with the general level.

A consistent theme between the Wars was the increasing need of main drainage. The rapid increase of population made dependence on wells, so liable to pollution, most undesirable. Even before Grayshott became a separate civil parish local residents felt concern, and at a meeting of Headley Parish Council there was a suggestion of adopting bye-laws to regulate uncontrolled growth. The Council appointed a sub-committee to examine the Bramshott sanitary bye-laws with a view to their adoption by Headley—in particular with reference to Grayshott. There is perhaps relevance in the fact that Canon Capes of Bramshott had taken over responsibility for the spiritual care of Grayshott, and that a curate of Bramshott resided in Grayshott. The reason for the Headley decision was given in the local paper:

"Owing to Grayshott having become so thickly populated and there being so much building going on in that district, in many cases the sanitary arrangements are very bad indeed. It was felt that if these were not improved an epidemic would break out."

Progress was slow, but in October 1898 Dr. Lyndon, writing in the Grayshott and District Magazine, was able to summarise the proposed bye-laws, which have been quoted fully in Chapter 10.

In the same month the bye-laws were submitted, as a result of a Headley Parish Meeting, to the District Council. They came into force in 1900.

The new Grayshott Parish Council discussed the need of main drainage towards the end of 1903. There were difficulties in the way—the main ones being the heavy cost of installing and maintaining a system which caused ratepayer resistance and technical problems arising from the configuration of the parish. In September 1903 the District Council received a report from a civil engineer on water supply and drainage in Grayshott. It was clear that the

Wey Valley Water Company would shortly be allowed to lay water mains in the village. The engineer said a main water supply would make a drainage system "highly desirable and before long absolutely necessary," since the wells were liable to pollution and a public water supply would lead to increased use of water for WCs and baths. He had considered various sites for sewage disposal works, e.g. Whitmore Bottom and the present Golden Valley, but they all involved putting in pumping stations in parts of Grayshott. He estimated that a system would involve an annual local rate of between 2s.5d. and 2s.8d. In November 1903 a Parish Meeting resolved: "That this meeting is of opinion that a water supply is urgently required but that there is no present necessity for a drainage system."

In 1904 some wells in the village were known to be polluted, and the Parish Council asked the District Council to arrange for a general inspection of them. That Council would not undertake this, but would inspect any specified individual wells. This ended the matter, as nobody was prepared to report his neighbour's well.

The War years had highlighted the sewerage problem, particularly when troops were billeted in the village, and after the War there was a resumption of house building. The problem was resurrected by Rev. A. E. N. Simms at the Annual Parish Meeting of 1923, in a resolution: "Believing that both for health and convenience a system of main drainage would benefit the village, this meeting asks the District Council to consider the desirability of preparing a scheme as soon as the cost of the same would not be likely to be prohibitive and would suggest that the Farnham Rural District Council might be approached as a combined scheme with Hindhead should lessen the cost for both authorities." In seconding, Dr. Lyndon said, "The problem might at any time become dangerous to health." The resolution was carried 35 to 6, perhaps because of its expressed desire to avoid excessive cost. The idea of a joint scheme became the basis of all future proposals, but they were dogged by misfortune, since joint schemes inevitably meant very lengthy negotiations between participating authorities and, as often as they seemed to reach a solution, something entirely out of local control — such as financial stringency or the outbreak of War — caused the abandonment of successive schemes.

The Alton and Farnham Councils consulted, but Farnham did not intend at that time to deal with Hindhead: but they evidently changed their mind and in 1924 resumed talks. By 1925 the Councils discussed getting a professional report at the cost of £150, but Alton jibbed at the cost, until the professional firm reduced their charge to £100. The Councils authorised the production of drawings and estimates, and the former showed that in Grayshott only the two main streets on the higher ground would be included, and the roads in the valleys would not. At this point the discussions were postponed, and eventually abandoned in 1927 "owing to the cost to the parish." But after a report of their Medical Officer of Health, the Alton Council were enquiring as to the feasibility of a cheaper scheme based on alternative sites of disposal works. Apparently a joint scheme with Bramshott was mooted, but the Ministry of Health considered it would not be viable. In all, four schemes were examined and turned down on cost, the least expensive based on outfall works "below Frensham Great Pond" being not less than £35,000. The Annual Parish Meeting of 1929 resolved, somewhat in despair, to form a small local committee in Grayshott to consider its sanitary conditions and take steps to urge the local authority to "remedy existing defects." The report of that committee led the Alton Council to prepare a scheme, concerning which the Parish Council in January 1930 urged Alton to proceed with any practical scheme, as it was thought the scheme already prepared could be merged into a larger scheme later, and the Council considered "the need of drainage is so urgent that it cannot be left till the larger scheme." By the end of the year a Ministry of Health Inquiry had rejected the Grayshott scheme, but in March 1931 Mrs. Lyndon thought another scheme could be prepared, perhaps in conjunction with other areas. A suitable outfall site had been selected at Headley, but progress depended on the "unemployment grant" being available—and the country was in a financial crisis. A further Inquiry was held into a joint scheme, but the whole thing petered out when the District wrote that they were unable to take any active steps. The Council resolved that Mrs. Lyndon should discuss the position with the Ministry of Health.

Meanwhile Major Wessel presented a Memorandum recommending that, as an interim emergency measure, the Alton Council should arrange with the Haslemere Urban District Council for the latter to undertake a "night soil" collection in Grayshott. That Major Wessel had a gift of picturesque expression the following extracts from his document will illustrate: Referring to the efforts of the last 20 years, "Nothing has been done with the result that your village is now on the verge of becoming a pestilential centre with disastrous results": To the Avenue, "where the smallholder has no room in his little plot in which to empty his night soil, as his ground is more than polluted and saturated, and the atmosphere is perfectly poisonous:" To the ratepayers who "should be entitled to the sanitary service of a professional instead of ruining their gardens and their health by their amateurish efforts in unnecessarily manuring their own ground." In default of main drainage which never seemed to eventuate, he argued, "There is no alternative but the old-fashioned night soil bucket system." A scheme of collection from 100 houses in the worst areas might cost a 4d. rate, but "your inhabitants would be glad to pay as an insurance against their health and happiness, not to mention the relief of having to give up a repulsive manual labour." Finally, "It has been suggested to me that night-soil carts are dreadful to meet at night. Granted—but this need only affect the revellers who should be in bed or our local policeman who, I'm certain, will put up with a problematical temporary scent as against a perpetual odour."

The District Council thought that removal of night soil should be paid for privately, but the Annual Parish Meeting pressed for immediate implementation and sent a copy of the resolution to the Ministry of Health, who arranged for a meeting of representatives of the Alton, Hambledon and Haslemere Councils. The night soil collection by Haslemere Council started in January 1935. But it was only in parts of the village and did not deal with liquid refuse. So the Annual Parish Meeting of that year again resolved that "the need for main drainage in Grayshott is still essential, especially in regard to two or three special areas." In the same year the area of night soil collection was extended to Jubilee Lane and Hill Road, and the Ministry of Health made an Order for the collection in Grayshott to be paid for by a parish rate, to meet an annual charge of £271.

The meeting of the three local Councils arranged by the Ministry resulted in the setting up of a Join Drainage Committee. The scheme proposed would include the Headley, Crossways and Glen Roads, Church Lane, Beech Hanger, and possibly the top of Hill Road and Whitmore Vale. This and all other schemes provided for main sewers to go down Whitmore Bottom. Considerable delay was caused by the hesitation of the Haslemere Council who were considering draining their own areas themselves, but by 1939 the prospects for the joint scheme were considered good. A perverse fate stepped in, and the scheme was abandoned on the outbreak of War. So the night soil collection continued for many years during which only the bold of heart and stomach, or those who resided there, ventured into the relevant areas on collection night.

A cognate subject exercised the Parish Council somewhat spasmodically — that of the provision of a public convenience. The question of providing one for both sexes was first raised in the Parish Council in October 1922, when the Village Greens Committee was asked to consider a site and make necessary arrangements with the Chairman: but the Committee was unable to make recommendations and the Chairman said the matter "should not be lost sight of." In July 1924 it was reported that the People's Refreshment House Association were in fact providing such accommodation for ladies behind the Fox and Pelican, and this "should partially solve the present difficulty": but only three months later it was considered that "this did not meet the need." The problem went into cold storage until July 1935, when Mrs. Lyndon said this was a recurring suggestion, but approaches to the District Council had achieved nothing, though she reported that the Fox and Pelican had improved their accommodation. During the War the problem became more acute on account of the number of troops in the area, mainly Canadians at Superior Camp on Ludshott Common. The Fox and Pelican convenience was used outside licensing hours by soldiers getting liquor from an off-licence house, and had been damaged. In consequence the landlord kept it locked, except in licensing hours. The Parish Council decided to approach the District Council for a temporary arrangement, if a permanent one was not practicable. That Council suggested a site on the Children's Recreation Ground, but the Parish Council rejected it as unacceptable. They asked the District to approach the owner of land adjoining the Village Green, but the latter refused consent and the scheme was dropped.

The Silver Jubilee of King George V and Queen Mary in 1935 was, of course, celebrated by the parish. Rev. E. G. Ireland got together a local committee, and Mrs. Lyndon pointed out that the King had asked that celebrations should be simple and inexpensive. The Council resolved to rely on voluntary house-to-house collections for finance. The committee arranged for a tea and sports for the children, a supper (at 2s.6d. a head) at the Fox and Pelican for pensioners, and a dance in the Village Hall — free, except for refreshments. This was all carried out, and there was a balance of £25 in hand which was used to improve the front of the Village Hall, by building a stone and brick wall with four piers connected by a wrought iron chain. In addition, the women of Grayshott gave a heather-thatched shelter (still there, but not now heather-thatched) on the north side of the Children's Recreation Ground, and the Girl Guides planted a flowering cherry at the Church Corner (trees there have been unlucky), which the Mother's Union, as a Coronation commemoration, fenced in with ornamental wrought iron railings made by Mr. Venning, and a fine example of craftsmanship in that medium.

In 1936 the celebrations of the Coronation of Edward VIII, as it was then expected, but actually of George VI as it turned out, began to be planned. They took the form which had become traditional in Grayshott, and used the same method of finance. A balance of £30 from the voluntary fund was used for apparatus on the Children's Playground at Philips Green.

After the Munich Agreement, War began to loom, and in the spring of 1938 Major Wessel was recruiting men and setting up an organisation in connection with Air Raid precautions. During the War, people in Grayshott— as elsewhere—were concentrating on the War effort, salvage, cultivation of allotments for which extra land was found, air raid trenches, garments for the Forces, food storage in the Village Hall, and requisition of iron railings for which the Parish Council did not seek compensation. All told, 10,261 garments were made, including 867 jerseys, 2,392 pairs of socks, 664 overcoats in oiled wool, and were sent to the Royal and Merchant Navies, the Royal Air Force, the Women's Auxiliary Air Force, and the Royal Artillery. In national War efforts the village did well: Alton War Savings Week 1941—£4,856: Warship Week 1942—£8,527: Grayshott adopted H.M.S. Eglinton: Salute the Soldiers Week 1945—£47,177. For the rest, the Parish Council could only mark time. Major Wessel's Report to the Annual Parish Meeting 1942, attended by only five members of the Parish Council and no member of the public, said quite simply, "I am afraid that I have very little to report to you as, due to the war, nothing but essentials have been dealt with during the year.

Between the Wars the social life of the village flourished. The new Playing Field and Tennis Courts provided permanent homes for the Cricket, Football and Tennis Clubs, and to the I'Anson Competition Cricket Cup was added the Miller Cup, intended for mid-week teams on early closing days. The Dramatic Society functioned for some years after the First World War, but in the latter part of our period drama was fostered mainly by the Women's Institute. For the men of the village there were three clubs, the Village Hall Men's Club, the Working Men's Club and, in 1932, the British Legion Club: and, in connection with the first, the Grayshott Bowling Club on the site of the present Fire Station. A Branch of the Church of England Men's Society had been formed in 1909. It lapsed during the War years and was re-founded in 1924, but it was replaced by a Men's Society in 1928 which ran discussion meetings based usually on papers by visiting speakers. It continued for some years under the inspiration of Mr. C. Beere, Manager of Lloyds Bank.

Youth work tended to be spasmodic, as everything depended—as it does now—on being able to secure devoted and efficient leaders. A Club for older boys had been started in 1906 by Miss Morgan Brown and Mr. Ivo Bulley, both of St. Edmund's School. After the First War a Boys' Club was founded in 1925, but had to be re-founded in 1928 under Mr. Lewis Robinson, and again in 1938 under Mr. R. E. King of Grayshott Primary School. Similarly a Scout Group started in 1912 by Captain Molyneux of Downleas was re-founded in 1915.

We have noted the appointment in 1908 of Grayshott's first District Nurse. There was a succession of nurses who did splendid work until Nurse Margaret Cuff was appointed in 1934. She held the post until her retirement in

1969, giving devoted and unstinting service to those in need of it: and, to the pleasure of all, she settled in the village on her retirement.

A village character intimately associated with the formation of Grayshott, Mrs. Hannah Robinson, died at the age of 93 in 1929. Known as "Granny Robinson," she had been born in the district but had been a widow for many years. She and her husband, Henry, had—as we have seen in an earlier Chapter—kept a shop at "Mount Cottage," and then established the first shop in the present village, in Crossways Road in 1877. Her shop was a little general shop, but from a small boy's point of view she was a purveyor of sherbet bags, sticks of liquorice, aniseed balls and striped humbugs.

Finally, it was in this period that Grayshott became increasingly protected by large stretches of common and National Trust land. In 1908 "Miss James' Walk" on the western lip of Nutcombe Valley was given to the public. Much of Ludshott Common and the Golden Valley became public property, and the National Trust was extending over the Hindhead Commons. This has been of the greatest value in preserving the village character of Grayshott.

Chapter 15

Recent Years

After the end of the Second World War the question of a War Memorial again came up for consideration. The pattern of discussion was much the same as after the First War, the formation of a local committee representative of the Parish Council and village organisations, to make suggestions for submission to a Parish Meeting. Early in 1949 ideas put forward by the British Legion were approved – that iron railings should be erected along the wall and at the back of the War Memorial enclosure, the old railings having been requisitioned during the War: and that a new block, inscribed with the names of those who died on service in the Second War should be added to the Memorial. The cost of the work was put at £300, which had been guaranteed by a few persons, and a committee under the chairmanship of Major Wessel was constituted to organise an appeal fund, towards which the Lyndon Trustees gave £50. The money came in somewhat slowly – largely, no doubt, because it was being collected some time after the War ended. However, by July 1950 all the accounts had been settled. The maintenance of the Memorial proved to be a problem, in particular to the British Legion who had taken great interest in it, but found it to be beyond its resources. In the years 1953/55 they spent £44 on it. Recourse was made in 1960 and 1966 to the Lyndon Funds, after the Legion had spent £120 in putting the Memorial in good order. In July 1973 remedial work costing £240 became necessary, towards which the Legion had raised £43. The Lyndon Trustees contributed £75, and the rest was met by the Parish Council from the general rate fund. The Council took over responsibility for the Memorial, though the Legion continue to maintain the small lawn and flower beds in the enclosure, and so contribute much towards the dignity and beauty of the Memorial at the heart of the village.

In the last thirty years the work of the Parish Council has constantly increased, particularly after the comprehensive reorganisation of Local Government in the early seventies. The number of councillors, eight in 1902, had risen to ten: pressure of work has led to the setting up of Standing Sub-Committees, each dealing with particular spheres of work. Each councillor serves on one or more of the Sub-Committees, which have limited powers to act but usually report to the full Council with recommendations for action. The additional burden and complexity of work is not peculiar to Grayshott. It is general. It is worth noting that the Hampshire Association of Local Councils (formerly Parish Councils) has in recent years organised valuable training courses and conferences, of particular service to new councillors, which Grayshott councillors have often attended.

The population, which was under 700 at the time of the formation of the civil parish grew in the next 70 years to over 2,400. This, together with rising costs and special projects, has meant increasing parish rate precepts, e.g. from

£230 in 1945/46 (excluding street lighting), to about £4,000 in the mid-seventies. This did not mean a great increase in rate poundage since the rateable value of the parish has also greatly increased.

Grayshott has not been immune from the pressure suffered by many rural communities, threatening increasing urbanisation and commercialisation, and flowing from the buying up of land for development, the proliferation of chain stores and supermarkets, sometimes the ambition of neighbouring larger communities to absorb them, and the ever-widening extension of the London commuter belt. In facing these tendencies Grayshott has important advantages. It is to a considerable extent protected by its extensive surrounding belt of National Trust and common lands, the former due in large measure to the generosity and foresight of inhabitants of the district. Its outstanding natural beauty, particularly the three wooded valleys which intersect it, led to its inclusion in the Hampshire County Council Country Conservation Area: and, above all, it has a strong sense of community and of separate identity as a village, which proved to be a great source of strength in the efforts which had to be made to preserve that identity. It is right to say that when the two major developments at Kingswood Firs and Waggoners Wells Estate were in course of construction it was feared that its newcomers might not integrate freely and happily with the village community, as they were likely to be elderly retired people or commuters to and from daily work elsewhere. It is equally right to acknowledge that these fears proved gradually but decidedly to be groundless, new and old fusing into one community. As early as 1962 the Annual Report of the Parish Council remarked: "The longer resident section of the community welcome the newcomers to the parish, and it is pleasing to note that in increasing numbers they are joining and strengthening the village societies and taking part in local affairs."

In the struggle to maintain the village as a village, two strands emerge: preservation of its beautiful environment, and therefore resistance to undue development: and preservation of the parish as a separate unit of local government.

In the late fifties Kingswood Firs Estate was being developed as 80 building plots. The planning lay-out was attractive and rural, and the developers built in a system of road lighting, the Planning Authority and developers consulting the Parish Council on both points. Also the developers confined themselves to the higher flat land between Kingswood Lane and Stoney Bottom, and did not spread down those valley slopes: and they respected the existing public footpaths.

The strong desirability of Parish Councils being consulted by the planning authorities in applications arising within the parish was raised in 1962 in a Circular Letter of the National Association of Parish Councils. At its May meeting in that year the Grayshott Council passed a resolution of wholehearted support and sent it to the National Association and to Alton Rural District Council, which was the local planning authority, "and who, it was understood, are opposed to any notification procedure." At the same meeting the need for such procedure was underlined when it was reported that both the District and County Councils had rejected a planning application for about 100 houses on 43 acres of land opposite Grayshott Hall. Although the Grayshott Council had not been consulted, it supported the rejection on the grounds that "It would constitute over-development of this area not in keeping with the rural amenities."

This became a constant theme from 1962 onwards. In July 1962 the Parish Council requested the District Council to set up machinery of consultation, but received a discouraging reply which they referred to the National Association.

The owner of the Grayshott Hall land appealed against the rejection of his application and a local enquiry was ordered. The Parish Council, supported by a Special Parish Meeting, drew up a reasoned resolution in support of the rejection, the main points being that it was a threat to scenic beauty: The Kingswood Firs Estate was not yet fully developed: speculative buying of the appeal site and also adjoining land (on which the Waggoners Wells Estate was subsequently built) for profit motive: the development might be a step towards ribbon development along the Headley Road: the application plus the Kingswood Firs Estate would add some 200 houses to the parish, and this would have a detrimental effect on the character of Grayshott: and the desirability of deferment of major developments until the production of a village plan. A number of residents subscribed to a fund to employ legal representation at the appeal, which was in fact withdrawn by the appellant, but we shall see that the problem came up again in a few years' time.

In January 1963 the Clerk of the Parish Council had an "amicable conversation" with the Clerk of the District Council and was told that Grayshott was a "white area" in which large-scale development would not be allowed, only limited in-filling on suitable sites. In the event of appeals against rejection of large-scale developments the District Council would consult the Parish Council. There the matter was left for the time being. In July 1964 came the first instance of the Parish Council being consulted on an initial major application, viz. for the demolition of "New Place," Headley Road, and the development on that site of a shopping precinct of two-storey buildings—which the Parish Council thought "undesirable at the present," mainly on account of traffic congestion. Nevertheless the application was approved.

In the same year the County Council divided Hampshire villages into three categories, of which Grade A consisted of "local service centres" providing comparatively sophisticated services such as extensive shopping and transport facilities, resident police, a fire brigade, and an adequate village hall. Grayshott was one of these, for which Village Plans would be drawn up. This did not have a definite result for Grayshott until much later, when the matter was dealt with over a wider area.

Meanwhile, a Commission appointed to review Local Government Boundaries was proceeding in 1963 to deal with South-eastern England, and Haslemere Urban District Council submitted a detailed case for the absorption of Grayshott by Haslemere. There is little doubt that Haslemere felt its Urban status, acquired in 1933 by the absorption of Shottermill and parts of Chiddingfold, Elstead, Frensham and Thursley, to be threatened by the growing tendency towards larger units of local government. It was in fact one of the smallest Urban Districts in the country, and an increase in size—particularly of population—might well ensure its continuance as a second tier authority. It had submitted in 1947 to the then Boundary Commission a case for absorbing Grayshott, but nothing came of it. The Haslemere case in 1965 was so detailed that it scraped the barrel very hard indeed, and, in the view of the Parish Council, produced some curious and irrelevant results to which the Grayshott Council replied point by point, and even proceeded to suggest that there were parts of Haslemere which might with advantage be annexed to Grayshott, particularly the developed area over the Surrey border lying to the north of the A3 road as far as its junction with the B 3002 road. The Parish Council document was sent to the Boundary Commission and to the District and County Councils. A Press statement, issued by the Parish Council, stated: "the Parish Council is firmly of the opinion that the interests of the parish and its inhabitants will be best served by the parish remaining within Hampshire and retaining its identity as a Civil Parish with an elected Parish Council in the Alton Rural District; and that its proposal to incorporate small areas of Haslemere and Bramshott would be in the best interests of the inhabitants both of the present parish and of the areas proposed to be taken in." The County Council strongly supported Grayshott's remaining in Hampshire. As it happened, the Boundary Commission did not proceed with its South-eastern England survey, being superseded by a Royal Commission on Local Government with the task of reporting on the boundaries, organisation and functions of all local authorities, with the advantage of having the documents of the Boundary Commission. Then followed much discussion in the Press and voluminous submissions of evidence by local authorities at all levels. A disturbing feature of this was that some senior local authorities made it clear that they had little use for Parish Councils and would gladly see them go. The really important argument for the retention of Parish Councils, and even for some extension of their powers, was as expressed in the 1967 Report of the Parish Council: "The possibility of the setting up of larger higher authorities makes the continuance of Parish Councils even more vital. The members of a Parish Council are known to and daily accessible to the inhabitants of the parish, and this ensures that local but important matters affecting village life are subject to uninterrupted and sometimes critical democratic control. It is at this level that the relationship between electors and elected is most close and the operation of democracy most apparent." Grayshott was one of the large minority of parish councils throughout the country to submit detailed evidence to the Royal Commission, often named from its chairman the Redcliffe-Maud Commission. The recommendations of the Commission in 1969 and the Government White Paper based on them contained serious implications for Hampshire.

For the local set-up in north-east Hampshire the proposal was to transfer the whole of the Alton Rural District, including Grayshott, and the Parish of Bramshott, from Hampshire to a new "unitary authority" of West Surrey. So the struggle had to start again, and on this occasion the attitude of the County Council seemed more ambiguous than in 1965. The Parish Council were most anxious to resist absorption into West Surrey, and at a crowded Special Parish Meeting in June 1970, after careful explanation and discussion of the issues, the following resolution received unanimous support: "The Parish Meeting welcomes the proposal for preserving the greater part of Hampshire as one Local Government Area, opposes the implication that the Parish should be excluded from the County and expresses its strong desire to remain within a Hampshire unit of Local Government in order, in the words of the Redcliffe-Maud Report, "to maintain the common interests, tradition and loyalties in the present pattern." There was a spontaneous suggestion from the floor of the meeting to organise a petition to the Minister of Housing and Local Government. This was enthusiastically agreed. In a week about 70 per cent of the local electors signed the petition, which was sent with the resolution and a reasoned document to the Minister and to the local M.P. (Miss Joan Quennell) who supported the Grayshott cause. The Parish Council continued to watch matters closely, but in the final outcome the Local Government Act 1972 left Grayshott and the whole of the Alton Rural District in the County of Hampshire.

For the purpose of representation on the County Council the county is divided into Electoral Divisions, Grayshott being in the Headley Division. In 1969 the County Council reviewed its Divisions and, in the interests of roughly equalising them in number of electors, proposed that Grayshott while remaining in the Alton Rural District — should be linked with Bramshott which was in the Petersfield Rural District for County Council Election purposes. The Parish Council joined with the Alton Rural District Council in resisting this. One grave objection was that Grayshott had not been consulted by the County Council, another was that the result would be very inconvenient when one County Councillor represented two parishes in different Rural Districts. A public enquiry was held at Winchester on 30th April and 1st May. The Parish Council was represented by Messrs. H. Buck and J. H. Smith, the latter giving evidence on the second day. The County Council proposal was rejected.

Another main theme in recent years was the preservation of Grayshott as a genuine village. Under the Local Government Act 1972 the Alton Rural District Council and its successor, the East Hampshire District Council, have been obliged to submit all planning applications for comment to Parish Councils, although the actual decision remains firmly with the District Council. From 1965 the Parish Council has had a standing planning sub-committee. It would be infinitely tedious to detail the applications and decisions. Generally speaking, the efforts of the Council to preserve the rural setting of Stoney Bottom and Whitmore Vale have been successful. Within the village itself the comments of the Council have often resulted in the rejection or substantial modification of applications which the Council have considered objectionable. In the majority of cases the Council have had no adverse comment to make. Examples of modifications of planning applications are the eventual development of The Square, the blocks of flats on the Hurstmere Estate, and the development of shops and offices on the former Continental Garage site. Examples of applications which were rejected are on the St. Ann's land, where development threatened the lower Stoney Bottom valley: behind Rockdale in the upper Whitmore Bottom valley; and, above all, on the fields to the west of the Waggoners Wells Estate and opposite Grayshott Hall.

We have already noted the rejection in 1962 of an application in the last of those areas. In 1972 another application was made for 172 houses on the same site. The Parish Council totally opposed this, and it was rejected by the Planning Authority. The applicant appealed, and a two-day public enquiry was held in the Village Hall in July 1973. The applicant appeared with several "expert" — and, no doubt, expensive — witnesses. The County Council contested the appeal and were represented by the District Council, as did the Waggoners Wells Estate Association with legal representation. The Parish

Council was represented by the Vice-Chairman: their case was centred entirely on the protection of rural amenities and the threat to the character of the village presented by such a large development. The appeal was rejected. It is interesting to note that the residents in the newly-developed Waggoners Wells Estate, about which the Parish Council had originally been dubious, sprang to the defence of the area of natural beauty in their own vicinity.

Since the Parish Council has been consulted in planning matters, its policy has been not to oppose reasonable applications for improvement of individual dwellings, but to oppose — or, alternatively, to suggest modifications of developments which, in the view of the Council, would threaten the character of the village or the beauty of its natural surroundings. In the latter context the Parish Council have obtained from the planning authority Tree Preservation Orders on the Hurstmere and St. Ann's estates, and in the fields on the north side of the B3002 road opposite Grayshott Hall.

An important area of discussion has been the designation of particular areas or buildings for Conservation Orders. In December 1974 the District Council consulted the Parish Councils. After much consideration the Grayshott Council asked for designation of the whole parish as such an area, a decision which was unanimously supported in September 1975 at a meeting of the Council with representatives of appropriate local organisations. The case was submitted to the District Council, even though the Parish Council realised that this might be difficult to achieve. The reasons why the Parish Council made such a sweeping request were also included. The District refused the Grayshott request, but further discussions may follow.

In the wider field of planning policy for the whole of Hampshire, Grayshott was also compelled to take a keen interest. Broadly speaking, the County was divided into three belts running from east to west. In the north was a belt of rapidly growing development arising from the Reading, Basingstoke and Blackwater towns, and in the south a similar area along the coast arising from Portsmouth, Fareham, Southampton and their hinterlands. Between these two lies a mid-Hampshire belt, still largely agricultural with country villages and small towns such as Alton and Petersfield. The general policy is to preserve this large area of scenic beauty and agricultural value for its own sake, and also as an outlet for refreshment in the wider sense, and recreation for the heavily urbanised belts to the north and south. This meant that careful planning of the mid-Hampshire area must be undertaken. For this purpose the belt was divided into convenient areas for each of which interim planning policies must be formulated in order to safeguard the main aim.

Grayshott was included in the Whitehill/Grayshott area, i.e. the parishes of Whitehill, Headley and Grayshott. The East Hampshire District Council produced the "Whitehill/Grayshott Study" as a discussion document. This paper divided the area into areas of "Higher Growth" and "Low Growth," and included illustrative maps. While it is fair to say that the document seemed to favour "Low Growth" for Headley and Grayshott, one of the maps showed what would be the effect of treating Grayshott as an area of "Higher Growth" — nothing less than development of the whole of the slope between Headley Road and the Stoney Bottom Lane, a prospect which the Parish Council thought would go far to destroy Grayshott as a country village. Consequently the Council entered a detailed memorandum of objection to this possibility. They were relieved to find that the final result, issued in the

"Whitehill/ Grayshott Interim Planning Policy," left Grayshott as an area of "Low Growth," in which only limited in-filling would be permitted. It is worth appreciative notice that at a consultative meeting of the three Parish Councils and the District Council in November 1973, and at a public meeting at Headley a year later, there was general agreement that Grayshott and Headley Should remain genuine villages, while Whitehill might develop considerably.

Immediately after the War, efforts started again to secure more council houses. The first, though minor, possibility was a site on the "Searchlight Field" (now the most easterly part of the Waggoners Wells Estate) where a Searchlight Station had operated in pretty solid buildings which the Parish Council thought were suitable for conversion into at least temporary accommodation. They informed the District Council of their views, but nothing came of it. In any case the resultant housing accommodation would have been minimal. The Parish Council then urged the District Council to consider acquiring land on the Kingswood Firs Estate, then undeveloped, but this proved impracticable. A more extensive opportunity seemed to open up when the War Office released Superior Camp, the military camp housed in semi-permanent buildings on Ludshott Common. Unfortunately, while council housing in Grayshott was the concern of the Alton District Council, the camp site was in the Petersfield Rural District, which had its own housing problems. Discussions between the two District Councils produced no houses for Grayshott, and Superior Camp became temporary housing accommodation for Petersfield. The main result on Grayshott in succeeding years was that Grayshott School was crowded with the child population of Superior Camp.

Meanwhile Grayshott had to be satisfied with 16 new houses in Beech Lane, completed in 1947, though the District Council were considering other sites. In 1953 they considered buying Philips Green from the Parish Council for housing, but the County Council were also interested in that site for a new school – the old one being overcrowded and with abysmal sanitary provision. Delay by the District Council resulted in the County Council buying it: ironically, the new school was not started until 1976. In 1953, all other sites having proved unsuitable, the District Council were still considering the eastern strip of the Searchlight Field, but a Government squeeze put an end to it in 1954. In 1961 the Grayshott Council considered a site at the Beech allotments for cheaper houses, either by council or by private building, but the developers of the Searchlight Field were not interested in the allotment ground. So the Parish Council, at a meeting in November 1961 attended by Dr. R. C. Droop (who was pressing for more housing for Grayshott people), decided to apply for planning permission for two houses with garages on the northern edge of the Sports Field which was Council property. Permission was refused, owing to unsatisfactory lay-out and inadequate access. The Council then turned to consider possibilities at Philips Corner, which was also parish property. This piece of land had been so named to perpetuate association with Philip I'Anson, when Philips Green was sold to the County Council. Both pieces of land were parish property given by the I'Anson family. Meanwhile an appeal decision had authorised 103 houses on the Searchlight Field.

In January 1962 Mr. F. L. H. Harris, Chairman of the Parish Council, suggested an approach to the Hampshire Old People's Housing Society to see if it would be interested in erecting suitable accommodation at Philips Corner, if that site could be made available by the Parish Council. A little later Mr. Peter Martin, the then Secretary of the Society, visited Grayshott and found the site entirely suitable for a flatlet scheme such as the Society already had near the county coast. By November 1963 planning permission had been sought from the Alton District and granted in principle.

Then came long and often frustrating negotiations with the Ministry of Housing and Local Government as to the possibility of selling the land to the Alton Council at a nominal figure (so as to avoid high site cost and hence excessive rents), or of leasing it to that Council at a peppercorn rent, so that in turn the District Council could lease it to the Society at a purely nominal figure. It was eventually ruled that the land being parish trust land, could be sold only by a compulsory purchase order served on the Parish Council by the District Council, as the housing authority: and could be sold at less than the official valuation of over £6,000 only with the approval of a Parish Meeting and the consent of the Ministry—which, in this case, required Parliamentary approval. A Special Parish Meeting in October 1965 agreed to sell at a price of £500 (to meet the cost of renovating and transferring the children's playground equipment to the adjoining Playing Field). The consent of the Ministry was obtained.

Equally prolonged negotiations then ensued to secure the capital needed to erect Philips House. Alton Council were not able to make the money available, owing to the financial squeeze then in force, but by the middle of 1967 the Hampshire County Council had agreed to make a loan to the Hampshire Old People's Housing Society. Meanwhile an architect, Mr. J. H. Orchard of Haslemere, had been appointed and a local committee had been formed of the Officers of the Housing Society and members of the Parish Council, with Mrs. D. Brooking as Hon. Secretary. Her correspondence and minutes and other records proved invaluable. In the autumn of 1967 the sale of the land to the District Council and its lease to the Society at a nominal rent had been completed. By May 1968 the local House Committee had finally been set up with a formal constitution and terms of reference. It consists of persons nominated by the Parish Council, the Housing Society and the Rural District Council, together with four Officers of the Housing Society. Its main functions are to select tenants, to supervise the day-to-day administration of the 27 flatlets in Philips House, and to raise money for communal facilities and amenities in the building. In all these negotiations, and in making constructive suggestions, the Clerk to the Parish Council (Mr. D. P. Lawson) made a great contribution,

The preparation of plans by the architect was technically difficult and complicated since a Government annual housing subsidy on the project depended on keeping the cost per unit of accommodation (i.e. the total cost of the building divided by the number of flatlets) below a very restricted figure. However, this was achieved in time, though there was an unfortunate and substantial delay when the plans, having been exhaustively examined and approved by the Ministry, were found to have been dealt with by that section of the Ministry which dealt with Surrey, whereas Grayshott was in Hampshire—an instance of confusion caused by the postal address. At last, in the late summer of 1969, a contract was awarded to a builder and work commenced.

189

It was hoped that Philips House would be completed by September 1970, and the House Committee got down to compiling a list of applicants and to fund-raising for such things as furnishing the communal lounge, the guest room and laundry, and the installation of a lift. A Spring Fair in 1970, organised by the ladies of the House Committee led by Mrs. Hicks-Beach, raised nearly £600, and soon the total fund had reached some £1,300. In addition, a gift of £5,000 to the Society was made by an anonymous local resident, as well as three gifts of £100 by others: and over £1,800 was subscribed by local residents in interest-free loans to the Society. By this time Mr. George Whitmarsh had joined the House Committee as its energetic Hon. Treasurer. Much thought and time were given by the House Committee especially the ladies — to the internal decorations and furnishings of all kinds to make the House both efficient and attractive.

Everything seemed to be set fair when suddenly, in July 1970, the building firm went bankrupt, leaving Philips House far from completion. This was a shattering blow which involved a long delay and serious additional cost. As soon as possible a new contractor was appointed and work on the building was resumed. It was now hoped to open the house in September 1971. In July of that year Mrs. Dyer was appointed as Warden and the final selection of tenants was completed, for occupation in mid-October. Then came a further blow when a serious defect in the water system caused extensive damage by flooding to some of the flats, and it became necessary to postpone still further the admission of the tenants, with all the inconvenience resulting for them. The first tenants took up residence in November, and Philips House was formally opened on 8th December 1971 by the Lord Lieutenant of Hampshire, Lord Ashburton.

The project, which was initiated in 1961 in the faith that it would be of great social benefit to the community, has been amply justified — not only by providing elderly residents of Grayshott and Hampshire with the means of continuing to look after themselves in comfortable independence, but also by releasing, in doing so, accommodation for other age groups. Philips House is an outstanding example of local authorities at all levels working together for the common good — the Parish Council in making the site available, Alton Rural District Council as the housing authority, and Hampshire County Council in advancing the necessary capital. Grayshott owes a great debt to the Officers of the Hampshire Old People's Housing Society (now the Hampshire Voluntary Housing Society) and, above all, to Mr. F. L. H. Harris for his vision, patience and persistence from the inception of the enterprise to its completion.

With Mrs. Dyer as Warden, and her husband looking after the beautiful garden, Philips House continues to succeed in its purpose. When Mrs. Brooking left Grayshott, Miss Faith Porter took her place as a very effective Hon. Secretary. The present Secretary of the Housing Society is Mr. Richard Warner.

In the previous Chapter we have seen that under the Fire Brigade Act the local brigade came under the control of the Rural District Council. Under the Fire Services Act (1947) control passed to the County Council. In 1956 that Council wished to extend the existing small Fire Station in order to provide larger and more effective appliances. Then the suggestion was made of making available the Small Village Hall either by lease or sale. This matter is dealt with in some detail in a previous Chapter. The modern Fire Station was erected on the Bowling Green site on Village Hall land and was handed over to the village Fire Service in the summer of 1964. Though the Grayshott Brigade is now incorporated in the County Fire Service, it continues — to the great satisfaction of the village — to operate keenly and efficiently, as has often been demonstrated in Fire Brigade competitions, and to be manned by local volunteer firemen on a part-time basis from a Station which is continuously operative. It is often greatly overworked in periods of dry weather, when common fires abound as a menace to house property and to the beauty of Grayshott's beautiful countryside. It is renowned locally and beyond for its rapid turn-out and arrival at points of danger. Its normal activity in summer months accelerated to climax in the drought conditions of the summer of 1976, when for many weeks it was in almost continuous action. It was appropriate that the village should co-operate enthusiastically, in recognition of its arduous and devoted service, at a large party organised in the Village Hall by Mr. S. Jefferys and a band of helpers.

Finally, we may note that the Grayshott Brigade has been outstanding in raising annually large sums of money for the Fire Service Benevolent Fund, e.g. £500 as a result of the party mentioned above, which helps firemen who are injured on duty and their families who suffer in cases of death on duty.

During the more recent period, after so long a succession of hope raised and then deferred, main drainage came at last to the village. An outfall site had been found at Lindford, suitable for taking sewage from Whitehill, Headley and Grayshott, and the 1947 Annual Parish Meeting sent a resolution to the District Council asking it "to expedite in every possible way the proposed drainage scheme" and reminding them "that the question has been before them for the past 42 years" and that "the need grows more and more urgent every year." By October the District Council asked the Parish Council for its approval of the scheme, which, owing to local configuration, could not cater for the whole area of the parish. The Parish Council gave approval with the hope that the village school could be included. A public enquiry was held at Grayshott in March 1948, to arrange for a loan, and it was hoped that the scheme would soon begin — but meanwhile the night soil collection continued. The Annual Report of 1950 stated: "It is noted that drainage has started in Whitehill. Grayshott lives in hope."

A difficulty about installing this large scheme was that, since the sewerage works were at Lindford, Whitehill and Headley would have to be drained before Grayshott, and the country was again in a period of financial stringency. However, the Parish Council, fortified by a letter in the local Press from a visitor who compared hygiene in Grayshott with that in Persia, continued to press the District Council, who sent a Grayshott resolution to the Minister of Health with an expression of its own concurrence. In the autumn of 1952 the Parish Council tried to arrange a joint deputation of the Parish and District Councils to the Minister, but in the prevailing economic climate the latter declined. Not until 1955 was the financial ban lifted to the extent of Government sanction for the Headley part of the scheme, and the Clerk of the District told the Grayshott Annual Parish Meeting that his Council would try to get sanction for the Grayshott section as soon as the Headley section was nearing completion. At last, in 1957, the Grayshott section was put to tender, and just over a year later the work was actually started. In March 1960 the

Parish Meeting was told that it was nearly completed, and that thus "a long-standing grievance is coming to an end" — after agitation by Grayshott for more than half a century.

The perennial problems of road safety and traffic congestion continued to demand attention.

A request in 1945 to move the 30 miles per hour speed limit signs in Headley and Whitmore Vale Roads a little further away from the actual village, though approved by the District Council, was rejected by the Ministry of War Transport. Similar requests were frequently made, and these, though frustratingly slowly, had some useful results. The attention of the police was drawn on occasions to the need to enforce the limits. Unfortunately their efforts produced only sporadic improvement, and the general impression remains that the speed of traffic as it approaches and passes through the village is often dangerously excessive, compelling pedestrians to panic-stricken and goat-like agility. In July 1973, after a police check in Headley Road to the west of the village, the Clerk was asked by the Parish Council to report that "matters were worse rather than better, and to enquire how many charges had been brought and what further action would be taken." As a result, certain prosecutions were undertaken and fines imposed. Towards the end of our period an application was made, in the interests of safety, for pedestrian crossings at the points where the path across the Children's Recreation Ground gives access on to the Headley and Crossways Roads. A traffic census was taken, but the result did not justify the application, and there the position has remained.

Frequently the dangerous access from Crossways Road on to the main road (the A3) came up for discussion, mainly in the case of pedestrians and cyclists. The danger spot is in Surrey, but it was of great concern to Grayshott. The problem was not solved until the "Halt" signs were eventually installed.

In 1973 Hampshire County Council asked all Parish Councils to make recommendations for Width (of Vehicles) Restriction Orders on narrow roads in their parishes. The Parish Council recommended Whitmore Vale Road and Hammer Lane. Haslemere Urban District Council and Headley Parish Council made similar recommendations for the stretches of these roads in their areas. The Orders have not yet been made, as this is inevitably a slow process demanding systematic consideration over the whole county.

In 1950 the condition of the pavements in Crossways Road led to negotiations between the District Council and the various businesses, whereby the latter should dedicate their sections as parts of the public highway, thereafter to be maintained by the District. The process took some years to complete, and the position cannot yet be considered satisfactory. In fact the pavements and the kerbing in both the main village roads still give cause for complaint: the activities of the public utility authorities do not always help matters.

In 1951 the Council requested "No Parking"-signs on the north side of Crossways Road between the War Memorial and the entrance to the Children's Recreation Ground where there was a severe bottle-neck, but the District Council countered by suggesting taking into the road a strip of that Ground. That suggestion was rejected by the Parish Council. The most the County did was to put a central white line near the Memorial. Another area of traffic congestion was at Fiveways Corner, aggravated by that being a turning-point for buses. The Parish Council sought to alleviate this by pressing for bus bays and shelters on both sides of the road, a little to the east of the actual corner. These were provided in 1960 on small areas of the Children's Recreation Ground and the Village Green which the Parish Council sold to the highway authority. A few years previously the Parish Council suggested unilateral parking on one side of Headley Road for an experimental period, but nothing came of it. Towards the end of our period the County Council put a white-painted traffic "island" at Fiveways Corner in an effort to persuade motor traffic to slow down when taking the corner.

In 1953 the Parish Council asked the District Council to adopt Beech-hanger Road as it served council houses in the main, but the District merely replied that the road was "fairly up the list for adoption." Eight years later the County Council were prepared to make up the road, including the section running past the tennis courts to an access on to Headley Road. There was at that time a children's corner where Philips House now stands, and the Parish Council were concerned that the making up of that section would encourage additional motor traffic which would be a hazard to children using the playground equipment: and, moreover, that—since the land on both sides was parish property—a heavy charge for making up would fall on the Parish Council and hence on the parish rate. After much correspondence and consultation the Parish accepted the County's offer to bear the whole cost of a footpath, and half the cost of making up, leaving the Parish Council to bear a total charge of just under £1,500. In 1974 Avenue and Glen Roads, in 1975 The Avenue, were adopted and made up and road lighting and, where possible, footpaths were provided, much to the safety and comfort of the residents. In the mid-sixties official street names were agreed with the District Council, which in due course erected the street name signs.

As early as 1954 the Parish Council were pressing the County Council on the need for a footpath along Whitmore Vale Road, owing to a large increase of traffic and in the interests of the safety of children going to and from the village school. The County replied that this was number 33 on a list of 53 footpaths to be made in the next three years. The financial position delayed this even longer. In 1969 the Parent Teachers Association expressed anxiety and the Parish Council again raised the matter with the County Council, both by letter and site meetings with the Divisional Surveyor and Colonel Digby, the local County Councillor. As a result, financial provision was made for construction in 1971/72. The main problem was on which side of the road the path should be. All sorts of suggestions were made, until, after several meetings and much discussion, it was agreed that it should be on the west side of the road which involved taking in a strip of churchyard land for almost the whole length of the path: and this posed a problem, owing to the proximity of some of the graves to the proposed path. The Parochial Church Council were entirely co-operative and agreed to give the land on condition that a suitable wall or fence, to provide privacy for the churchyard, should be erected by the County Council, which also agreed to make one section of the path a little narrower than the standard width, and to plant some trees on the churchyard side of the fence, a stone wall being prohibitively expensive. There was understandably a strong difference of opinion in the village, since the footpath would detract from the rural nature of the road, and the high oaken fence extending to such a length would look very stark, particularly before it began to weather. On the other hand, many people felt that the safety

193

of children must be paramount. A kind gift from a parishioner enabled roses to be planted along the inside of the fence, which would grow to a height above it. These, together with the trees to be planted, would break the line of the fence.

In recent years it has become increasingly obvious that the village needs adequate car parking, in the absence of which unrestricted parking at the road sides has led to increasing congestion and, on occasions, chaos—when, for instance, a bus is endeavouring to get through a road with cars parked nose to tail on both sides, and a delivery van or lorry delivering to a shop is standing stationary near the middle of the road alongside the parked cars. In the absence of reasonable off-road parks it has not been possible to devise an acceptable scheme of street parking restrictions—in spite of suggestions, conferences, and discussions too numerous to detail.

As early as October 1947 the local Superintendent of Police suggested to the Chief Constable and Alton Rural District Council a car park on part of the Village Green at the junction of Headley Road and Whitmore Vale Road, but a petition of protest was signed by over 350 local government electors, and the Parish Council voiced its own objection, suggesting instead parking at the road sides on alternate days.

Nothing further was done until 1956, when the bus bays being on the way, the Grayshott Council suggested the site next to the Fox and Pelican. Adjoining landowners objected, and the Parish Council took refuge in again suggesting unilateral parking—but nothing came of it. There were ideas from time to time of making the Village Hall car park public, but, although it was used by a few motorists, it was too far from the shops to be a real solution, and was itself often congested when functions occurred at the Village Hall.

The first tiny improvement came in 1960, when the ditch along Apley House opposite St. Luke's Church was filled in to form a lay-by for general use. Thenceforward the main effort was to secure the present car park between the Village Green and the Fox and Pelican. All sorts of difficulties— legal and financial—delayed the acquisition of the site, and it was not until 1970 that the car park was constructed. At each important stage the approval of a Parish Meeting was obtained: for instance, the Parish Council wished to sell a small piece of land at the eastern side of the Village Green to the District Council for £425, the price at which the Parish Council had acquired it— instead of £1,300, the price fixed by the District Valuer. This stage in itself took two years to complete, as it was legally necessary for the District Council to serve a compulsory purchase order on the Parish Council, and for the consent of the Minister of Housing and Local Government to be obtained for a sale at less than the price fixed by the District Valuer. The lay-out of the car park is pleasantly rural, and, after a slow start, it is extensively used. In 1972 the District Council purchased land in Hill Road, below the shops at the end of Crossways Road, for a car park which has not yet been constructed.

Another amenity sadly lacking was, as we have seen, a public lavatory. In 1949 a suggestion that the Fox and Pelican might withdraw consent for the public use of their lavatories turned out to be a false alarm, but the District Council was approached to provide a public convenience. They agreed to consider it if a suitable site could be found. This must obviously be near the centre of the village. In October 1950 a Parish Meeting voted in favour of a site on private land between the Village Green and the Fox and Pelican, but the

District Council preferred one on the Children's Recreation Ground. The well-attended Annual Parish Meeting of 1951 again voted for the former, and the Parish Council bought a strip of the private land to add to the Village Green, on part of which the public convenience could be placed. National financial stringency and legal processes imposed further delay, but by the end of 1953 an agreement had been reached whereby the Parish Council leased the site to the District Council at a nominal rent, the District to be responsible for cleaning and maintenance. In 1955 the building was constructed.

Towards the end of 1955 the Parish Council, supported by a Parish Meeting, decided to substitute electric for the original gas street lighting, and to re-organise the placing of the lamps at a cost of £1,750, to be funded by a Public Works Board loan. This was carried out in 1957. As the new housing estates at Waggoners Wells and Kingswood Firs were built, the developers were required to install street lighting which thereafter became the property and responsibility of the Parish Council. This also applied to smaller and later developments at Hurstmere, Chestnut Close and Vicarage Gardens. In 1974, when Glen Road and The Avenue were being made up, there was some confusion as to which authority — the Parish or the County Council — had the responsibility for street lighting in the parish. It was eventually agreed that control remained with the Parish Council on the basis of footway, not highway, lighting. The parish now has about 100 street lamps, and a councillor acts voluntarily as Lighting Officer — by no means a sinecure.

The demand for allotments declined after the Second World War. Grayshott had two allotment grounds, at The Beeches and Stoney Bottom. Lack of tenants caused the closure of The Beeches and the transfer of the few tenants there to Stoney Bottom. By 1957 the process was complete, and the Beech allotments were let for the grazing of horses. At Stoney Bottom the story is much the same. There were only four allotments used for their original purpose, and the rest of the land was leased for horticultural use to one of the village businesses. But one can never tell. In 1976 there seemed to be a revival of interest, and consideration was given to the possibility of re-opening the Beech allotments.

The spirited warfare between the Parish Council and the Post Office died away in this most recent period. Agreement was easily reached on increased provision of telephone kiosks and letter boxes; on the Post Office closing on Saturday rather than on Wednesday afternoons; and on daily closing at 5.30 p.m. instead of 6 p.m. There was an attempt to eliminate the occasional confusion arising from the official postal address of "Grayshott, Hindhead, Surrey," but the Post Office gave reasons why — because of mail sorting technicalities — there could be no change.

We have seen that the Children's Corner was moved to the Playing Field when Philips House was built. Later, on public demand, an additional Children's Corner was provided on the Children's Recreation Ground. Though this was somewhat controversial, experience has proved that it is extensively used without additional safety risk.

For a few years after the Second World War there was a Cadet Unit and a Rifle Club on the Playing Field, but these organisations proved to be comparatively short lived.

The Playing Field was administered by a Recreation Club with a representative Committee. In the autumn of 1947 this body was in financial difficulty and wished to hand back its responsibility to the Parish Council. The latter asked the Club to continue as a co-ordinating link between the Council and the Clubs renting the ground, but agreed to take responsibility for paying the groundsman's wages, while the Club raised the rents of playing pitches. Even so, the Recreation Club—facing expenditure of over £1,200 on the Tennis Courts and enlarging the Cricket Table, and foreseeing the urgency of providing a new Sports Pavilion—resigned and was replaced by a Sports Committee formed from the user clubs, with Mr. Harry Buck as Chairman and Miss Muriel Hartwell as Hon. Secretary. With the aid of a Ministry of Education grant of over £1,000 the work on the Tennis Courts and Cricket Table was carried out, but, owing to Government restrictions, no grant was available for a new pavilion. So the Parish had to go it alone. It was agreed to purchase materials from the wartime Witley Camp, the cost of which—together with erection and completion—was slightly over £1,000 towards which the Sports Committee had £700. The balance of £300 would be met by a Bank Holiday Fete, and £50 from the Lyndon Trust. Later a small grant and an interest-free loan came from the Playing Fields Association. The new Pavilion was completed by May 1952, and was opened by Major Tommy Whitaker.

After doing yeoman service for some twenty years this pavilion needed renewing, because it was not of a very high standard to begin with and adequate maintenance had not been possible. Accommodation problems arose, particularly when a ladies' Hockey Club became a permanent user club. Moreover, better facilities were required by local sports leagues.

When the Parish Council considered the matter in March 1972, Mr. D. Brooking suggested that the existing Village Hall and its site should be sold and the proceeds used to build a new Village Hall and Social and Sports Centre on the Playing Field. This soon became the subject of controversy between those who favoured retaining the existing Village Hall, and thorough modernisation and modest extension of the existing Sports Pavilion—and those who supported the much wider scheme. This difference of opinion led to a very long series of Parish Council meetings, consultative meetings between the Sports Clubs and the Council, and Parish Meetings. Quite early on the Parish Council, who had ultimate responsibility, came to the conclusion that it would be undesirable to sell the Village Hall, which by the nature of the building would have little selling value, while the value of the site for development would depend on the kind of planning permission which could be obtained. In the opinion of the Council these factors raised doubts as to the financial viability of the wider scheme. Moreover, negotiations were in progress for providing permanent accommodation for a branch of the County Library in the Village Hall premises. The adoption of the wider scheme might well lead to an interim period when there would be no Village Hall at all. For these reasons the Council thought it wiser to proceed expeditiously with the smaller scheme, particularly in a period of rapid inflation, leaving open the possibility of a larger scheme if, in future years, that should seem desirable and financially possible.

Meanwhile the advocates of the larger scheme went into action. The Sports Clubs, including the Badminton Club which used the Village Hall, formed themselves into the Associated Sports Clubs, which, under the energetic leadership of Mr. S. Jefferys, organised a lottery to raise a Pavilion

Fund. The proceeds of the lottery eventually amounted to about £2,300. For a long time there was doubt as to whether this Fund would be handed over to the Parish Council to help finance the smaller scheme. This difficulty was not removed until early in 1975.

There was difference of opinion, too, on the method of improving the existing pavilion. There were advocates of doing it by voluntary labour, but the Council, having legal responsibility for the building, turned the suggestion down and decided to employ a qualified architect and a building firm. That this was a wise decision was confirmed by experience. The work involved gutting, radical internal modification, and rear and side extensions (including a committee and refreshment room) of the original pavilion, which had been erected out of square—a fact which itself caused serious technical difficulties of planning and construction. The new Pavilion was completed in the summer of 1975. As an integral part of the general scheme of improving sports facilities, a new Tennis Pavilion was erected at the Tennis Courts at a cost of about £1,200. The delay caused by controversy resulted, owing to rampant inflation, to an unfortunate and serious increase in the cost of the main Pavilion. This had been estimated in 1973 as about £9,900, but turned out in 1975 to be over £18,000. The cost of the two pavilions was funded by a Public Works Board loan, an additional parish rate precept for 1976/77 only, grants from the Hampshire Playing Fields Association and Tennis Association, the substantial sum raised by the Associated Sports Clubs, an advance from Grayshott Sports Committee, and by the Parish Council liquidating their Philips Green Account and utilising the Lyndon Trusts. But a considerable sum remained to be refunded in respect of the advance from the Sports Committee.

At every stage of this long and controversial matter the Parish Council sought and obtained the support of a Parish Meeting, although after March 1974 there was no legal obligation, under the Local Government Act (1972), to do so. Grayshott Sports Clubs now have first-class Pavilions, and it will be for the village to decide in future years whether any further addition is required. It should also be mentioned that the Sports Committee receives an annual grant from the Parish Council.

Of the rural public footpaths, that through Stoney Bottom had always been troublesome owing to springs near Waggoners Wells. Technically this path is an ancient public highway for which the District Council are responsible. Over the years the western end had become practically impassable, and efforts by the landowners did not produce lasting results. The problem was eventually solved in 1963 by agreement with the National Trust, whereby the path at the western end was diverted to a higher level along the bank which was their boundary, and the District Council provided a small bridge to connect the diversion with the road near the ford.

In the 'fifties, purchase by the Parish Council secured the fine clump of beeches to the immediate north-east of the Playing Field. There were also some magnificent beeches bordering the footpath along Whitmore Hanger and behind the Playing Field. Some of them blew down across the path during a gale, and expert examination revealed that all of them had rotted at the heart and were in a dangerous condition. Reluctantly it was decided that they must be felled, but young trees—mainly larch and copper beech—were planted as replacements. Though the felling was very sad, it must be admitted that a splendid view across the valley to Beacon Hill was opened up. In the early sixties, when Wealden Woodlands was afforesting Flat Wood in Hammer Lane, they were most co-operative in keeping open and signposting the public foot and bridle paths which cross their land.

The path opposite the Headley Road end of Boundary Road, which runs down into Woodcock Bottom, though used as a public footpath was not officially designated as such. It is in fact in Surrey, but is largely used by Grayshott people. Haslemere Urban District Council, at Grayshott's request, agreed to give it official designation.

Footpath No. 8, leading north from Headley Road near the boundary of Bede Cottage to join the path running along Whitmore Hanger to the north of the Sports Field, caused some anxiety when the development of Waggoners Wells Estate began in 1965. The developers desired to close the southern end of the path in order to extend their development. They offered to plan the estate roads so that some of them could be used in substitution for that section of the path, and the Ministry of Transport issued a draft Order for the diversion of the path. The Parish Council decided to resist this, and secured the support of a Parish Meeting. In the end a sensible compromise was negotiated whereby the footpath was moved westwards to just inside the developers' boundary, as a dedicated footpath which was to be put in good order by the developers.

A short footpath which linked Whitmore Vale and Whitmore Vale Road, just west of the ford, was rescued in 1973 by the vigilance of a local resident.

A very useful safeguard for public paths was provided under the National Parks and Access to the Countryside Act 1949, which set up machinery for surveying and recording them on definitive maps, all Parish Councils being consulted. Early in 1955 the first such map for Grayshott was issued, the second and current one in 1964.

In the matter of keeping the village greens in good order and the public footpaths in good condition and free from obstruction, the village has been fortunate in having the services of Mr. Peter Burrows. Born at Langley, near Weavers Down, he comes of a family of Hollywater in the Parish of Headley.

During the Second World War he was at first in the reserved occupation of timber cutting, but in 1943 he joined the Royal Army Veterinary Corps and served overseas. Apart from expert skills in country crafts such as cutting hop poles and making chestnut fencing—and, particularly, brooms, both heather and birch—he is a mine of information on rural matters such as rights of way, public paths, common rights and local enclosure awards.

Many of his brooms have found their way to Canada and the U.S.A., especially California where they seem to be used as much for decoration and illustration of the broomsquire's craft as for practical purposes. When the Jane Austen bicentenary was celebrated at Steventon, Peter Burrows was requested to spend a day there demonstrating the art of broom-making. He has an avid interest in local history, and has built up a collection of books on the subject, as well as an arsenal of the tools of his trade, modern and—even more interesting—traditional. He was appointed by the Parish Council in January 1965.

In the early seventies a Best Kept Village Competition was organised through the Hampshire County Magazine. Grayshott entered in 1971 and a by-product was a sudden proliferation of litter bins and the unusual spectacle of Parish Councillors, equipped with litter prongs and plastic sacks, walking the roads and bye-ways with an intent—if somewhat distracted—gaze. Grayshott reached the semi-final, and the Vice-Chairman of the Council collected the resultant certificate at an open-air ceremony in the middle of a field at Greywell on a wet, cold and windy day in September. In the next two years Grayshott entered again, but with no success owing to some public apathy—but even more to the litter deposited by shoppers from near and far, and large-scale building operations in Headley Road, which inevitably detracted from general appearance and tidiness. Thereafter Grayshott has not entered.

In 1971 the County organised a Survey of Hampshire Treasures, and Mrs. G. Cooper compiled an exhaustive list, mainly scenic and ecological, for Grayshott.

In the post-war years, after the short Chairmanship of Dr. A. E. Western (1947–48), the Parish Council had only two Chairmen in nearly 30 years. Major L. I. T. Whitaker served between 1948 and 1959. He was a shrewd, brisk but kindly Chairman. In 1969, when Grayshott celebrated its Diamond Jubilee as a civil parish, Major Whitaker was High Sheriff of Hampshire, an office which his father—Mr. A. Ingham Whitaker—had held in 1919. Father and son appointed the Vicar of Grayshott, Rev. A. E. N. Simms and Canon A. R. Winnett respectively, as their Chaplain during their year of office. Major Whitaker was a Deputy Lieutenant of Hampshire in 1968. After a long illness he died in February 1971 to the unfeigned sorrow of all who had known him. Mr. F. L. H. Harris was Chairman from 1959 to 1976, and gave the wise and patient leadership which was needed in a period when the work of the Council was increasing greatly, both in quantity and complexity. Mr. Harris also holds positions of responsibility in the Hampshire Association of Local Councils, in the Hampshire Council of Social Service, and in the Hampshire Voluntary Housing Society. A great debt of gratitude is owed to Mr. Harris, and also to Mr. D. P. Lawson, the Clerk of the Council. They were a most successful partnership. Although Mr. Harris ceased to be Chairman in 1976, he remained on the Council. His successor is Mr. A. Weston.

The social life of the village has continued with unabated vigour, and has been strengthened by the more recent newcomers in Kingswood Firs and Waggoners Wells Estates.

The Women's Institute, founded in 1925, continues with great effect and commendable stability, making its jams, cakes and home-made wines. indulging its capabilities for decorative and useful craft work, displaying its histrionic gifts, and enjoying informative talks and discussions.

The Good Companions Club was founded in the autumn of 1960 and has proved an enduring organisation, encouraging companionship and mutual enjoyment among the more elderly residents under the leadership of such people as Mr. E. Sopp, Major Hills and Mr. T. Tanswell.

The Horticultural Society is a resurrection in the fifties of a former similar body which operated continuously up to the Second World War. It has wonderful outings to beautiful gardens and erudite sessions devoted to the culture in most unpromising circumstances of fruits, flowers and vegetables, the success of which is a source of wonder and envy to less skilful gardeners at its annual Flower Show, which is a popular village event. The Society is most efficiently run and involves the work and interest of a wide section of village life.

The Grayshott Stagers is also a revival of a pre-War dramatic society. The founding members in 1951 included Wing-Commander Chalmers, Mr. and Mrs. R. E. B. Meade-King, Mr. and Mrs. K. Baldock, Mr. and Mrs. W. Cowell, Mrs. Harry Buck, Mr. Max Reese, Mrs. W. Larkham and the late Mr. L. Larkham, and Mrs. J. Bicknell. From 1951 until 1963, beginning with "John Marlow's Profession," it put on two plays each year. In 1954 it broke fresh ground by producing a musical, "The Quaker Girl," and this was followed by a long series of such productions, broken only by a one-year gap in 1972. Memory is bright of eighteen successive musicals produced jointly by Mrs. Larkham and her husband, Leslie—which, if not always musically perfect or choreographically exact, certainly conveyed a strong impression of enjoyment, even of exuberance, greatly appreciated by audiences both at Grayshott and Haslemere: for, after the first few years, the Grayshott performances were duplicated at the Haslemere Hall. After 1963 the usual pattern was one straight play and a musical each year. Audiences were regularly large for straight plays in the earlier years, but that was in the days before the ubiquitous television, and it is sad—and perhaps a reflection on modern social custom—that audiences have been getting smaller. This has even, although to a lesser extent, applied to the musicals. In addition, there was usually a "Summer Show," run mainly as a social event with entertainment of the cabaret type, to which—as well as experienced members—the younger and less experienced were able to contribute. As might be expected from men and women possessing or aspiring to histrionic talent, committee meetings tend to be long, lively, and sometimes keenly contentious.

Another recent re-birth has been the Grayshott and Hindhead Choral Society, although after a much longer period than in the other cases. In its modern form it grew from a combination at services of the choirs of the United Reformed Church and St. Luke's Church, under Mrs. Jean Spry and Mrs. Irene Hartland. Its Christmas Coffee and Carols evenings became a popular event at Grayshott and at Beacon Hill. Other concerts were given at St. Luke's Church. Under its more recent Musical Director, Dr. Chalmers Burns, who is patient and long-suffering although this is not always immediately evident at practices, the Society has become more ambitious, with performances of great works which have tended to alternate between St. Luke's and St. Alban's Churches.

Epilogue

In this book an attempt has been made to trace in some detail, though not exhaustively, the development of Grayshott—its life and institutions, from the early outlying hamlet of Headley parish, remote from the present village, through its growth and vitality in the last decades of the nineteenth century and its formation as a separate parish, both ecclesiastical and civil, at the opening of the present century, to its strong development as an organised community in little over seventy years. We have seen how much it owes to those far-sighted residents who laid the foundations, and to those of all classes and creeds who have succeeded them and continued their work.

That Grayshott has and will continue to have serious problems cannot be doubted. Perhaps the most important in the more immediate future will be the preservation, in face of many pressures, of its lovely countryside and its village characteristics. We may be confident that the spirit of friendliness and public service which have served it so well in the past will continue unabated in the future.

Acknowledgements

I gratefully acknowledge my indebtedness to the following for their ready co-operation.

The Officials of: —

   The Public Records Office.
   The British Museum Reading Room.
   The British Library Newspaper Library.
   Hampshire Public Records Office.

To the following for access to local records: —

   J. McGhee, Esq., Clerk to Headley Parish Council.
   The late Canon Tudor Jones, Rector of Headley.
   Revd. S.F. Hooper and Grayshott Parochial Church Council.
   Grayshott Parish Council & D.P. Lawson, Esq., Clerk to that Council.
   D.H. Roberts, Esq., and Managers of Grayshott Primary School.
   The Proprietors of *The Haslemere Herald* for permission to quote from
      their paper.

To the following for valuable information: —

   The late Major L. I. T. Whitaker and Major Jeremy Whitaker for
      information on Grayshott Hall and correspondence between the
      late A. Ingham Whitaker, Esq. and George Bernard Shaw.
   Revd. F. M. Hodges Roper, United Reformed Church.
   Revd. G. Crosby, Methodist Church.
   Revd. P. J. Hartnett and Mother Superior, St. Joseph's Church and the
      Convent of the Cenacle.
   L. Franks, Esq., The Kingswood Firs Estate.
   Mrs. E. N. Bickerdyke, The Grove School.
   D. E. W. Spencer, Esq., Amesbury School.
   P. C. Weeks, Esq., St. Edmund's School.

To the late Dr. Rolston for indicating certain source material.

To the following for permission to print extracts: —

Messrs. John Murray: extracts from *For My Grandson;* 1933: Sir Frederick Pollock

Messrs. Hamish Hamilton: extract from *Purely for Pleasure;* 1966: Margaret Lane

Messrs. E. W. Langham, Farnahm, Surrey: extracts from *Frensham Then and Now;* 1938: H. J. Baker and H. C. Minchin

The Society of Authors and the Bernard Shaw Estate: extracts from letters written by George Bernard Shaw to the *Haslemere Herald*

The Haslemere Herald; extracts from letters from George Bernard Shaw and other extracts

Associated Newspapers Group Ltd: extracts from *The Morning Leader* and *The Star,* August 1899

The Contemporary Review: extract from an article 1899

The Spectator: extracts from issues of August and September 1899

To many individuals for information on the early years of the modern village — in particular, the late Mrs. G. Cane, the late Mr. Tom Johnson, and the late Mr. B. P. Chapman.

Heatherley

by Flora Thompson

Her sequel to "Lark Rise to Candleford"

... about her time in Grayshott

'Heatherley' picks up the story a year after Flora left 'Candleford
Green' and arrived in Grayshott, Hampshire, to take up her first
permanent job.

**She completed the typescript, but never submitted it for
publication before her death in 1947.**

*Many years later, it was included in a posthumous collection of her
writings by Margaret Lane—but this is now out of print.*

In a new edition, we have gone back to review her original typescript and also added historical notes and some fresh material
found in her archives.

Introduction by Anne Mallinson of Selborne
Chapter illustrations by Hester Whittle
Historical notes by John Owen Smith

ISBN 1-873855-29-X (paperback)

Published by John Owen Smith
19 Kay Crescent, Headley Down, Bordon, Hampshire GU35 8AH
Tel/Fax: (01428) 712892
sales@headley1.demon.co.uk

Web-site for information on Flora Thompson:—
www.headley1.demon.co.uk/flora/

Laura goes farther

One hot September afternoon near the end of the last century a girl of about twenty walked without knowing it over the border into Hampshire from one of its neighbouring counties. She was dressed in a brown woollen frock with a waist-length cape of the same material and a brown beaver hat decorated with two small ostrich tips, set upright in front, back to back, like a couple of notes of interrogation. This outfit, which would no doubt appear hideous to modern eyes, had given her great moral support on her train journey. The skirt, cut short just to escape contact with the ground and so needing no holding up except in wet weather, was, her dressmaker had assured her, the latest idea for country wear. The hat she had bought on her way through London that morning. It had cost nine and eleven-pence three farthings of the pound she had saved to meet her expenses until her first month's salary was due in her new post, but she did not regret the extravagance for it…

Start of the first chapter of 'Heatherley' by Flora Thompson

Other books relating to the history of Headley and Grayshott

One Monday in November…and Beyond
—the story of the Selborne and Headley Workhouse Riots of 1830
During the 'Swing' riots of 1830, according to the famed historians
J.L. and Barbara Hammond, "the most interesting event in the
Hampshire rising was the destruction of the workhouses at Selborne
and Headley." If these riots had succeeded, "the day when the
Headley workhouse was thrown down would be remembered ... as
the day of the taking of the Bastille." Here a local historian traces
the dramatic events of two days of rioting and its aftermath in the
villages and beyond. *ISBN 1-873855-33-8*

All Tanked Up*—the Canadians in Headley during World War II*
A story of the benign 'invasion' of Headley by Canadian tank
regiments over a period of four years, told from the point of view of
both Villagers and Canadians. Includes many personal
reminiscences and illustrations. *ISBN 1-873855-00-1*

On the Trail of Flora Thompson*—beyond Candleford Green*
The author of *Lark Rise to Candleford* worked in Grayshott post
office from 1898–1901. A local historian investigates the people and
places she would have seen here at that time. *ISBN 1-873855-24-9*

Headley's Past in Pictures *— a tour of the parish in old photographs*
Headley as it was in the first half of the 20th century. In this book
you are taken on an illustrated tour of the parish by means of three
journeys – the first around the centre of Headley and Arford, the
second to Headley Down and into Grayshott, and the third along the
River Wey and its tributaries. In doing so, we venture occasionally
outside today's civil parish boundaries – but that too is all part of the
history of Headley. *ISBN 1-873855-27-3*

John Owen Smith, publisher:—
Tel/Fax: (01428) 712892
E-mail: wordsmith@headley-village.com
Web Site: www.headley-village.com/wordsmith

Index